CASE STUDIES IN SCHOOL LEADERSHIP:

KEYS TO A SUCCESSFUL PRINCIPALSHIP

KAREN HESSEL

JOHN HOLLOWAY

EDITED BY NEIL SHIPMAN

SCHOOL LEADERSHIP SERIES
VOLUME 2

Educational
Testing Service

Educational Testing Service (ETS), headquartered in Princeton, New Jersey, is the world's largest private educational testing and measurement organization and a leader in educational research. A nonprofit company, ETS is dedicated to serving the needs of individuals, educational institutions and agencies, and governmental bodies in 181 countries.

ETS's Teaching and Learning Division is committed to supporting learning and advancing good teaching through a coherent approach to licensing, advanced certification, and professional development for teachers and school leaders.

In response to the national movement towards standards-based education and assessment, the division is collaborating with national organizations, states, school districts, and accomplished practicing teachers and administrators to develop exemplary, research-based professional development products and services for educators.

Included are the PATHWISE® Framework Induction Program for beginning teachers, the PATHWISE Framework Leader Academy, the PATHWISE Framework Observation System, the PATHWISE Framework Portfolio Program for experienced teachers, the PATHWISE Teacher Evaluation System, Assessment Wizard, and the PATHWISE School Leadership Series.

For more information, visit www.teachingandlearning.org.

Educational Testing Service

Teaching and Learning Division

Educational Testing Service
MS 18-D
Rosedale Road
Princeton, NJ 08541-0001
Web site: http://www.ets.org/pathwise

ISBN 0-88685-225-0

Printed in the United States of America

07 06 05 04 03 02   10 9 8 7 6 5 4 3 2 1

TABLE OF CONTENTS

LIST OF FIGURES

ABOUT THE AUTHORS

Karen Hessel is the Principal in Residence at Educational Testing Service (ETS®), located in Princeton, New Jersey. As Principal in Residence, Karen is the program director for the School Leadership Series of licensure assessment in the Teaching and Learning Division at ETS. As program director, her main duties include test development and assisting states throughout the country in the adoption and implementation of the licensure series. Prior to coming to ETS, Karen spent 30 years as a teacher and administrator in public schools in Pennsylvania and New Jersey. In addition, Karen co-authored Volume 1 in the School Leadership Series entitled, *A Framework for School Leaders: Linking the ISLLC Standards to Practice* (ETS, 2002).

John Holloway is the program director for the Teacher Quality Initiatives in the Teaching and Learning Division at ETS. As director, his main duties include creating professional development programs for teachers and school leaders based on the principles of evidence-centered teaching. Prior to joining ETS, John served as a high school science teacher for several years and then as a high school principal for 25 years. In addition, John was an adjunct professor, teaching graduate courses in school leadership and administration. John is a contributing columnist to the ASCD (Association for Supervision and Curriculum Development) monthly journal, *Educational Leadership*, as well as co-author of Volume 1 in the School Leadership Series.

ABOUT THE EDITOR

Neil J. Shipman, an educational leadership consultant and clinical associate professor in the department of leadership at the University of North Carolina — Chapel Hill, was the director of the Interstate School Leaders Licensure Consortium (ISLLC) from May, 1996 through January, 2001. Areas of special interest to Professor Shipman that are reflected in his numerous publications include the principal's role in improving instruction; his/her redefined role in light of school reform efforts; professional development for school leaders; and the impact of the ISLLC Standards for School Leaders on the reform movement. Dr. Shipman approaches consulting and his duties as a professor using his broad background as a practitioner and his perspectives on reform efforts gained while leading ISLLC in the development of standards, assessments, and a collaborative professional development process for school leaders. Serving a very large, suburban school system as a principal for fifteen years, and then as a supervisor of instruction, an area director for instruction, an acting associate superintendent, and an acting coordinator of early childhood education, has enabled Dr. Shipman to use his wealth of experiences in developing aspiring leaders for schools and school systems. Professor Shipman has been instrumental in affecting program reform in higher education programs for school leaders as well.

Dear Reader,

Never before have our schools been in greater need of the strong, visionary leadership only a well-prepared principal can provide. The testing provisions of the *No Child Left Behind* Act sharpen the focus on the school as the fundamental unit of scrutiny for student performance. Now driven by the mantra of "adequate yearly progress" and the threat of sanction or reconstitution, schools must accelerate and amplify their efforts to close achievement gaps and guarantee every student's ability to perform on state tests. Now, more than ever, we need principals who can lead teaching and learning and transform their schools into 21st-century learning communities.

The continued development of such principals is central to the mission of the National Association of Secondary School Principals (NASSP). As part of our commitment to principal development, NASSP participated in a consortium formed in 1994 to develop a set of standards to define and guide the practice of school leaders. The Interstate School Leaders Licensure Consortium (ISLLC) produced the ISLLC Standards for School Leaders in 1996. These standards are not meant to be all-inclusive, but are focused on indicators of knowledge, dispositions, and performances that are important for effective school leadership. The challenge for principal preparation programs, then, has been to place the standards in context—translate the standards to the principal's day-to-day professional life—and programs around the nation have been meeting the challenge head-on. NASSP is proud of its success, in this regard, with its Center for Principal Development programs, and proud as well to be associated with *Case Studies in School Leadership: Keys to a Successful Principalship*. This volume lifts the standards from the printed page and drops them in schools around the country to explore how the ISLLC Standards apply to real principals in real situations. As we identify with our colleagues in the case studies, we're reminded of our common call to refocus the school leader's role on what matters most—teaching and learning.

It is my hope that school leaders throughout the nation will find *Case Studies in School Leadership: Keys to a Successful Principalship* an effective tool in their continued professional development.

Gerald N. Tirozzi
Executive Director
NASSP

National Association of Secondary School Principals

The National Association of Secondary School Principals (NASSP) is the preeminent organization of middle level and high school principals, assistant principals, and aspiring school leaders. NASSP promotes improvement of secondary education and the role of school leaders by advocating high professional and academic standards, addressing the challenges facing school leaders, building public confidence in education, and strengthening the role of the principal as instructional leader.

Recognizing that successful schools require leaders who are able to perform at optimum levels and who have the knowledge and skills necessary to meet present and future challenges, NASSP's Center for Principal Development offers a variety of assessment and development programs designed to identify and develop leadership talent.

NASSP works with school districts, regional service agencies, boards of cooperative services, universities, professional associations, state departments of education, and other providers of programs and services to establish assessment/development centers. These centers provide local facilitators with the knowledge, skill, and support to deliver NASSP professional skill development or assessment programs that meet the needs of all school leaders.

National Association of Secondary School Principals, 1904 Association Drive, Reston, VA 20191-1537. Phone: (703) 860-0200. Fax: (703) 476-5432. Web site: www.principals.org.

Dear Reader,

During the last decade of the 20th century, major stakeholder groups recognized that school leadership was a crucial factor in any conversation about school reform. One result of this recognition was the formation of the Interstate School Leaders Licensure Consortium (ISLLC) in 1994. Comprised initially of 23 states and eleven national leadership organizations, the primary task for ISLLC was to develop a set of standards for principals and superintendents.

Supported and encouraged by the National Policy Board for Educational Administration (NPBEA); conceived by Scott Thomson, then executive secretary of the NPBEA; conceptualized by Professor Joseph Murphy of Vanderbilt University; and organized by Neil Shipman as project director for the Council of Chief State School Officers (CCSSO), the first-ever national set of common standards for school leaders was developed by the ISLLC and published in 1996.

Standards, in and of themselves, are relatively useless. They must be applied in order to have any true meaning. The key to standards-based reform lies in how standards are put to use. Since publication of the *Interstate School Leaders Licensure Consortium Standards for School Leaders* (CCSSO, 1996):

- Over two-thirds of the states have adopted or adapted the ISLLC Standards.

- Licensure examinations for principals and superintendents, developed by Educational Testing Service (ETS) in partnership with ISLLC and CCSSO, are being administered by ten states, with ten more recently completing standard settings in 2002.

- The National Council for Accreditation of Teacher Education (NCATE) has developed new *Standards for Advanced Programs in Educational Leadership* using the ISLLC Standards as the framework.

- Anecdotal evidence indicates that many university preparation programs are aligning their curriculum with the ISLLC and with the new NCATE Standards.

- ETS is publishing the School Leadership Series (based on the ISLLC Standards) to help aspiring and practicing principals develop and improve their practice.

While ISLLC has been the catalyst for the conversations that inspired all of the aforementioned implementations, ETS is now taking this conversation to the next level with first, the publication of *A Framework for School Leaders: Linking the ISLLC Standards to Practice* (ETS, 2002), and now, *Case Studies in School Leadership: Keys to a Successful Principalship* (ETS, 2003).

The three **Keys** that make this book a necessary part of life-long learning for school leaders are:

- Volume 2 of the School Leadership Series is based on Volume 1, *A Framework for School Leaders: Linking the ISLLC Standards to Practice*, thus assuring *standards-based* practice;

- the twelve case studies in Chapters 3 through 8 are *authentic and performance-based*; and

- the cases are all written *by practitioners for practitioners*, for aspiring school leaders, and for professors who are responsible for developing these leaders.

The authors of Chapters 3-8 (the twelve case studies) are real, active, on-the-job school leaders who are practicing their skills in real schools with real parents, students, staffs, and communities, all of whom are faced daily with very real challenges. They represent all levels of schooling, grades pre-K through 12; urban, suburban, and rural settings; and from states across our nation. They have "been there, done that." As seen through their eyes, these case studies help readers to constantly focus on issues of teaching and learning and school improvement.

From a detailed description of decision-making processes through multiple indicators about how to progress from being a principal with rudimentary skills to being an accomplished principal, Karen Hessel, John Holloway, and their practitioner colleagues have created a book that is to be used, not simply read once and then stored on a shelf. This case studies book should be written in, underlined, highlighted, dog-eared, and kept easily accessible for reference by every practicing and aspiring principal.

Not every case will be needed by every reader every day. A principal could very well be accomplished in one ISLLC component and rudimentary in another and, thus, want to pick and choose when and what parts of the book to reference. After initial reading, *Case Studies in School Leadership: Keys to a Successful Principalship* should truly become a set of keys for opening doors to effective leadership.

Volume 2 is not a cookbook filled with recipes and prescriptions that will automatically make one successful. But it will stimulate thinking and aid in reflection. Thoughtful reflection of one's actions and the relationship of those actions to the Volume 2 text will extend and enrich the principal's role in implementation of the school's vision. For example, it could be helpful during reflection time to consider how certain decisions are linked to keys described in one or more of the case studies in this text. Or the case studies could be stimulants for discussion among job-alike support groups. Volume 2 could also be valuable as a resource or text in school leader preparation programs, as a guide to professional growth activities for practitioners, or in development of board of education members and teacher leaders. Let the reader's imagination be the guide.

It is difficult to write a book by committee, but Hessel and Holloway (both experienced and successful principals), with the help of a dozen practitioners from the field, have pulled it off. This book is a "...definitive source in identifying those competencies that best describe the actual work done by effective school leaders" (ETS, 2003).

Neil J. Shipman
Chapel Hill, North Carolina

ACKNOWLEDGMENTS

In the completion of this book, sincerest appreciation is expressed to Educational Testing Service for giving us the opportunity to create this second volume of the School Leadership Series, designed to promote the success of all students through advancing school leadership. Many individuals supported our efforts; most significantly, however, we must recognize Mari Pearlman, Vice President of the ETS Teaching and Learning Division, who provided the inspiration for the project. Cindy Tocci and John Williams, the management team of the ETS Teaching and Learning Division professional development, provided us the encouragement and resources needed to continue this important work. In addition, there would be no framework without the initial research and work done by Joe Murphy and Neil Shipman, who continue to guide and support our efforts. Additionally, as the book's editor, Neil proved invaluable in guiding our writing, keeping our thoughts focused on the task, and keeping us true to the tenants of the ISLLC Standards.

Several other individuals and groups played vital roles in the creation of this book. These included:

- Jennifer Cathcart, who provided excellent technical support services throughout the entire process

- Christian Hilland and Gina Page who provided support services

- Salli Long , editorial project manager

- Kathy Benischeck, publications project manager and the ETS Publications Department Staff

- Janet Brennan, ETS Regional Director, who helped edit the draft document

- The principals and educational leaders from around the United States who contributed to Chapters 2–8, who have experience using the Standards in their practice and who contributed to the book by providing their personal views about the meaning of the Standards and how they define practice. These effective school leaders include Ed Baumgartner, Richard Benjamin, Kathleen Carr, Floyd Crues, SueAnn Gruver, Robert Hicks, Peter Holly, Maureen Madden, George Manthey, Angela Olsen, Michael Schlar, Laserik Saunders, and Wayne Yamagishi.

We are deeply indebted to the National Association of Secondary School Principals (NASSP) as they continue to provide us guidance, support, and inspiration in undertaking this project. Supported by their leadership and vision, we proudly offer this book to all who have a stake in successful school leadership.

Finally, we continue to be deeply indebted to our professional colleagues, both teachers and administrators, with whom we have had the pleasure of working over the many years as school principals and now as directors of the School Leadership Series at ETS. And, as in our first book, we are most indebted to all the students who attended our schools, delighted and inspired us, and helped to mold our vision about what is most important about public education—teaching and learning and the success of all students.

CASE STUDIES IN SCHOOL LEADERSHIP:

KEYS TO A SUCCESSFUL PRINCIPALSHIP

A fresh vision for school leadership is emerging in the new millennium. The ISLLC Standards have laid a solid foundation. Now, a framework for school leaders provides a blueprint for redefining and refocusing the role of the school leader by linking the Standards to practice. This framework presents a common vocabulary for describing various levels of performance as the school leader attends to the business of school leadership and ensuring academic success for all students. The resulting structures, as well as the case studies described within this book, are intended to help develop, support, and nurture the current and succeeding generations of school leaders.

PREFACE

> Some are born great; some achieve greatness,
> and some have greatness thrust upon them.
>
> Shakespeare's *Twelfth Night*. Act II, Sc.5, 157–159.

Out of 1,435 Fortune 500 companies studied by renowned management researcher Jim Collins, *only 11* achieved and sustained greatness for 15 years after a major transition period.

What did these eleven companies have in common? Each had a Level 5 leader at the helm. Level 5 leaders blend the paradoxical combination of *deep personal humility* with *intense professional will*. This rare combination also defies our usual assumptions about what makes a great leader. See Figure 1 below.

So, just what does it mean to be a Level 5 leader? Can you develop Level 5 leadership? More importantly, just how does this concept transfer to the accomplished school leaders described in Volume 1: *A Framework for School Leaders: Linking the ISLLC Standards to Practice*, and further defined here in Volume 2, *Case Studies in School Leadership: Keys to a Successful Principalship*?

FIGURE 1: YIN AND YANG OF LEVEL 5

The Yin and Yang of Level 5

PERSONAL HUMILITY	PROFESSIONAL WILL
Demonstrates a compelling modesty, shunning public adulation; never boastful.	Creates superb results, a clear catalyst in the transition from good to great.
Acts with quiet, calm determination; relies principally on inspired standards, not inspiring charisma, to motivate.	Demonstrates an unwavering resolve to do whatever must be done to produce the best long-term results, no matter how difficult.
Channels ambition into the company, not the self; sets up successors for even more greatness in the next generation.	Sets the standard of building an enduring great company; will settle for nothing less.
Looks in the mirror, not out the window, to apportion responsibility for poor results, never blaming other people, external factors, or bad luck.	Looks out the window, not in the mirror, to apportion credit for the success of the company—to other people, external factors, and good luck.

Harvard Business Review*

* From "Level 5 Leadership: The Triumph of Humility and Fierce Resolve" by Jim Collins, *HBR OnPoint (From the Harvard Business Review), 2001 (Product Number 5831)*. Copyright © 2001 by the Harvard Business School Publishing Corporation; all rights reserved.

What is a Level 5 leader?

A Level 5 leader is a study in duality.

A Level 5 leader is

modest and willful;

shy and fearless;

timid and ferocious;

rare and unstoppable.

A Level 5 leader combines personal humility with professional will. In terms of humility, "they routinely credit others, external factors, and good luck for their companies' success. When results are poor, they blame themselves. They act quietly, calmly, and determinedly—relying on inspired **standards**, not inspiring charisma, to motivate."

Inspired standards demonstrate Level 5 leaders' unwavering will. Utterly intolerant of mediocrity, they are stoic in their resolve to do whatever it takes to produce great results—terminating everything else. And, they select superb successors, wanting their companies to become even more successful in the future.

FIGURE 2: LEVEL 5 HIERARCHY

THE LEVEL 5 HIERARCHY

The Level 5 leader sits on top of a hierarchy of capabilities and is, according to our research, a necessary requirement for transforming an organization from good to great. But what lies beneath? Four other layers, each one appropriate in its own right but none with the power of Level 5. Individuals do not need to proceed sequentially through each level of the hierarchy to reach the top, but to be a full-fledged Level 5 requires the capabilities of all the lower levels, plus the special characteristics of Level 5.

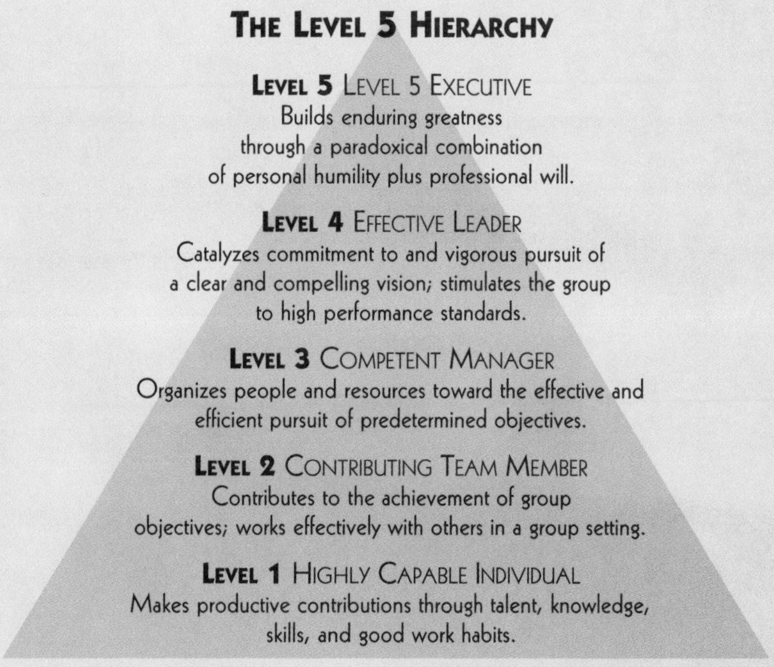

LEVEL 5 LEVEL 5 EXECUTIVE
Builds enduring greatness
through a paradoxical combination
of personal humility plus professional will.

LEVEL 4 EFFECTIVE LEADER
Catalyzes commitment to and vigorous pursuit of
a clear and compelling vision; stimulates the group
to high performance standards.

LEVEL 3 COMPETENT MANAGER
Organizes people and resources toward the effective and
efficient pursuit of predetermined objectives.

LEVEL 2 CONTRIBUTING TEAM MEMBER
Contributes to the achievement of group
objectives; works effectively with others in a group setting.

LEVEL 1 HIGHLY CAPABLE INDIVIDUAL
Makes productive contributions through talent, knowledge,
skills, and good work habits.

*Harvard Business Review**

There are very few **strong natural leaders** (SNL). "To grasp this concept, consider Abraham Lincoln, who never let his ego get in the way of his ambition to create an enduring great nation. Author Henry Adams called him "a quiet, peaceful, shy figure. But those who thought Lincoln's understated manner signaled weakness found themselves terribly mistaken—to the scale of 250,000 Confederate and 360,000 Union lives, including Lincoln's own" (*Harvard Business Review*, 70). Those who study Lincoln know that Abraham Lincoln represented quintessentially that paradoxical combination of humble yet willful leadership (Level 5).

Level 5 leaders sit atop a hierarchy of four more common leadership levels—and these leaders possess the skills of all four lower levels. See Figure 2 on the previous page.

FIGURE 3: LEVELS OF PERFORMANCE

The **RUDIMENTARY** level typically describes that "little or no evidence" exists for the set of behaviors called for by the specific component. It is important to note that the designation of "rudimentary" does not necessarily mean that the school leader is not capable overall or not capable of the specific set of behaviors found within the component. Instead, this designation simply means that there is little or no evidence of achievement of the component judged by performance.

The **DEVELOPING** level typically describes "limited" evidence. The evidence may not address the component in its complexity, may be lacking in breadth or depth, or may be less effective than is expected. For example, the school leader may be aware of the fact that stakeholders should be involved in the decision-making process, but there is only limited evidence that the leader knows when or how to get them involved, or is consistent with this fundamental practice over time.

	LEVEL OF PERFORMANCE			
Central Themes	**Rudimentary**	**Developing**	**Proficient**	**Accomplished**
A Vision for Success	There is little or no evidence that the school leader either collects or analyzes data about the school's progress toward realizing the vision.	There is limited evidence that the school leader collects data on the school's progress toward the vision or uses this information to promote student success in any meaningful way.	There is clear evidence that the school leader collects data periodically on the school's progress toward the vision and uses this information to make decisions that promote the success of students.	There is clear, convincing, and consistent evidence that the school leader collects and analyzes data on the school's progress toward realizing the vision throughout the school year and continually uses this information to make decisions that promote the success of all students.

The level of **PROFICIENT** typically describes "clear" evidence. The evidence is specific and reasonable, and addresses the complexity of the component. At times, the evidence may be somewhat uneven, with specific features within the component addressed more effectively than others. In general, the evidence shows that the school leader knows what to do and does it.

The level of **ACCOMPLISHED** typically describes "clear, convincing, and consistent" evidence. The evidence is very specific and credible. It is comprehensive and thoughtful, presenting an integrated, highly effective approach to the behaviors specified in the component.

If you examine the Level 5 Hierarchy Diagram (see Figure 2) level descriptions against the descriptions of the four levels of performance taken from Volume 1: *A Framework for School Leaders: Linking the ISLLC Standards to Practice* (see Figure 3), consider these similarities:

1. As one proceeds up through each hierarchical level, the needs of the company or institution supercede the individual needs of its members. Likewise as one proceeds across the levels of performance in the framework for school leaders, the focus is on the contributions of all members of the school community (staff, students, parents, community stakeholders) to do whatever it takes for all students to succeed. "The role of the principal in today's successful school has transcended the traditional notion of functional management, power, behavioral style, and instructional leadership. The best schools have principals who consider their most important task as establishing a school culture. Whether through collaboration, consensus building, personal influence or modeling, the principal is able to promote a school's vision for success by promoting a culture where students, staff and community members have school goals that become more important than their self interests" (Ogden, pp.27, 28).

2. Both models focus on enlisting a commitment and vigorous pursuit of a clear, compelling vision.

3. Both models value self-reflection that leads to enhanced performance. Collins calls this the "seed" within you. "Leaders **without** the seed tend to have monumental egos that can't subjugate to something larger and more sustaining than themselves (i.e., their companies). But for leaders **with** the seed, the right conditions can stimulate the "seed" to sprout" (p.65). Joan Richardson (2001) writes, "At the heart of reflection is the belief that, given opportunities to carefully consider their work, educators possess the necessary knowledge to improve their practice. Reflection is the process through which educators tap into that knowledge." Self-reflection allows the leader to view his/her current practice through the lens of the ISLLC Standards and identify immediate changes than can be made to one's practice.

Considering the concept that there are relatively few strong natural leaders, it is our belief that through self-reflection and mentoring, the skills, traits, actions, dispositions, or beliefs that characterize Level 5 leadership (accomplished leadership) can be nurtured in aspiring or practicing school leaders. Some of the characteristics of successful leaders are: determination, intensity, drive, confidence, forward thinking, and risk-taking. These leaders are believers in shared leadership and they believe that their work is about building, creating, and contributing.

Collins states, "We would love to give you a list of steps for getting to Level 5 — but we have **no solid research data** that would support a credible list." The inner development of the person is necessary for "Level 5 leadership." In short, Level 5 is a very satisfying idea, a truthful idea, a powerful idea, and, to make the move from good to great, very likely an essential idea. But to provide "ten steps to Level 5 leadership" would trivialize the concept.

So, too, in this book, we would love to provide all the keys to move leaders from the rudimentary level of performance to the accomplished level of performance — but similarly we do not have any solid research data that would support this list. To say that we have included all the necessary keys for successful movement would also trivialize the highly complex and challenging job of the principalship. However, what we DO HAVE is the voice and real life experiences of twelve accomplished school leaders who have lead outstanding schools and districts. They have been successful in terms of increasing student achievement. They have distinguished themselves as National Blue Ribbon Principals or as principals of schools defined by Craig Gerald in *Dispelling the Myth Revisited: Findings from a Nationwide Analysis of "High Flying" Schools* (Education Trust, 2001). Despite the odds, they have shown ALL students CAN learn and that ALL students CAN be successful.

Collins says, "Whether we make it to Level 5, it is worth trying. For like all basic truths, what is best in human beings, when we catch a glimpse of that truth, we know that our own lives and all we touch will be better for making the effort to get there" (p.76).

Effective school leadership is becoming more critical than ever. In our first book, *A Framework for School Leaders: Linking the ISLLC Standards to Practice* (2002), we created a framework to define professional practice as viewed through the lens of the Standards.

> Exciting and challenging changes in the landscape of school leadership are at hand. Imperatives for new standards-based assessments and programs, new ways to allocate resources, and new visions for professional development all figure prominently in that landscape. In the quest for professionally powerful ways to bring about these changes, when used responsibly, the framework and ISLLC Standards, it is hoped, will be an important means for promoting and sustaining a new vision of leadership.

> Used constructively and thoughtfully, the framework can serve to remind us of our commitment to our children, and to serve as a kind of roadmap to help us find our way through that new landscape of school leadership. We take the journey for our students, all our students. Despite the roadblocks and potholes and stop signs, taking the journey is a noble effort (Hessel and Holloway, p. 123).

But what does this journey look like in actual practice? Can the ISLLC Standards and the framework provide the roadmap to a successful principalship?

Notes

INTRODUCTION

Why Volume 2?

As a result of numerous requests and the positive feedback we received on the publication of *A Framework for School Leaders: Linking the ISLLC Standards to Practice*, it became clear that there was a need for a Volume 2 in the School Leadership Series. Principals were eager for more specificity in applying the rubrics in Volume 1 to their positions.

The Link to Volume 1

Volume 1 was designed to be rather general in description and dependent on the position of leadership held in the district. It was designed to provide for a close examination and understanding of the Standards; to encourage job-alike groups to examine the areas of focus, knowledge, and skills that frame each Standard; and then to finally challenge the reader to further interpret the rubrics using the narratives that accompany each Standard.

Volume 1 was also written with the intent of assisting institutions of higher education in the preparation of school leaders, by introducing them to the national Standards developed by the Interstate School Leaders Licensure Consortium (ISLLC) under the auspices of the Council of Chief State School Officers (CCSSO). Students in preparation programs have made excellent use of the book and its rubrics as another tool to be used to prepare before taking one of the licensure assessments in the School Leader Series of Tests: the School Leader Licensure Assessment (SLLA) or the School Superintendent Assessment (SSA). The language of each of the component rubrics in Volume 1 purposefully reflects the language of the rubrics used in the scoring of these licensure exams. These rubrics are familiar to the students and thus allow them to anchor their thinking and response to each of the exercises.

The Purpose of Volume 2

The purpose of Volume 2: *Case Studies: Keys to a Successful Principalship* is to focus on the role of the school principal and, through a case study approach, describe specific ways to improve performance in the leadership areas defined by the ISLLC Standards. The specific ways to improve performance are entitled "Keys" in Volume 2. In order to accomplish this goal, the redefined role of the principal is discussed per the ISLLC Standards. The focus is on the most relevant elements of the Standards:

- Teaching

- Learning

- Success for all students

Volume 2 specializes in further defining and examining how the levels of performance for each component table translate to the work of the principal. Each chapter is designed to answer the following essential questions:

What does the principal's performance look like at the rudimentary level?

What does the principal's performance look like at the accomplished level?

What are the "keys" to move from one level to the next?

The Organization of the Book

Volume 2 is divided into nine chapters as follows:

Chapter 1 provides the purpose, overview, and multiple uses of the book.

Chapter 2 focuses on the principal's role in the data-based decision-making processes. It investigates the research model of evidence-centered design (ECD); it describes how Educational Testing Service (ETS) has focused the application of ECD to the field of education. It also stresses the importance of data-driven decision making in the actions of the school principal. Practical examples of effective use of data-driven decision making and its impact on student achievement within a school district are described in this chapter.

Chapters 3–8 are designed as case study investigations. These chapters reflect the national interest in the standards movement and the involvement of twelve top school leaders, many from schools that have been defined as "dispelling the myth" (Gerald, 2001). These twelve leaders from rural, suburban, and urban schools across the country have created authentic case studies connected to front-burner issues in the nation's schools.

Each of these six chapters is formatted to address one of the six ISLLC Standards. The focus of Chapter 3 is on Standard 1, Chapter 4 on Standard 2, and so on. Each chapter includes a description of the Standard and its four components as defined in the associated framework for school leaders table.

In each chapter there are two case studies, one that presents a dilemma in an elementary school setting and another in a secondary school setting. The case studies are constructed to include general background on the school setting, several documents that further define the issues, and two questions. In each case, the authors have provided the reader with the response from two fictitious principals: one at a rudimentary (or beginning) school leader performance level and the other at an accomplished level (one we all aspire to reach). The authors have included in their responses essential concerns that must be addressed in each setting. Their responses focus on the four central themes of the Standards (i.e., Vision for the Success of ALL Students, Focus on Teaching and Learning, Involvement of Stakeholders, and Ethical Decision Making).

The final section of each chapter includes the "Keys," or steps, that describe how a principal can improve his/her level of performance moving from a rudimentary to an accomplished level.

The final chapter, **Chapter 9**, discusses how the lessons learned from the field are aligned to current views and research on effective school leadership. Chapter 9 outlines next steps for the principal who wants to improve his/her leadership performance. It also challenges the practicing school leader to gather support for reform that results when others understand the true role of the school principal as defined by the ISLLC Standards. The principal is the Instructional Leader in the building and this is his/her most important role. Accountability for school reform and the improvement of student achievement ultimately rests with the principal, the educational leader in each school.

Uses for Volume 2

Graduate Level Educational Leadership Courses. Institutions that prepare school leaders for the job of the principalship will find the framework and case studies invaluable in structuring their course offerings as well as their clinical experiences.

Professional Development for Practicing School Leaders. As school leaders constantly seek to improve their practice they will discover that this book offers guidance on where to best focus their efforts.

Self-Reflection. Through self-reflection, school leaders can discover where their greatest needs lie and plan accordingly. "It's the ability to look back and make sense of what happened and what you learned. But it's also the ability to look forward, to anticipate what's coming up and what you need to do to prepare for that," explains Bill Sommers, executive director of instructional services for the Minneapolis Public Schools. Reflection is an element of inquiry-focused professional learning, such as action research, classroom observation and feedback, and book study.

Administrative Study Groups. Using Volume 2, job-alike groups formed from district administrative teams can collaborate with their colleagues and pursue joint goals that lead to improved performance of both the principals and their schools.

Orientation of New School Board Members. Introducing new board members to the redefined role of the school leader can be done effectively and efficiently through the use of both volumes of the School Leadership Series. This new view of the role of the school leader allows for a more valid appraisal of the principal's work by the local board of school directors.

The research is clear, convincing, and compelling — *the leadership of the school principal is the key to student achievement*.

Notes

EVIDENCE-CENTERED DECISION MAKING

The Principal's Role in Data-Based Decision Making

As stated in Chapter 1, our intent is to show how a principal at the rudimentary level and a principal at the accomplished level each respond to situations created in a series of twelve case studies. In each case, our fictional principals respond to situations within the context of the ISLLC Standards. It is through these living examples that we gain an understanding of how principals react to a variety of situations in a way that reflects the underlying premise of the Standards by "promoting the success of all students." But how does the principal, or even an observer of the principal's actions, know if these solutions ultimately promote success? Effective principals measure gains in pupil achievement and school success factors by collecting evidence from a variety of sources. By analyzing the evidence, or data, effective principals are able to monitor their practice, decide on courses of action, and plan for the efficient allocation of resources.

One way to collect such evidence is through a carefully planned and implemented pupil-assessment process. According to Mislevy (1999) and others, the key ideas in educational assessment include:

- identifying the aspects of skill and knowledge about which inferences are desired

- identifying the relationships between targeted knowledge and behavior in situations that call for their use

- identifying features of situations that can evoke behavior that provides evidence about the targeted knowledge (p.4)

In *Tomorrow's Teachers* (Wang & Walberg, 2001), the authors assert that well-developed curricula include strong and functional assessment components. These assessment components are aligned with the curriculum's major purposes and goals, so that they are integrated with the curriculum's content, instructional methods, and learning activities and designed to evaluate progress toward major intended outcomes. They contend that effective principals insist that teachers use assessment to evaluate students' progress in learning and plan curriculum improvements, not just to generate grades. Good assessment includes data from many sources besides paper-and-pencil tests, and it addresses the full range of goals or intended outcomes (not only knowledge but higher-order thinking skills and content-related values and dispositions). In addition, learning activities and sources of data other than tests should be used for assessment purposes. Everyday lessons and activities provide opportunities to monitor the progress of the class as a whole and of individual students, and tests can be augmented with performance evaluations using tools such as laboratory tasks and observation checklists, portfolios of student papers or projects, and essays or other assignments that call for higher-order thinking and applications (pp. 33–34).

Mari Pearlman (2001) supports the underlying foundations of the ISLLC Standards. Her research has shown that, while student successes are often measured by assessment results, accomplished principals understand that assessment is just a part of a more important and larger whole, which is learning. To gather the data necessary to make claims of successful student learning, principals and teachers frequently use a construct known as the Evidence-Centered Design Model (ECD). This model asks these questions:

- What is being measured? What claims do we want to make **on the basis of the assessment score**?

- What are the characteristics of the person(s) being assessed?

- What is the purpose of the measurement?

- What, specifically, do we want to measure?

- What evidence would credibly support these claims?

- How can such evidence be gathered, given constraints of time, energy, cost, and measurement methodology?

In today's climate of educational accountability, educators strive to ensure that the content of standardized and teacher-made tests are aligned with the standards. Fiero (2001) supports Pearlman's fundamental beliefs about the importance of valid and reliable data-gathering systems. Using the evidence-centered approach, he asks:

- What evidence do we need to collect in order to support the claim that a student who performs well actually meets the relevant standards?

- Which kinds of evidence and how much of it do we need to obtain?

- If, for example, we wanted to claim that a student can "convey and organize information, using facts, details, and illustrative examples, and a variety of patterns and structures," what would be the form of the evidence and how much of it would we have to collect?

- Or, if we wanted to claim that a student can "formulate, ask, and respond to questions to obtain, clarify, and extend information and meaning," what evidence should we collect?

- What kinds of developmentally appropriate evidence would make us confident that a student could meet these standards?

While effective principals make use of the goldmine of information collected through student assessment, these same accomplished school leaders also rely on data from a variety of other sources to make informed decisions. As we will see in our case studies, accomplished principals make informed decisions by collecting and analyzing data from these multiple sources.

There is ever-increasing literature on the importance of committing to data-based decision making in schools and school districts. Noyce, Perda, and Traver (2000) have encouraged the creation of "data-driven schools." Bernhardt (1994/1998) and Schmoker (1996/2001) have done likewise. The *Journal of Staff Development* (2000) devoted an entire issue to "data," as has the Wisconsin Center for Education Research ("Using Data for Educational Decision Making," 2001). The NASSP's journal, *Principal Leadership* (March, 2002), focused on "Teacher Talk: Conversation that Improves Practice" and recommended the use of action research for making informed, data-driven decisions.

Interestingly, however, none of the above have much to say about the role of the principal in data-based decision making. This may be attributed, in part, to the emphasis currently being placed on the shared nature of decision making — the implication being, perhaps, that the principal does not have a prominent role in such a scenario. Calhoun (1999) and Forsythe (1997), however, not only argue the case for data-based decision making but also underline the crucial role played by the school principal in data-driven school improvement efforts. Indeed, in a published conversation with Dennis Sparks, Calhoun (1999) concludes by saying,

> In my 28 years of experience, there is nothing as critical to school implementation of new teaching strategies as the principal's full participation in learning the strategy, practicing in the classroom, sharing with his or her peer coaching group how students responded, and building the next lessons together. I can almost map a school's level of implementation by how engaged the principal is in modeling what is happening (p. 58).

The same is true, we would argue, for the implementation of data-based decision making as an essential ingredient of school improvement. The principal has to demonstrate his or her engagement by practicing and modeling the necessary skills and processes. Forsythe (1997) adds to this point.

> The emphasis on the initiative of teachers in successful school improvement does not in any way diminish or supplant the role of the principal in that process. In fact, the importance of the principal is increased, not decreased, by the engagement of teachers in the school-improvement process (p. 101).

The principal, then, has to demonstrate engagement while creating opportunities for others to become engaged.

Quadrant Thinking

In her article, Forsythe uses "quadrant thinking" to describe the process that principals experience when they attempt to develop their leadership skills. "Quadrant thinking" is an organizer for thoughtful action designed by Holly and Forsythe (1996). They used two intersecting continua to produce four quadrants that can be used to guide the growth/development/change process (see Figure 4). Taken together, the quadrants produce a developmental cycle that can be used for planning, implementing and reflecting about any particular change process. In terms of this model, therefore, principals involved in school improvement efforts such as data-based decision making have to traverse the cycle at least twice—once for personal change and development and a second time in order to involve others in the same learning process. Forsythe's article focuses on the first process—a principal's personal change journey—while this chapter concentrates on the second process in which the principal, having experienced the journey of personal change, now involves others in the implementation of effective school improvement by committing to shared, data-based decision making.

> The principal must believe and act in the role of partner and participant with the teachers and must do so in a caring and nurturing community. For many principals this requires a shift in both thought and action. Quadrant thinking frames thoughtful action (Forsythe, 101).

Charles Handy (1989) has always maintained that change and learning are much the same process. "Quadrant thinking" is a frame for understanding and applying change and learning. As an organizer for thought and action, it borrows from learning theory, stage theory, and development theory and has much in common with the staff development model introduced by Joyce and Showers (1988). Other similar approaches are the team development model that involves "forming, storming, norming, and performing" (Tuckman, 1965) and the Concerns-Based Adoption Model (Hall and Hord, 1987).

FIGURE 4: QUADRANT THINKING*

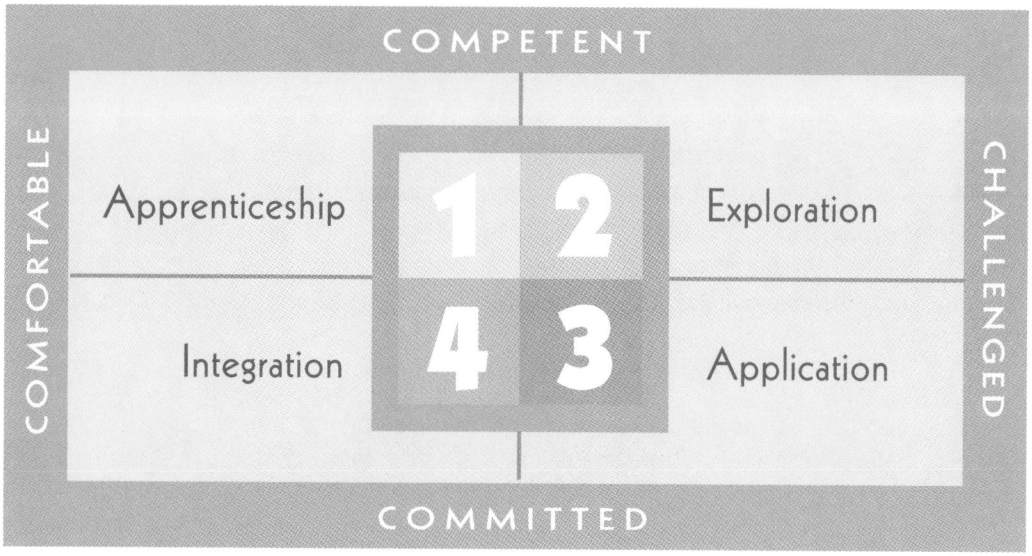

* Used by permission of author, Kay Forsythe.

APPRENTICESHIP QUADRANT

This quadrant involves participants becoming comfortable with the new ideas (in this case, data-based decision making) and working to acquire the knowledge and skills required to perform effectively in this new fashion. They are led to understand the purpose of the changes (teachers so often say that no one bothered to explain the "why" of the changes in which they're involved) and watch demonstrations of the skills in action. Inevitably, they are not yet believers, but they are "in the picture." They have a basic knowledge and are beginning to understand what is expected of them.

EXPLORATION QUADRANT

At this stage, participants move from basic competency to being challenged in practice. It is the time for guided practice. As they make their first, tentative steps — probably in workshop-type, simulated settings — they need to receive sensitive, constructive guidance. A supportive climate is crucial at this stage of their learning. As the challenge increases, it is time to use the newly acquired skills in the work context — with colleagues acting as guides and mentors.

APPLICATION QUADRANT

While coaching and critical friendship are still required, application is the time when those involved branch out and try the ideas for themselves — and , in so doing, put their own personal stamp on the changes. As their skill level increases, so does their ownership and, indeed, their commitment. The participant acquires the sense of power that comes with efficacy and becomes his/her own critical friend. Forsythe refers to this as the "merging of mind and heart into self-actualizing and self-assessment" (p. 104).

INTEGRATION QUADRANT

This stage is akin to being on auto-pilot. The change has become integrated in the participant's repertoire. It is just something that the person does — habitually and almost without thinking. It is the prime time to consolidate the learning by the learner becoming the teacher or mentor of others who are setting out on the same learning journey. As Forsythe concludes:

> The pinnacle of integration is achieved when the principal encourages teachers (and other staff members) to take the same journey through the quadrants: to gain knowledge and skills, explore new strategies, apply them in deep ways, and integrate them into their daily teaching and learning (p. 104).

So when the principal has experienced his or her own personal learning journey concerning the application of data-based decision making, what has to be done by the principal to lead others through the same learning process? In answering this central question, what is certain is that the principal's role changes over time. Actually, it's a multiplicity of roles that the principal has to play—adopting different roles at each stage of the change cycle. Again, "quadrant thinking" is helpful in explaining why and how these changes of principal behavior have to take place—and in what sequence. Like all models, however, the linearity built into "quadrant thinking" is not always followed in practice. Learners who grow up in this digital age, for instance, often learn the basics during the exploration stage—through trial and error. Whatever learning sequence is adopted, however, basic knowledge and skills have to be learned and the learning reinforced experientially.

Setting the Stage (Quadrant One)

In Quadrant One—the Apprenticeship Quadrant—the principal is the instigator-in-chief of other people's learning. At this stage the principal is up-front and leading by example—the teacher and instructor, the "master" in what amounts to a master-apprentice relationship. The principal's main task is to set the scene by explaining the expectations and defining what is meant by the innovation, in this case, data-based decision making. Setting the scene involves drawing both the big picture (how this particular change fits within the overall vision of the school) and the small picture (how each colleague fits into the new scenario). Experience tells us that educators need both. They also need to hear that some elements of the innovation are already being practiced and that it is quite appropriate to combine the best of the old with the best of the new. In fact, there are three areas in which staff need to be reminded of the valuable foundational work already accomplished that will act as major building blocks for the new work.

1. Shared Decision Making

This is the first pre-requisite of successful decision making. If the school has developed what Calhoun (1994) refers to as a common public agreement about how collective decisions are made and implemented, then the staff needs to be reminded of this—and informed that the same agreed on process will be used as the basis for the new, amended style of working. Indeed, reflects Calhoun, one cannot see how a school faculty could begin to apply themselves to data-based school improvement efforts without preliminary work on decision making being in place.

Saphier et al., (1989, pp. 6–8) have described how to make decisions that stay made. They pointed out that in order to bind staff members together to make legitimate decisions, the process of decision making has to be improved. Leaders, they say, have to pay attention to decision-making processes if they expect to enlist the faculty in solving problems, changing instructional practices, and carrying out school improvement plans. As a result, Saphier, et al., identify twelve guidelines for making good decisions:

- Identify the issue or goal.

- Find out how much discretion is needed to take action in this area.

- Determine who will make the preliminary and final decisions:

  - an individual or group at a higher level in the organization

  - you, as administrator, unilaterally

- you, as administrator, with input from staff

- you, as administrator, and staff by consensus

- staff, with input from you, as administrator

- staff by consensus

- staff by vote

- subgroup of staff, with input from others

- subgroup of staff unilaterally

- individual staff members unilaterally

■ Communicate who will make the decision.

■ State the non-negotiables.

■ Determine the full consequences of the decision.

■ Involve all parties whose working conditions will be affected by the decision.

■ Make clear the timeline for making and implementing the decision.

■ Make the decision, then issue a statement containing the key points of the decision.

■ Provide for review, evaluation, and revision of the decision.

■ Close the loop — communicate the reasons for the decision to all affected parties.

■ Plan how to monitor and support the implementation of the decision.

These guidelines demonstrate how important it is to have clarity around decision making: *who* will make *which* decisions, *when*, and *how* the decisions will be made. Many schools have developed protocols that describe how decision making will occur. Indeed, as Calhoun (1994, pp. 26–27) counsels, much of the clarity needed to guide shared decision making should be encapsulated in a constitution or charter that describes how school-wide decisions are made and specifies the areas in which teachers and administrators will be equally responsible for decisions. Staff members also need to understand, however, that shared decision making is not an end in itself — it has to be *for* something else (e.g., data-driven school improvement). The same, of course, is true of data-driven school improvement — which is needed for increasing student achievement.

2. School Improvement

Every school has a history with school improvement—and staff should be reminded periodically of their track record with school improvement planning and implementation. Data-driven school improvement that builds on the foundational work of shared decision making denotes a certain kind of school improvement. Described by Holly and Southworth (1989) and Joyce, Wolf and Calhoun (1993), the "Developing School" is the self-developing, self-renewing school.

According to Joyce et al., (1993), the basic question has been how to blend research on organizational culture and innovation with experience in school improvement, and generate a design for an organization that is self-renewing (see Gardner, 1963, p. 4). The self-renewing school, they say, is the antithesis of the kind of educational workplace where so many new ideas are stillborn; where educators feel that they live in a torrent of change mandates, while little changes. The common experience is one of many changes, yet not much changing. Teachers, they say, have been virtually shell-shocked by the barrage of "semi-changes" that sap their energy but make few substantial differences. In the self-renewing school, however, all members will feel that they are making a difference. They will feel that they are in "an accelerated and richer state of growth, working together for school improvement" (Gardner, p. 5). Moreover, say Joyce et al., it is...collective inquiry concerning the effects of our actions on students—learning with and from each other and gaining in knowledge, technical skills, and interpersonal relations—(that) sustains school renewal (p. 5).

3. Strong Instructional Leadership

School principals, building on their past practice, have to explain how they will behave in this new scenario and, consequently, what colleagues can expect from them. They would do well to use material from recent national reports and publications. For instance, with the help of principals throughout the association, NAESP (2001) has identified six standards for what principals should know and be able to do. Taken together, says the report, they form a definition of what constitutes instructional leadership:

- Lead schools in a way that places student and adult learning at the center.

- Set high expectations and standards for the academic and social development of all students and the performance of adults.

- Demand content and instruction that ensure student achievement of agreed-upon academic standards.

- Create a culture of continuous learning for adults tied to student learning and other school goals.

- Use multiple sources of data as diagnostic tools to assess, identify, and apply instructional improvement.

- Actively engage the community to create shared responsibility for student and school success.

This NAESP report reinforces the central tenet of the ISLLC Standards that student learning must be the focus of schools and should drive all decisions school leaders make.

Hessel and Holloway (2002) have also summarized the kind of leadership required in the data-driven, self-renewing school.

> The effective school leader works for continuous school improvement achieved through a cyclical, or recursive, process in which the school's vision, mission, and strategic plans are developed, implemented, monitored, evaluated, and revised. The leader understands the change process, and knows that part of that process is the systematic examination of assumptions, beliefs, and practices and of the school culture and climate. The process includes also identifying, clarifying, and addressing barriers to achieving the school's vision. The effective leader assures that the process is inclusive, involving all stakeholders...He or she uses a variety of information sources, including assessment and demographic data, to make decisions (pp. 21-22).

Hessel and Holloway go on to say,

> As plans to implement the vision are put into action, the school leader must assure that these plans are monitored from the beginning and evaluated over time. The school leader systematically collects and analyzes data on the school progress towards realizing the vision. This monitoring and evaluation must be tied directly to objectives and strategies. Demonstrating a clear understanding of the link between effective teaching and student learning, the school leader also regularly collects data on both student achievement and teacher performance...Monitoring and evaluating the vision...is an ongoing inclusive process. It includes both informal and formal

methods. Stakeholders are afforded opportunities, through such strategies as surveys or questionnaires, open forums, and dialogues, to indicate how well they believe the implementation plan is working. The accomplished school leader invites the appropriate stakeholders to analyze and review this information during the year (pp. 42-43).

From the very beginning, then, the principal has to explain his/her role as "Keeper of the Vision." Indeed, from the outset, the principal is the conscience of the self-renewing school. In explaining this contribution to school improvement, the principal commits to tracking—with data—the implementation of the vision over time. This is the new version of strong instructional leadership.

However, caution Joyce, Wolf, and Calhoun (1993), strong leadership should not be equated with "a strong man or woman who manipulates others" (p. 29). Strength in the context of the self-renewing school, they say, lies in the ability to generate a productive, collaborative community that is bound together in a democratic framework and process. The most effective leaders "do not simply follow established formulas for getting things done, but are effective diagnosticians, problem solvers, and leaders of others to find needs and create solutions" (p. 29).

The same authors point out that "leadership" is a collective term and that leadership can be generated at all levels of the local system. Staff members, therefore, need to be reminded of the importance of continuing the use of a school improvement team that crosses all role groups within the organization and coordinates all school improvement activities. This central team is the first step toward, and the fulcrum of, the establishment of an infrastructure for data-based decision making within the school.

In an introductory session for all staff members, it is essential that the principal reminds those present of their previous efforts in the three areas described above. The school leader should also give witness to his or her continuing commitment to the work. In Dubuque Schools in Iowa much of the script for such an occasion comes from district-wide Data Coach Training. These sessions involve small teams (the principal and at least two colleagues) from each building who are expected to replicate the training experiences with colleagues back at school. The idea of creating Data Coaches was first suggested by Tom Bellamy after helping to implement the "Cycles of School Improvement" (see Bellamy, Holly, and Sinisi, 1997). It is a question of building capacity within the system and as the title "Data Coach" suggests, it is a two-sided concept. It involves having a facility with data and being an enthusiast, an advocate, and a mentor for its use. As the leading Data Coach for the building, the principal has to exhibit the necessary knowledge and skills, while being the champion—and coach—for the use of data-based decision making by others. According to Noyce, Perda, and Traver (2000), "When districts and schools use data to make decisions, they have the makings of a data-driven school culture... (but) data-driven school cultures do not arise in a vacuum. They need a *major motivator* and technical and financial support" (p. 54).

The same authors also understand the importance of beginning to build capacity for growth and development. Two factors are foundational:

- An institutionalized willingness — epitomized by the principal's positive attitude — to use numbers systematically to reveal important patterns and to answer focused questions about policy, methods, and outcomes;

- An in-house search for interested colleagues. This may be the 'one person who has a quantitative bent, enough curiosity to look for patterns, and most important, a willingness to share with colleagues' (pp. 54–55).

At this early stage, then, the principal is already looking to widen the circle of technical expertise and enthusiasm. Having the other data coaches in the building is a move in this direction. Yet the principal is the one who has to convince the staff-at-large that this particular change vehicle is neither a bandwagon nor a hearse.

In Dubuque, it is emphasized that, in introducing the work to colleagues, the right mix of Content (knowledge), Process (skill acquisition), and Relationships (involving the establishment of a climate conducive to collaborative learning) has to be applied. Indeed, this balanced approach (referred to as CPR) is used throughout the training. In the initial stage, however, it is the knowledge component that has to take precedence. Consequently, the Data Coaches are provided with six pieces of content to share with the members of the Site Council, the school improvement leadership team, and with colleagues generally. The six areas covered are: Why Data-Based Decision Making; Data-Driven Continuous Improvement; Different Kinds of Data to Collect; System Levels of Data-Based Decision Making; Processes Involved in Data Use; and The Importance of External Data. The actual material used is included below in summary form (Holly and Lange, 2000).

Establishing an Infrastructure for Data-Driven School Improvement (based on Data Coach Training in Dubuque Schools)

1. Why Data-Based Decision Making

Experience tells us that, whenever any major change is promulgated, educators have a need to know "the why." In the case of data-based decision making, what needs to be said is that it is an activity (or set of activities) that serves multiple purposes. Indeed, in a very recent AASA report entitled, "Using Data To Improve Schools: What's Working" (2002), several purposes are listed. Data, it is stated, are used to

- measure student progress;

- make sure students don't fall through the cracks;

- measure program effectiveness;

- assess instructional effectiveness;

- guide curriculum development;

- allocate resources wisely;

- promote accountability;

- report to the community;

- meet state and federal reporting requirements;

- maintain educational focus;

- show trends (p. 3).

Above all, the report emphasizes, data are used to make smart decisions. As Holly and Southworth (1989) and Joyce, Wolf, and Calhoun (1993) have pointed out, data-based decision making is a *process* innovation that helps us deal more prudently with all other innovations. By grounding their work in data, staff members will be sufficiently informed as to the nature of their real needs such that they will be able to focus on a shared—and less extensive—change agenda. "Less is more" is the important concept here—by avoiding change overload and unnecessary fads and fashions, the staff will be able to concentrate on less things, do them better, and, therefore, achieve more. *Focus* is the key term to use. As Holly (1997) has written elsewhere,

> It is better to *focus* on less change but base it on more information—changes should be needs-based and data-driven (Holly, 1997).

Calhoun (1999) agrees. She advocates the use of data in order to focus on a few, important needs. Data helps to get specific, she says; it is a case of narrowing the focus to broaden effectiveness. Moreover, once these specific needs are identified, staff members have a common agenda to gather around by working together on a collective but now limited study. Noyce, Perda, and Traver (2000) point out that data-based decision making helps with prioritizing and allocating resources—another benefit of the "less-is-more" approach. It is worth reminding colleagues at this point that, without data-based decision making, there is no rhyme or reason to change selection. Indeed, according to Joyce, Wolf, and Calhoun (1993), of all the decisions that are made in self-renewing organizations, none is more important than the selection of initiatives that will pay off in terms of student learning. To increase capacity for innovation, they say, and then select weak initiatives would border on the tragic. The goal is to avoid fragmentation and superficiality of our change efforts (pp. 44–45).

2. Data-Driven Continuous Improvement

During the process of continuous improvement, there are four stages of data collection:

- Collecting *needs assessment data* in order to establish priorities and set goals

- Collecting *baseline data* to identify the current performance level in each goal area, prior to implementation

- Collecting *up-close data* (Calhoun's apt description) in order to formatively monitor progress over time and be able to make 'in-flight adjustments' during implementation

- Collecting *trend-line data* (baseline data re-visited) to show more summatively that progress has been achieved in each of the goal areas

3. Different Kinds of Data to Collect

Bernhardt (1998) maintains that there are four kinds of data that can be collected in schools and their communities. She talks about:

- Student Learning Data—standardized tests, criterion-referenced tests, teacher observation, and performance assessments

- Demographic Data—the disaggregation of information regarding enrollment, attendance, discipline referrals, dropouts, ethnicity, gender, grade level, safe and drug free schools, language proficiency, and so forth

- Perception Data—perception surveys, stakeholder perceptions, community attitudes, and observations

- School Process Data—the major programs being implemented in the school and the quality of teacher performance

Relative to student learning data, Calhoun (1999) has argued that there is a need to go beyond test scores:

> Of course, schools need to look at general information such as grade promotion and retention rates, attendance, standardized test scores, and so on. In their focus area though— which could be writing informative prose, reading comprehension, non-routine problem solving, or whatever—they need to regularly

collect what I call up-close data, data as close to the student performance as possible. That data may be collected weekly on some goals, or gathered monthly or every six weeks. For example, if the school were seeking to improve informative writing, teachers would bring samples of student writing to their work groups at least once a month. To facilitate this work, teachers might study very closely and share with their peer coaching group just three students: a student with low fluency in writing, one with moderate ability, and a third who seems very skilled (p. 58).

These are important words to put in front of educators. Calhoun's down-to-earth approach makes the ideas very accessible to teachers and their everyday classrooms. By suggesting that teachers track and share the development of just three students, she makes it all sound so possible.

4. System Levels of Data-Based Decision Making

It is important for teachers to hear that, although there are different system levels for data use (state, district, school, classroom, and student), their purview is localized—to some extent the school, but mainly the classroom and the students. Moreover, they also need to hear that the other system levels are being mobilized in support of their in-house efforts. In Dubuque, for example, the Data Coaches receive not only the training but also regular site visits by either central office support staff or external consultants.

5. Processes Involved in Data Use

Data have to be collected, analyzed, interpreted, reported on, and the emerging lessons used to guide some action steps. This cycle of data use is another constant factor in all data-based decision making efforts. Again, the recent AASA report is a useful reference. In answering the question, "What is data-driven decision making?" the following steps are listed:

- Collecting data

- Analyzing data

- Reporting data

- Using data for school improvement

- Communicating through data (p. 3)

6. The Importance of External Data

In Data-Driven School Improvement, it is crucial to consult both internal data (data collected within the school community that speak to the school's current performance) and external data (the world of ideas outside the school). While internal data are used to identify internal needs and problems, it is external data from which the solutions will emerge. Indeed, in a school with a data-driven culture, staff members are continuously trying to match internally identified needs with externally generated possibilities. As Calhoun (1999) reminds us,

> Teachers also must reach out to the knowledge base to interact with the ideas of others. A lot of time must be spent in study so faculty will select classroom strategies that are likely to yield increases in student achievement and to learn how to use them to a high level of skill (p. 55).

The task, she says, is to teach people how to access and screen the external knowledge base. Indeed, many schools are using her SAR (School-Wide Action Research) Matrix (see Calhoun, 2002) to map out both internal data and external data in a particular goal area—for collaborative reflection and action planning. Calhoun describes the matrix as a guide for structuring inquiry and action. By using this process, she says, educators will be able to "see through and beyond" the data to the changes that are necessary and to the specific student performances required (Calhoun, 1999 p. 55).

The six areas listed above represent the content of the training sessions in Dubuque and elsewhere in Iowa (Holly, 2002). Taken together, the content of the six-item agenda provides a shared language for data-driven school improvement. In order for the participants to start processing the content, however, the principal has to play the role of resource manager. Colleagues need to be able to follow up the initial training by using the kind of resources that will strengthen their learning. Fortunately, there are several handbooks currently available that contain practical exercises, activities, and visual tools. Holcomb (1999) explains in laymen's terms the importance of "Getting Excited About Data." Her useful book contains "A Design for Data Day" which can be used by administrators at both district and school levels to introduce the whole question of how to go about using data. Her carousel idea for data analysis has been used most effectively by educators in Iowa in such introductory sessions. Wahlstrom (1999), Bernhardt (1998), Schmoker (2001), Garmston and Wellman (1999), and Levesque, et al., (1998) have also produced worthwhile workbooks that teachers can use to supplement their training. The point here is that, by being aware of these excellent resources, the principal can support the training efforts from the outset. Indeed, nothing will happen, concludes Calhoun (1999), "...unless the principal and a core of leaders are fully engaged and willing to use all they know ... to help everyone move forward" (p. 56).

One school leader who totally understands this message is Barb Shoenauer, principal of Irving Elementary School in Dubuque, Iowa, and an original participant in Data Coach Training. Irving School is a National Blue Ribbon School of Excellence, largely because everything that happens there is driven by data. This is definitely a school that experiences what Noyce, Perda, and Traver (2000) refer to as a "data-driven culture." Reading the principal's reflections concerning her role in data-based decision making over several years reminds us that, while principal leadership and drive are essential in Quadrant One, in order to transition to Quadrant Two, ways have to be found to bring colleagues more on board. According to Ms. Shoenauer (2002),

> As with any new program or initiative it is so easy, as a principal, to "do it yourself." Principals see this "do it yourself" strategy as a timesaver and also as a way to assure that there is a high quality end product. Data-based decision making is so vital in today's educational scene that principals must understand it is not effective or internalized until staff members learn about it, practice it, and see how it directly benefits individual classrooms and students. It cannot belong only to the principal. Also, teachers are on a continuum with some using only basals to drive instruction while others are using data in a very sophisticated manner for educational decision making. The challenge for the principal is to help teachers find the middle ground where data drives decisions within the parameters of district/state adopted curriculum based on standards and benchmarks utilizing both district- and school-based data.

> To begin the process of school-wide decision making based on data I feel that it is especially important to model the process for staff. As a first step in this process I worked with the staff in two areas of data collection, one academic and the other related to school climate. In the area of climate we developed a survey and I administered it to students in grades 3 through 6 to gain their input regarding several topics that had been identified by the school community as important to nurture positive school climate. The results of this survey were shared with staff and students. The discussions that followed really helped the school community identify several areas that needed to be addressed and

develop programs that have improved the school community. Academically, a process was designed to utilize the data from the Iowa Test of Basic Skills item analysis to determine grade level and individual student strengths and weaknesses. This data was then matched to student needs to determine if appropriate programming was presently available. At this point the total staff saw the benefit of using data to make decisions regarding these specified areas. They had not made the transition to personally acquiring and utilizing data for their own instructional improvement. (Personal correspondence)

What is clear from these illuminating reflections is that, in order to transition to the next stage of development, Quadrant Two, the principal's role has to change, however subtly.

Guided Practice (Quadrant Two)

In Quadrant Two, the Exploration Quadrant, content is joined in importance by process (skill acquisition) and then, in succession, by the strength that comes with supportive relationships. The principal's first—and major—task in this quadrant is to ensure the transfer of skills to colleagues. In passing the baton, principals now have to work with and through others to be successful. While still the orchestrator of the work, the principal increasingly becomes the facilitator of other people's learning. Three factors—that are all part of capacity-building—come into play at this point. The first is staff training, the second is the establishment of facilitating structures, and the third is systemic alignment.

With staff training, organized by the principal, comes the transfer of skills. With the transfer of skills comes the beginning of the transfer of ownership. The more colleagues are trained in the necessary skills and methods, the more they own the initiative. The more they feel the skills are theirs, the more they are likely to use them. According to Noyce, Perda, and Traver (2000):

> Training those at the building level is a powerful approach because it puts information analysis directly in the hands of those most responsible for making and effecting decisions at the instructional level... Administrators, faculty, and other key stakeholders support this work by allocating resources to establish and maintain a data collection system and by training personnel who are as close to the classroom as possible (p. 56).

Potentially powerful, perhaps, but, as Calhoun (1999) points out, it is the quality of the training and learning experience that makes the difference:

> Many school leaders are familiar with the Joyce and Showers training design model and can be quite articulate about it. But when I look at the staff development provided by the school or district, that's not what I see happening. When I look at school and district improvement plans, provisions have not been made to support staff in expanding their curriculum and instructional repertoire. So through dialogue, I try to activate their knowledge about learning theory. We discuss what we know about changing cognition and behavior. We talk about the need for information, multiple demonstrations, and regular practice with the skills. I try to help them tap into what they know about good learning theory, and then to get them to use it on themselves.

> It's also important that principals and teacher facilitators, school district staff, intermediate service agency staff, and state department of education staff—all of us who have accepted the responsibility of leading other adults—must model whatever we are supporting or promoting (p. 58).

Multiple demonstrations, regular skill practice, the application of good learning theory, and modeling are all required to be successful in Quadrant Two. Indeed, everything we have learned about effective staff development (see Joyce and Showers, 1988, and Sparks and Hirsh, 1997) has to be applied to these learning experiences. During this quadrant, participants have to travel from basic competency to the new challenges that come with personal practice. Guided practice helps initially, as does mentoring and the "non-feedback" approach to peer coaching that encourages the learner to observe the master practitioner in action. Demonstrations are best supported by simulated practice in workshop settings. During the Data Coach Training sessions, for instance, participants are encouraged to work with other schools' data first, to get the feel of data analysis before beginning to use and make sense of their own data. Using their own data, however, does add a powerful degree of authenticity and excitement to the proceedings.

The best training, however, has to be accompanied by the establishment of facilitating structures. These include the provision of time-institutionalized procedures, and working within a team structure. In arguing for time for teachers to look at data and study the external knowledge base, Calhoun (1999) wonders why this rarely happens. "It shouldn't be so hard for people to work together, study student learning, and to apply good learning theory to themselves. It's almost impossible to be a learning community if you don't have time to work together regularly" (p. 56).

Common planning time for collaborative data use is essential. This provision becomes part of the institutionalized procedures demanded by Noyce, Perda, and Traver (2000). The development of a data-driven culture, they say, "...requires a few knowledgeable staff members, supportive administrators, and institutionalized procedures for distributing data collection instruments, retrieving data, writing reports, and informing decisions" (p. 53).

The creation of data using teams is another major support. Noyce, et al., (2000) advocate for the establishment of a central data team at the school level that is linked to the teachers on one side and the school's administration and the district's central office on the other. What Joyce, Wolf, and Calhoun (1993) refer to as a cross-role leadership team (of which the principal is a full or ex-officio member) becomes the centerpiece of a data-using infrastructure. Study groups, learning teams, and action research teams are other examples of school-based teamwork for data-processing. In Dubuque, the Data Coaches, including the principal, are encouraged to link first with the school's Site Council (which serves the purpose of a central data team) and then with the members of the school improvement action teams. These action teams are usually assembled in line with the building's school improvement goals. In this way, data use is placed at the disposal of school improvement and distributed throughout the school. Moreover, argues Calhoun (1993), the principal, as the organizational and managerial facilitator, is best placed to provide these teams with resources, information, and technical assistance. The importance of this facilitator role should not be overlooked. As Calhoun (1994) concludes, "Alone, the principal cannot make action research a successful experience; but without the principal as organizational and managerial facilitator, teachers find it almost impossible to successfully pursue school-wide inquiry" (p. 119).

In terms of systemic alignment, Noyce et al., (2000) support the idea of establishing similar data-use networks both within the school and within the school system. The goal is to generate a capacity for data use throughout the local system so that the system itself embodies data literacy. This requires, they say, a free flow of data within schools and within the same school district. Again, it is the school principal in his or her boundary role that is best placed to make these connections.

In the self-renewing educational organization envisioned by Joyce, Wolf, and Calhoun (1993), the principal is *the* link between what happens at the school level and at the local system level. To be site-based alone, they say, is to be deficient of all the power that can be harnessed throughout the local system. This is why site-based decision making lacks the power that comes with system-wide, shared decision making.

The role played by Nancy Bradley for Dubuque Schools is a good example of how central office staff can support school principals within the self-renewing local organization. In her role as Director of School Improvement and Staff Development, Bradley works alongside school principals and Site Council members to find and organize professional development opportunities that match the needs identified in the school data. According to Joyce, Wolf, and Calhoun (1993), the three spheres of the organization—the teacher, the school, and the district—are responsible for improving instruction and supporting one another. In Dubuque, Nancy Bradley is a pivotal figure within this support nexus. For instance, she has been an unstinting supporter of Data Coach Training and has been instrumental in the involvement of other central office support staff. Indeed, at the training sessions, each school team is accompanied by one of her district-level colleagues in their School Liaison role. Moreover, in a recent article, Calhoun (2002) describes how a state department can become a partner in such a support network. She cites the "Every Child Reads" initiative in Iowa in which the state department, school district personnel, school principals, and teachers are working together to improve student learning. Central to this initiative is the concept of action research for data-driven school improvement.

Reflecting on the activities in this quadrant, Shoenauer (2002) makes the point that the development of teacher expertise is inevitably differential:

> The next step in the process for principals is to cultivate those staff leaders who show that love for use of data and a willingness to share their learning with their colleagues. This is when the importance of patience in the process is vital. To bring the entire staff on board is a multiple year process. It involves identifying the training time and technology applications vital to use for this type of decision making. Staff members also have to become comfortable in their ability to find appropriate data. Without these skills staff members may get so caught up in only the data collection that they do not see the wonderful applications they can make with the information they acquire.

> Principals must accept that the range in staff interest and skill level will be broad. While several staff members might design a complex school-wide database, there will also be staff members who are experimenting with the personal use of simple data as a resource for teaching their students. This is OK. Just as we accept the strengths and interests of students so we also must do the same with staff. The goal should be to see continuous improvement in staff learning and application in the area of using data in decision making. (Personal correspondence)

These words from a very experienced principal reflect the wisdom that comes with years on the job. They remind us that faculty members are always going to be at different stages of personal development and, indeed, at different points in the four quadrants model posited in this chapter. While this phenomenon may have some disadvantages, there is one huge advantage — those faculty members who are at a more advanced stage of development can be positioned to mentor and coach their other colleagues who are experiencing the earlier stages of growth. At this point the approach to peer coaching that involves critical feedback from more experienced observers comes into its own. This, of course, signifies a departure from the non-feedback model of peer coaching that fits Quadrant Two activities so well. It also signifies that the learner has transitioned into Quadrant Three.

Trying It Out (Quadrant Three)

In Quadrant Three, the Application Quadrant, all the new learning is applied by individuals, small teams, or the whole faculty on a much more everyday, on-going basis. Daily practice replaces simulated practice; dependent learning is replaced by more independent and interdependent learning. Being an independent learner, however, entails accepting more personal responsibility and, in turn, part of being personally responsible is to accept the challenge of accountability.

As Fullan (1993) has observed, as the pressure increases during implementation, so must the level of support. And this is where the principal comes in. Once again, the principal plays a crucial dual role in Quadrant Three. It is the principal who has to keep up the pressure and make sure people are keeping on track. This involves setting, and keeping to, deadlines, ensuring that task expectations are clear, and issuing the challenges that come with increased accountability. On the other side of the pressure coin, however, has to be all the psychological and technical support needed by those making changes happen.

This is not the time for the principal to stay in his or her office to clear the seemingly ever-increasing in-tray. This is the time to be out there among colleagues acting like some unofficial cheerleader, exhorting and challenging, helping and supporting. The kind of principal whose leadership style can best be described as "formal hands-on" (as opposed to "formal hands-off" or even "informal hands-on" and, in comparatively rare cases, "informal hands-off") thrives in this dualistic scenario. He or she has enough formality to be respected (and, therefore, heeded), but is sufficiently "hands-on" to be right there with colleagues in the cauldron of implementation. Neither a monarch nor a push-over, this principal gains in respect by rolling up his or her sleeves and working alongside colleagues on the same tasks and to the same deadlines.

What does this quadrant look like in terms of data-based decision making? According to Shoenauer (2002),

> As the process becomes more complex in application the level of data compilation will become more specialized and more meaningful to staff. This is the time when the staff needs to use data compilation to make decisions based

on the needs of the school, the classroom and the individual child. You should also begin hearing informal conversations among staff regarding data and how they will use it. (Personal correspondence)

Becky Taylor Harris is a teacher colleague of Barb Shoenauer's at Irving School. It is fascinating to read her reflections as a fellow recipient of the Data Coach training and as a member of the "Data Coach Team" in the school. While not a principal, she is clearly part of the (albeit unofficial) leadership of the school and her teacher leader perspective highlights not only the complexities of this stage of development but also the rigors of having to play a leadership role.

As a participant in the data coach training and a member of our data coach team, I have benefited from the discussions, which helped set a direction for our school team. The role of the data coach in the building may be one of the most challenging aspects of the program. There is much resistance to being expected to do more paperwork. Collecting data entails more paperwork, so this data collection must be meaningful for people to cooperate. The data coach may be seen as a harbinger of more work, rather than a resource to support action research and school improvement as well as student learning.

The data coaches need to encourage the staff in this work and constantly keep the flow of data in front of the staff. This cannot be a venture that is kept out of sight. The data needs to be discussed on a regularly scheduled basis. Data coaches need to help provide ways to efficiently analyze data in the most useful way for teachers. The discussions need to take place at Site Council, with the whole staff, at grade level team meetings and individually in a reflective way. Of course, making adequate time available to do this will be the biggest challenge of all. New habits will need to be established for some people, and these people will need a lot of support and encouragement to see the importance of this effort.

Data coaches need to be overall guides in this process, helping to coordinate the information, presenting it in useful formats and keeping it accessible. Action teams will need to be purposeful in setting aside time to discuss the collected data on a recurring basis. In our building, a large portion of the data is related to the area of language arts. The responsibility of dealing with data may need to be redistributed so the language arts action team isn't overwhelmed by the quantity of information.

Finally, the action teams will need a way to disseminate the data and discuss it with the stakeholders. Trends, evaluations of interventions and the effectiveness of strategies will provide endless material for discussions. As a member of the language arts action team, I see this as a daunting, but necessary task for our school to take the next step toward providing effective instruction for all our students. (Personal correspondence)

Arising from these insightful reflections are so many issues both for principals leading data-based decision making efforts and for data-based decision making itself. Both participants mention the increasing need for specialization for the work to be meaningful to colleagues. In schools in Dubuque, action teams have been used extensively to perform this role. Action teams are aligned with the school improvement goals of the school, one goal per team, and all faculty members are strongly encouraged to join at least one of these teams, hopefully in terms of an interest-based decision on the part of each person.

At Irving, where there is a highly advanced structure of action team membership, all the teams are intentionally linked to each of the grade level teams, thus ensuring two-way communication on school improvement matters. The action team members are responsible for the collection, analysis, and dissemination of all the data internally and externally pertinent to their focus area. The grade level teams are charged with operationalizing the ideas emanating from the action teams, and providing feedback concerning the ideas in action. By the action team structure enabling staff members to "chunk" the work and to choose the goal area of most interest to each of them, inroads are made into the complexities of the work in two important ways. The sheer amount of school improvement work is divided, hopefully on a fairly equal basis, among the teams and, by being able to focus on an area of personal interest and investment, the work becomes that much more meaningful to individual members of staff.

As the orchestrator-in-chief of all these activities, there are lessons here for every principal to apply. An additional task for the principal, of course, is to make sure that no particular group is becoming too overburdened. This deployment issue is crucial for both staff logistics and motivation. There is another major benefit accruing from the deployment of staff action teams. They connect school-level operations and decision making with the everyday activities at the classroom level. They bridge the work of schools and the work of classrooms. What is decided at the school level, therefore, (say, in the Site Council where all action teams are represented) has much more likelihood of being implemented in individual classrooms. Conversely, classroom issues have much more chance of being aired (and acted upon) at the organizational level. It is the principal's task to attend to the maintenance and sustenance of these organizational and structural issues and staff dynamics over time.

On the data processing side, there are also several lessons to be learned from these reflective educators. First, when goals are truly needs-based and data-driven, working in goal area action teams becomes more meaningful to the participants — especially when they worked with the data, identified the needs and helped to select the goals in the first place. Data lend relevance, authenticity, and immediacy to the change process. Decisions that are grounded in data are not only informed decisions, they are *our* decisions. The more inclusive the process, therefore, the more staff ownership grows. Second, given the necessary time allocation, the ongoing collection of data replenishes all staff discussion and reflection at whatever level of the school. Data use is not a single event; it becomes a way of life. It is the way we go about our business. Third, data coaches are required to guide the continuing work and provide crucial support in terms of technical know-how — especially in areas like data analysis where educators initially lack confidence in their own abilities. Fourth, data speak to us at various levels of the school organization.

Given this, there seems to be a pattern of development with which staff members seem more comfortable. Acclimatization to using data seems to go more smoothly when teachers work initially with whole-school data (as when they study needs-assessment data prior to identifying whole-school goals). While these data may well speak to an academic area, they are school-wide data and not personal data (i.e., data related to my classroom, my teaching, and the learning of my students). Clearly the transition from school-level investigation to classroom study involves increasing accountability pressures. It will not happen overnight. In the meantime, it's the principal's task to establish a supportive context for the transition so staff members will feel safe enough to face being challenged. Again, it is useful to read the reflections of Becky Taylor Harris:

The process is needs-based and data-driven. A prime example of this is our spelling data, which was reviewed several years ago. Spelling scores on ITBS were significantly lower than they should have been. This provided an opportunity for a purposeful intervention, which differed from our current practice. Our school decided to collect baseline data through ITBS scores and the Test of Written Spelling. After the new spelling program had been implemented for a year, data was again collected using the same assessment methods. The data supported the effectiveness of the new intervention...

This step in the data collection process is wrought with difficulties, including buy-in by staff members and time to critically discuss the results. There is a need by staff to believe in the importance of the information being collected and analyzed. Without this buy-in, there can be sabotage of the process, either intentionally or unintentionally.

This last issue of buy-in leads to the importance of relationships. The relationships of the people involved in collecting, disseminating and sharing data are crucial to the forward progress of data collection implementation. Without a certain level of trust and a shared focus on what is important (student learning), there can be no forward progress. This still seems to be evolving at our school...Some staff may feel threatened by the availability of information about their students. They may feel it is a reflection of their teaching ability. The emphasis needs to be continually focused on student learning and how we, as teachers, can make adjustments to improve it. It is not a matter of competition, but a joint effort to better our teaching and our students' performance. (Personal correspondence)

Clearly, then, the transition from working with whole-school data (in Irving's case, spelling data) to focusing on individual classroom data is not an easy or straightforward one. Somewhat ironically, as the relevance of looking at specific classroom data grows, so does the degree of personal threat. Yet, while the focus stays at the whole-school level, it is possible for individual teachers to walk away from the data. Many commentators (including Lange, 1998) have pointed out that the change process and learning cycle are akin to the grief cycle. Learning always involves some unlearning. The resulting sense of loss is accompanied by feelings of anger, denial, and resistance. The onus is on the principal and other school leaders to nurture colleagues through this difficult period.

As previously mentioned, if Quadrant One activities are mainly focused on the imparting of *content* and Quadrant Two entails the *process* of skill transference, then Quadrant Three stands or falls on the strength of staff *relationships*. As Becky Taylor Harris emphasizes, trust and time for staff dialogue are crucial ingredients at this point. What also emerges from her critique is that the quality of the learning climate (which the principal has such an important role in creating) will have a direct bearing on the depth of personal analysis and conversation. Above all, however, the challenge is to find ways to embrace accountability at the classroom level. Currently, at Irving, some staff members are working on a school-wide database that will contain information student by student, classroom by classroom. As a consequence, the stakes are getting higher. According to Becky Taylor Harris,

> We have a database in development. Recommendations for the information to be collected and stored on the database have been gathered from all the constituents, including Site Council, teachers and staff. This improves the ownership of the information when staff deems the information to be useful and meaningful. The magnitude of the project seems daunting at this point and there have been illuminating discussions at staff and Site Council meetings about who will have access to this information on the database and how it will be shared, interpreted and stored. It seems like an immense issue. Every question opens another potential area for discussion. These discussions are very helpful, but I believe the database has to be easily accessible to teachers to use in instructional decision making to be worth the incredible amount of work and time involved. It shows great promise.

I hope to continue to be integrally involved in data collection at our school. My experience with this has been very rewarding in spite of the time and hard work involved in the process. I know that data is indispensable when making instructional decisions. I also think that this is the trend of the future and will continue to be important when making instructional decisions. We can no longer choose to teach something simply because we like it or we think our students will. It is imperative that our instructional decisions are based in solid teaching practices. (Personal correspondence)

Irving School continues with the struggle of how to use data in meaningful ways. The fact that it is a struggle would indicate to these authors that the school is at a critical juncture in its development and is making important headway. The faculty would seem to be moving from using data to *really* using data; and, in so doing, asking all the right, but difficult, questions and experiencing all the predictable emotional reactions. Encouraged by their principal, they are searching for the next, right moves. The product of their quest is the kind of activity called for by classroom action research. In teacher-based action research (see Holly, 2002, Calhoun, 1994, and Sagor, 2000), whether operating individually or in small teams, classroom practitioners confront the gaps in their practice between their espoused values and their current realities, as evidenced in their accumulating data. As Becky Taylor Harris observes,

The underlying need to be able to have successful trusting relationships between all stakeholders lies in the ability to self assess one's own teaching and its impact on student learning. The more a teacher can do this comfortably, in a non-threatening environment, the easier it is to discuss student learning with others.

Teachers must constantly question their own effectiveness and their teaching strategies. It is easy to get into a rut of doing what one has always done and failing to adjust as needed to meet students' needs. If the focus is kept on student learning, then discussion can take place about how best to impact this...

The implications for me have been apparent in my action research project. I am piloting the *Soar to Success* reading program with a select group of 6th grade students. I had the opportunity to receive training in this instructional approach, which is bound to benefit more than the current group of students. I am able to participate in a regularly scheduled group discussion with other special educators piloting the program. We have the opportunity to talk about how this project has impacted our students' learning, and any modifications we feel may be necessary for special education students. I have greatly appreciated the opportunity to have these discussions because they are immediately relevant to my situation. We share our up-close data, which we are collecting on a continuous basis. We have been able to discuss what we consider are reasonable expectations for our students. It has been very helpful to be able to receive and share feedback when branching out in a new instructional direction.

It seems to be the nature of special education to question the effectiveness of a particular teaching strategy. This questioning is essential to our students' progress. It is also healthy for us as special educators. Without this professional questioning, our students run the risk of failing to meet their potential. This is absolutely unacceptable. We have a responsibility to question our instructional practices to improve our effectiveness. (Personal correspondence)

When introducing Quadrant Three in this chapter, we used Forsythe's words, "...the merging of mind and heart into self-actualizing and self-assessment," to describe the essence of this stage. These teacher words quoted above provide rich testimony of what actually happens when a practitioner experiences this merger of mind and heart, reflection and commitment, in pursuit of data-based self-improvement. What started by being lodged in the heart and mind of the principal has been transferred to the person that interacts with children on a daily basis, the classroom teacher. Such commitment takes the form of a deep-set resolve to continue the pursuit of improving teacher effectiveness and student learning.

Calhoun (2002) describes experiences very similar to those detailed above. Indeed, in helping to initiate and sustain action research in schools, Holly and Calhoun play very similar consultant roles and are continually learning much the same kind of lessons. "My experience," says Calhoun, "is that regular use of multiple sources of data to inform us about student performance or our own performance is often threatening at first, because it requires that we juxtapose our practices and our students' performance against exemplary research-based practices and high levels of student performance attained in similar settings. The resulting confrontation and social turmoil, however, may be natural accompaniments to substantive change" (Calhoun, 2002, p. 20).

The confrontation and social turmoil referred to by Calhoun is exactly what Becky Taylor Harris has described. Ms. Taylor Harris herself is a wonderful example of the phenomenon, of teacher leaders emerging to help colleagues through the vicissitudes of school improvement. Again, based on her experiences, Calhoun (2002) is able to make this same point.

> The good news is that when groups have adequate organizational support in using data as a source of information to guide practice, leadership generally surfaces within the group. These leaders provide examples of using data to make instructional and curriculum changes and model informed decision making and problem solving in action. Their schools begin to use on-site data and the external knowledge base as sources for continually assessing the effectiveness of actions and current practices. This emerging leadership often signals a change in the social system of the school. It doesn't come easily in most settings, but with opportunity and leadership from school and district administration, it happens. Along with benefits for students, educators feel more professional (Calhoun, 2002, pp. 20).

With the likes of Nancy Bradley providing ongoing district support and Barb Shoenauer continuing to exercise leadership at the building level, it is up to all those teacher leaders like Becky Taylor Harris to translate the work into action at the classroom level, the essence of Quadrant Three activities.

By focusing on the very real experiences of those at Irving School in Dubuque, we have learned much about Quadrant Three:

- The going certainly gets tougher. Quadrant Three represents the stormy waters before the calmer seas of Quadrant Four.

- Educators, according to Noyce, Perda, and Traver (2000), begin to ask hard questions about the impact of curricular programs, staff development, and teaching and learning.

- Teachers understand that they can use data to improve their classroom practice and, therefore, student learning.

- Teachers are more likely to use data, however, when encouraged and assisted by teacher leaders and when given the protection and mutual support that come with working in teams. In a recent article, Bambino (2002) describes how Critical Friends Groups, by providing structures for effective feedback and strong support, are currently helping teachers commit to data-based improvement efforts.

- The work with data gradually becomes more sophisticated. As Noyce, Perda, and Traver (2000) concur, more advanced schools like Irving are currently experimenting with student information management systems that have a school-wide importance but also have the potential to inform instructional decision making in each and every classroom.

- Noyce et al., (2000) also point to the increased potential for rendering ourselves more accountable. Armed with data, they say, schools can respond proactively, rather than reactively, to demands for accountability. The Irving experience, however, while not invalidating this statement, would suggest that it's a process wrought with difficulties. Dealing with people's fears and sensitivities is clearly a major task.

- However, schools that overcome these obstacles and learn how to embrace accountability also find ways to share their data with the various stakeholder groups. While, in Dubuque Schools, the Site Council is often the first venue for such data-based conversations between teachers, administrators, parents, business partners, and community representatives, as Calhoun (1994) concludes, the principal is still best placed to be the spokesperson for the process of data use with parents, school board members, and the community.

- The role of principal becomes more important, not less. It is fascinating to contemplate how many role changes the principal has to undertake during the various quadrants and stages of development. In Quadrant Three, principals support teachers by giving them a voice, listening to them, and acting on what they say. Principals, in addition, encourage teachers' improvement efforts and protect them as they risk new behaviors.

According to Elmore (2002), schools that build their own internal accountability systems by opening up the black box of teaching and learning, demand a new form of instructional leadership. He says,

> Today's principals are the generation of principals who are going to reinvent the organization of schooling — much more so than superintendents and mid-level administrators in school systems. The notion of a school as a continuously improving organization with its focus highly concentrated on instructional practice and on the problems of how students learn and don't learn ultimately rests in the relationship between principals and teachers. This generation of principals is the generation that is going to lead us through this massive shift in the view of what administration is all about (p. 43).

Principals like Barb Shoenauer are definitely in the vanguard of this movement. She has the positional authority, the knowledge, the skills, and, above all, the kind of relationships with staff members that make her the leader of instructional improvement at Irving.

Internalizing the Process (Quadrant Four)

Quadrant Four is about integration. The learning is now integrated with previous learning experiences within the learner. It is now part of what this person is and does on an everyday basis. Habituation has been achieved. Application of the new ideas is continuing and grounded in deep personal commitment. The learner has come to believe in the importance of the change effort — through the gratifying experience of successful application. What began as an externalized set of ideas has been internalized. As Shoenauer concludes in her reflections:

> You know you have reached your goal when staff members are at your door asking for the most current test results so they can work with them. They might also stop by because they are so excited with their new database or some recent student results that they just have to share with you. This is when you know the school is truly making decisions based on data. Staff members see the benefit and the buy-in is now throughout the school. You no longer need to talk about the how-to of data collection since conversations have now moved to the next level

of decision making based on data. This may seem to be a simple difference but it is a major accomplishment for a staff because they have truly internalized the process of data-based decision making. (Personal correspondence)

Working on the principle that the best way to consolidate any learning is to teach it to others, this is the ideal moment to become the teacher—to have the responsibility of imparting the learning to others. As this number of 'teachers' grows and their learning permeates the collegial dialogue of the school, integrated learning leads to integrated relationships that, in turn, lead to cultural integration. The learning becomes embedded in the culture of the school. Data use becomes business-as-usual and the school is comfortable with the challenges that come with data-based decision making.

In Quadrant Four, far from being redundant, the principal has three major and connected roles to play: 1) leading the integration of vision and practice, 2) leading the integration of data use, and 3) leading system-wide integration. Let's examine each role more closely.

Leading the Integration of Vision and Practice

The principal's first task is to challenge colleagues by asking the big questions concerning the realization of the school's vision. What, and how much, progress has been made toward achieving the vision? What does the data tell us? Are there any remaining roadblocks? What are they and how can they be removed? Where should we be concentrating our efforts in the next developmental cycle? These are all major questions and answering them will fuel the next round of school improvement and organizational learning. Working together, staff members have to be able to provide the answers and be prepared to plan how to deal with the consequences. While the staff has to accept the mantle of accountability for accomplishing *their* vision, it is the principal who acts as the catalyst for their deliberation. The principal has to be detached and objective enough to be able to stand back and pose the critical questions, yet attached enough for colleagues to be willing to accept the challenge.

The focus in these conversations should be on the issue of alignment. Ideally, the school's vision, research-based "best" practices (found in the external data) and the current reality of the school's performance (as evidenced by internal data) should all be in close alignment. By committing to gap analysis, staff members are investigating whether there are any performance gaps between the ideal, the recommended, and the actual. This is a crucial dialogue that has to be instigated by the principal. As Hessel and Holloway (2002) have reminded us, contained within the first of the ISLLC standards is the exhortation that school leaders "...should facilitate the development, articulation, implementation, and stewardship of a vision of learning that is shared and supported by the school community" (CCSSO, 1996). In Quadrant Four, by challenging colleagues to integrate their beliefs and their everyday practices, the principal is acting as the steward of the school's vision. Schools improve, says Schmoker (1996), when purpose and effort unite. It is the principal's job to keep everyone's eyes on the prize of improving student learning and then reward success when it occurs. "Sincere, regular praise, plus recognition and celebration of accomplishment, may be the most overlooked ingredient in results-oriented leadership" (Schmoker, 1996 p. 104).

Echoing Wheatley (1994), Schmoker argues that leaders must be broadcasters, targeting praise and recognition to create a unified, purposeful culture in the local system (p. 107).

Leading the Integration of Data Use

According to Holly (2002), there are four levels of data use within a local system: the district, the school, the classroom, and the student. Those at each level, he says, can look at the same data (e.g., standardized test scores) and ask themselves the same basic questions. How are we doing as a district? How are we doing as a school? How are we doing in this classroom? How am I doing as a student? There is a symmetry to these arrangements that is essential in order to achieve the power of systemic congruence. As a consequence, in Dubuque Schools, Data Profiles are being established at all four system levels. The District Profile is used for reporting to the state department and the local community; each building includes a School Profile in the annual up-date of its School Improvement Plan; and Classroom Profiles and Student Profiles are currently under construction with pilot projects established in both areas. At Irving School, for instance, each teacher has been working on a Classroom Profile during the 2001–2002 school year as a launch-pad for classroom action research. In providing guidance and support for these initiatives, Holly (2002) points out that the same generic guidelines should be applied at any of the system levels (pp. 3–4). Data Profiles, at each of four system levels, should have the following attributes:

- Each profile is a database, a kind of data-bank account into which deposits and from which withdrawals can be made.

- Such transactions are ongoing; the profile is constantly in use.

- Once created and continuously updated, the profile can be used at all four levels to:

  - gain new insights and new learnings;

  - make 'in-flight' adjustments;

  - report to various audiences, both informally and formally;

  - check on progress toward the shared, long-term vision;

  - provide feedback;

  - identify changing needs;

  - re-work current goals and/or set new goals;

  - amend action plans;

- monitor progress;

- provide, at various times, baseline data, up-close data, and trend-line data;

- show growth over time; and

- provide the material for accountability (Holly, 2002).

By working on these four Data Profiles, staff members come to understand the importance of disaggregating the data. District data have to be disaggregated for each school; school data have to be disaggregated for each classroom; and classroom data disaggregated for each student. So when the members of the Irving faculty complete their item analysis of the Iowa Test of Basic Skills (ITBS), they can ask questions that embrace all four system levels:

- What is our contribution to the achievements of the district?

- How are we doing as a building? What are our strengths and challenges?

- How am I doing in my classroom? What are my strengths and challenges?

- How is each student doing? What are his or her strengths and challenges?

By starting at the school level, Barb Shoenauer is not only issuing a collective challenge to her staff but also modeling for them how to go back and respond accordingly at the classroom and student levels. Diagnostic school improvement is to be matched by diagnostic teaching.

Leading System-Wide Integration

According to Joyce, Wolf, and Calhoun (1993), "the self-renewing organization is integrated, and its work is integrative" (p. 26). Containing the three spheres of the teacher, the school, and the district, such a local system, they say, is neither controlled by district office personnel nor reliant on site-based management and school (or even classroom) autonomy. Within such a mutually interdependent community of learners, it is the principal's task to extend the learning in one part of the organization (his or her building) to all the other parts. The principal, therefore, is the conduit and the hub for integrated, systemic learning. By encouraging the free flow of data within the local system, the principal is making yet another major contribution to the creation of a data-driven culture in the local school organization.

Within the principal's leadership of system-wide integration, he or she has to worry about the connectedness and health of both the total system and every small piece of that system. As all commentators agree, data-driven school improvement efforts are for one thing only, the improvement of learning. In Quadrant Four, therefore, the principal has two final questions to ask of the accumulating data. Is student learning improving and, if so, is there improvement for all students? As steward of the school's vision, the principal, by asking these questions, is protecting those pockets of students that might not be faring so well — but whose lack of success may be hidden in data aggregation. Issues concerning gender, ethnicity, social-economic status, mobility, and at-riskness come into play here. Even in seemingly good data there may well be disproportionate achievement gaps between various groups of students. The ultimate questions, posed by the principal, need to be, "How are we doing?" (for these various groups of students) and, to each colleague, "How are you doing?"

By posing these questions, the principal is inviting staff members to continue their own learning journeys into new cycles of development. Integration is not a destination; it is the end of one cycle of learning. The next challenge is self-directed learning. According to Glickman (2002), the effective school leader facilitates the teacher's own progress toward reflective, more autonomous, action research. The principal's gift to his or her staff members is their growing realization that, as part of their self-actualization, data use is now their concern.

Contributor—Peter Holly

Chapter contributor Peter Holly was originally a teacher, then administrator, researcher, and school improvement consultant in the United Kingdom. Since 1990 he has worked solely with schools and school districts in the United States. He was one of the lead consultants for Schools for the Twenty-first Century in Washington State, the NEA's Learning Lab project, and the New Iowa Schools initiative. Currently, he is an independent school improvement consultant working mainly in the Midwest with school systems.

FIGURE 5: THE PRINCIPAL'S ROLE IN DATA-BASED DECISION MAKING

QUADRANT 1
APPRENTICESHIP QUADRANT

Defining Roles/Expectations/Need for Improvement

Explain how this innovation fits within the overall vision of the school

Explain how each staff member fits into the successful implementation of the initiative

Communicate reasons for the decision to initiate change

Connect current practice with change efforts

Identify parameters of change (non-negotiables, time line, key points in the process)

Identify plans for monitoring and supporting the initiative

QUADRANT 2
EXPLORATION QUADRANT

Capacity Building/Skill Aquisition/Guided Practice

Provide staff training to develop skills

Establish supportive relationships to ensure the transfer of skills

Provide time for data sharing and analysis

Establish a team structure to manage data (study groups, learning teams, action research teams)

Provide resources, information, psychological and technical assistance

Align data-based decisions with the goals of the school

Connect data to work at the classroom level

QUADRANT 3
APPLICATION QUADRANT

Use multiple sources of data as diagnostic tools to assess
    instructional improvement efforts in the classroom

Systematically examine staff assumptions, beliefs, and practices
    relating to implementation efforts, school culture and classroom
    climate

Identify, clarify, and address barriers to achieving the school's vision

Allow for formal and informal methods of data collection on
    multiple levels

QUADRANT 4
INTEGRATION QUADRANT

Sustain an attitude of self-renewal throughout the school

Invite innovative solutions to problems

Widen the circle of technical expertise and enthusiasm for
    collaborative learning

Conduct an in-house search for colleagues interested in serving in
    leadership capacities

Re-visit data on a regular basis to ensure accuracy in assessing
    current performance

Adjust implementation efforts as recommended by staff / leadership
    teams

CONTRIBUTORS TO CHAPTERS 3–8

We would like to thank the individuals introduced on the following pages who contributed to this collaborative project. These accomplished professionals were able to provide us with a national perspective on timely issues facing today's school leaders. We thank them for their ideas, and in many cases, their words which we have been able to incorporate into the text.

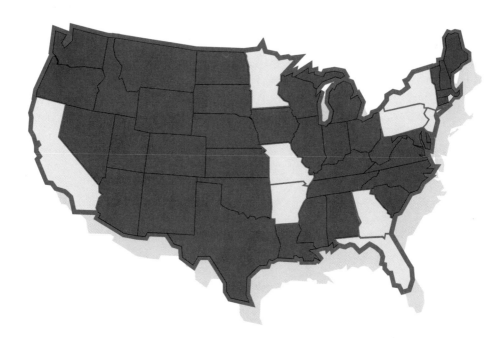

The shaded areas represent the states in which contributors to chapters 3–8 work.

MATRIX OF LOCATION OF AUTHORS, SCHOOL LEVEL, COMMUNITY TYPE

LOCATION OF AUTHORS	SCHOOL LEVEL	SCHOOL TYPE
North East ■ ■ ■ ■	Elementary ■ ■ ■	Suburban ■ ■ ■ ■ ■ ■
South ■ ■ ■	High School ■ ■ ■ ■ ■ ■	Rural ■ ■
West ■ ■ ■	Middle School ■ ■ ■	Urban ■ ■ ■ ■
Midwest ■ ■		

CASE STUDY

Jefferson Elementary
Suburban Elementary School
Grades K–8

Wayne Yamagishi is the principal for the Piner-Olivet Union School District in Santa Rosa, California. Wayne, as an educational leader, has developed schools characterized by successful educational change, high performance, community vision, and staffs that believe each child will succeed and is expected to do his/her personal best. He is a consultant for the Association of California School Administrators (ACSA) with a focus on developing instructional and leadership strategies for new and aspiring principals. His background includes experience at the elementary, middle, and high school levels serving as a counselor, assistant principal, and principal.

CASE STUDY

Lincoln High School
Urban High School
Grades 9–12

Maureen O. Madden is the principal of Toms River High School East in Toms River, New Jersey. Part of the Toms River Schools, a seventeen school district, Toms River High School East is one of the largest schools in the state. Maureen has been a school leader for five years after working as a high school English teacher for seventeen years. She is a member of the editorial staff of *Educational Viewpoints*, the professional journal of the New Jersey Principals and Supervisors Association. Maureen is active in the Middle States Commission on Secondary Schools. She lives in Toms River with her husband Bruce, a special education teacher, and her three children, Steven, Casey, and Taylor.

CASE STUDY

Washington Elementary
Rural Elementary School
Grades Pre-K–6

Kathleen Carr began her educational career as an elementary classroom teacher in a suburb of Buffalo, New York, and continued as a classroom teacher in Tampa, Florida. She moved from classroom to Primary Specialist to an Assistant Principal, assuming the principalship of Dover Elementary in the spring of 1995.

CONTRIBUTORS TO CHAPTERS 3–8

4 CASE STUDY

Adams High School
Suburban High School
Grades 9–12

Dr. Laserik Saunders successfully served the San Diego Unified School District for 36 years as teacher, vice principal, and principal before retiring from the senior high school principalship on January 31, 2002. He is a charter member of the Association of California School Administrators (ACSA) and, in retirement, he remains active with ACSA, as team leader for the Principal's Center Summer Institute held at UCLA each summer. He has received numerous commendations for his outstanding school leadership and service to youth.

5 CASE STUDY

Tyler Elementary School
Rural Elementary School
Pre-K–6

Edward Baumgartner is the Principal of Palisades Middle School in Kintnersville, PA. He taught World Cultures and Sociology in ninth and eleventh grades and has served in various administrative capacities at the high school, junior high, and middle school levels. He has also presented at numerous national conferences on the topics of New Standards and strategies to facilitate community involvement. He can be reached at Palisades Middle School, 4710 Durham Road, Kintnersville, PA 08865, USA. E-mail: ebaumgartner@palisades.k12.pa.us.

CASE STUDY  **6**

Monroe High School
Urban High School
Grades 9–12

Dr. Sue Ann Gruver has been the principal at Clear Springs Elementary in Minnetonka, Minnesota for the past five years. Previously she was a principal in the Anoka-Hennepin School District at Champlin Elementary in Champlin, MN. Prior to the principal role, Dr. Gruver was a Reading Specialist with the Hopkins School District in Hopkins, Minnesota. Dr. Gruver is a PATHWISE® certified national trainer for Educational Testing Service in the Teaching and Learning Division. Through on-site training she promotes the principles of good teaching described in Charlotte Danielson's *Enhancing Professional Practice: A Framework for Teaching* (ASCD, 1996). Dr. Gruver has a B.A. from St. Mary's College, Notre Dame, Indiana, a M.A. in Reading and a doctorate in Educational Leadership (Ed. D.) from the University of St. Thomas, St. Paul, MN. She currently resides in Eden Prairie, MN.

CASE STUDY **7**

Wilson Middle School
Urban Middle School
Grades 6–8

Michael A. Schlar has been an educator for 38 years at the William Alexander Middle School, Brooklyn, New York. He taught social studies for ten years, was the assistant principal for ten years and was the principal for the past eighteen years. During his tenure as principal, William Alexander Middle School became the Community School District 15 School of Distinction and Choice as a result of exemplary programs initiated by Michael — the Rainbow Academy for the Intellectually Gifted and Talented, the Academy of Arts and Creative Education, and the Academy of Environmental Sciences. Michael has received awards of recognition and excellence from Rudolph W. Giuliani, Mayor of New York City, the Council of Supervisors and Administrators and "Educator of the Week" (New York State Lottery). Michael is an adjunct professor in the Baruch College Public Affairs Department — Administrator/Supervisor Certification Program.

CONTRIBUTORS TO CHAPTERS 3–8

 CASE STUDY

Taft High School
Urban High School
Grades 9–12

Floyd Crues has been a teacher/administrator with the St. Louis Public Schools for approximately 25 years. His current assignment is Executive Director for Alternative Education/Student Concerns where he provides leadership for: Student Rights, Alternative Education, Summer School, Extended Day Programs, Charter Schools, Internship Programs, and the 21ST Century Program. Prior to this assignment, he served as Executive Director for Secondary Education for the St. Louis School District. Before becoming a central office administrator, Mr. Crues developed the district's alternative high school, and successfully served as its principal for six years. Mr. Crues also served as principal of one of the district's largest secondary schools for six years.

 CASE STUDY

Roosevelt High School
Suburban High School
Grades 9–12

Angela Olsen, Ed. S., is the tenth-grade assistant principal at Bryant High School in central Arkansas. Prior to taking this position, she was employed at the Arkansas Department of Education as the Administrator Licensure Program Advisor where she worked closely with ETS, the ISLLC Standards, and the state's school leadership preparation programs. Her experience includes teaching English and Spanish, serving as the English department chairperson, and serving as a principal of a 9–12 high school. She presently serves the Arkansas Association for Supervision and Curriculum Development as the newsletter editor and as a facilitator for the Arkansas Collaborative Network. She is currently pursuing a doctoral degree in educational leadership from Arkansas State University.

CASE STUDY **10**

Jackson Middle School
Suburban Middle School
Grades 6–8

George Manthey is the director of the California Curriculum Management Audit Center and a Professional Development Executive for the Association of California School Administrators (ASCA). A former teacher and elementary school principal, George now spends the majority of his time assisting under-performing schools to create action plans that will lead to meaningful improvements in student learning. His professional goal is to remove the achievement gap that exists between student groups. George writes a column for each issue of ACSA's *Leadership Magazine* and wishes that somebody, someday, will seriously call him a poet.

CASE STUDY **11**

Truman Elementary School
Suburban Elementary School
Grades Pre-K–8

Robert Hicks is superintendent of schools for the Exeter-West Greenwich Regional School District in southwest Rhode Island, a position he has held since 1992. He served as president of the Rhode Island Association of School Administrators from 1998–2000 and was Rhode Island's "Superintendent of the Year" in 1999. He earned a B.A. and M.A. from the University of Rhode Island, a Certificate of Advanced Graduate Study from Rhode Island College, and Ed.D. from Boston University.

CASE STUDY **12**

Grant High School
Suburban High School
Grades 9–12

Richard Benjamin is the Executive in Residence at Kennesaw State University, working on the start-up of a Teacher Center and a Center for Leadership, Ethics and Character. He is teaching in a new Educational Leadership program focusing on teacher leadership. He is a retired school superintendent who served in Ann Arbor, Michigan, Nashville, Tennessee, and Cobb County, Georgia. He was a Visiting Scholar at the Carnegie Foundation with Ernest Boyer and works with selected schools on school transformation.

FIGURE 6: MATRIX OF CASE NUMBERS BY STANDARD AND FOCUS (CHAPTERS 3–8)

Number / Title	Standard	Author, City and State
1. Jefferson Elementary	1	Wayne Yamagishi, Santa Rosa, CA
2. Lincoln High School	1	Maureen Madden, Toms River, NJ
3. Washington Elementary	2	Kathleen Carr, Dover, FL
4. Adams High School	2	Laserik Saunders, El Cajon, CA
5. Tyler Elementary	3	Ed Baumgartner, Kintnersville, PA
6. Monroe High School	3	Sue Ann Gruver, Minnetonka, MN
7. Wilson Middle School	4	Michael Schlar, Brooklyn, NY
8. Taft High School	4	Floyd Crues, St. Louis, MO
9. Roosevelt High School	5	Angela Olsen, Bryant, AR
10. Jackson Middle School	5	George Manthey, Burlingame, CA
11. Truman Elementary	6	Robert Hicks, West Greenwich, RI
12. Grant High School	6	Richard Benjamin, Kennesaw, GA

Focus	School Type	Community Level
Developing the vision	K–8	Suburban
How to monitor and keep on track with your mission	9–12	Urban
Valuing students and staff Sustaining a culture for learning	Pre-K–6	Rural
Monitoring and aligning a culture for learning	9–12	Suburban
Use of data to develop and implement a plan that supports teaching and learning	Pre-K–6	Rural
Creative ways of obtaining and allocating resources to support teaching and learning	9–12	Urban
Student/school community service opportunities	6–8	Urban
Community and school cooperative program for students at risk	9–12	Urban
Plagiarism	9–12	Suburban
Funding designed to meet the needs of students at risk	6–8	Suburban
Ability to seek new state and federal funding opportunities	Pre-K–8	Suburban
High school exit exam	9–12	Suburban

STANDARD 1: THE VISION OF LEARNING

In Chapter 3 we begin the actual case studies. The focus of the cases in Chapter 3 is on ISLLC Standard 1: The Vision of Learning. Chapter 3 introduces you to issues of concern at Jefferson Elementary School, a K–8 suburban elementary school and Lincoln High School, a 9–12 urban high school.

As you read through this chapter and each subsequent chapter, you will find each case structured in a specific way.

First, you will be introduced to a specific Standard and to the case study scenario and its accompanying documents. Secondly, you will be given two focus questions to keep in mind as you read the case and as you analyze the two fictitious principals' responses: one principal at the rudimentary level, the second at the accomplished level.

As a reader, you will consider the core of the ISLLC standard and then apply this understanding to the rudimentary and accomplished principals' responses. We also invite you to consider other factors that could be built into each principal's response.

STANDARD 1

A SCHOOL ADMINISTRATOR IS AN EDUCATIONAL LEADER WHO PROMOTES THE SUCCESS OF ALL STUDENTS BY FACILITATING THE DEVELOPMENT, ARTICULATION, IMPLEMENTATION, AND STEWARDSHIP OF A SCHOOL OR DISTRICT VISION OF LEARNING THAT IS SHARED AND SUPPORTED BY THE SCHOOL COMMUNITY (CCSO, 1996, P.10).

COMPONENT ONE **A**   Developing the Vision

COMPONENT ONE **B**   Communicating the Vision

COMPONENT ONE **C**   Implementing the Vision

COMPONENT ONE **D**   Monitoring and Evaluating the Vision

School leaders must believe that their mission is to educate all students and to give them the opportunities to acquire the knowledge, skills, and values that are essential for them to become successful adults. Effective school leaders develop and communicate this vision of high standards of learning within the school and the entire community. The vision promotes and fosters an attitude within each stakeholder, the need to commit themselves to high levels of performance and to foster personal areas of improvement.

Visions of learning are based upon essential values and knowledge that are the foundations to develop high expectations for student success. Visions of learning are essential to the school administrator's belief that all members of the school community are to be included in its development and implementation.

Visions of learning drive personal goals and program objectives. The vision becomes both a personal and professional goal. The role of the effective leader is to communicate the vision to students, staff, parents, and community. It is the bond that demonstrates our shared priority that powerful instruction will ensure that students possess the knowledge, skills, and values necessary to become successful adults. As the effective leader shares and promotes the vision, the implementation plan should be focused on all facets of the learning environment. The leader assures that the vision is connected to the strategies that will allow for:

- identification of what needs to be done

- what and how to accomplish the task

- identification of resources

- timeline and benchmarks

The educational leader must facilitate the monitoring of the plan from the beginning and evaluate it over time. Stakeholders are afforded opportunities to talk about the vision, think and reflect upon its success, and ensure that the data provides clear and convincing analysis that success is promoted for all students.

 CASE STUDY

Jefferson Elementary School
K–8 Suburban School

As you read this case, consider these two questions:

1. How should the principal of Jefferson Elementary prepare to address the administrative team regarding the Superintendent's directive to promote student success?

2. Just as the understanding and analysis of goals are an important element of success, student performance data is an essential component of working toward these goals. How would a principal use this data to promote effective instructional practice and student success?

Jefferson Elementary School serves 620 students in grades kindergarten through eight. It is one of four schools in the district and its eighth grade students transition to the local high school.

Jefferson provides a comprehensive program that includes School Improvement, Title I, English language development, Gifted and Talented, and an array of special education services that include resource specialists, a special day class (grades 4–8), a speech and language pathologist, a part-time occupational therapist, and a part-time adaptive therapist for physical education.

Students in grades K–3 enjoy a class size of 20 and each class has a full-time certificated teacher and a one-hour para educator to support the core academics. Students in grades 4–8 have class size averages of 29.5 with a certificated teacher and a 1.5 hour para educator.

Throughout the county this school has the reputation of being well-organized with facilities that are clean and well kept, and a community that honors education. The school has little to no vandalism, enrollment includes a high rate of incoming transfers, and the teaching cadre is proud to be in the field of education. The community acknowledges Jefferson with high regard and local realtors are zealous about opportunities to feature the school as a strong positive in their regular advertisements.

In spite of the many positives and "good feelings" about Jefferson Elementary, there are questions about the academic growth and achievement gains of its students. A data review of the scores in the areas of total reading, mathematics, and language have displayed a flat profile over the last three years. Almost all student groups, beginning in grade 2, have hovered between the 28th and 39th percentiles. Curriculum committees and school leadership reviews assert that the lack of growth is the result of change in adopted curriculum materials, higher level of students with a primary language other than English, and the fact that standardized tests allow for such normal curve expectations at various standard deviations.

Staff focus groups are stoutly convinced that nothing they can do would make a difference. Their perceptions are that as teachers they are the best of the best and have great facilities, a community that supports their school, and minimal student discipline issues. The community is telling them that all is well at Jefferson, enrollment continues to indicate growth, and the staff feels comfortably professional. The questions for Jefferson Elementary are:

"Why change if things are going well?"

"What are the factors that will make us a better school?"

"Who is telling us that they think we can improve?"

"What will a VISION do to improve our performance?"

memo...

March 20

To: Administrative Team

From: Superintendent of Schools

Recently, I was reading a book entitled *Leadership Jazz: the Art of Conducting Business through Leadership, Followership, Teamwork, Voice, and Touch* by Max De Pree (1993). It addressed the issue of the quality of life. It brought to my attention how each of us, as educational leaders, bring about change and improvement for our schools. Do we have a direction, a vision for our schools and programs? How do we evaluate this notion of quality and when do we adjust our path?

As we work towards our educational mission and goals, I want each of us to identify areas we prize that represent leadership qualities and how your school, staff, students, parents, and community demonstrate these characteristics.

I know that each of you understand the importance of providing your school with a focus that communicates how we are committed to the adherence of high student expectations, that there is convincing evidence that this focus is embedded in all of your educational programs, and that there is evidence that this commitment is shared by all.

Essential to this notion is that all information is based upon a variety of sources and that student data is an essential component that informs and directs this path.

Beginning at our next administrative meeting each of us will present our points of view on how we promote student success throughout our school programs and how we demonstrate our responsibility to all members of our community.

As we learn how to define our vision we will progress to the stages of implementation, communication, and evaluation.

I look forward to working with you to discover the *leadership jazz* within each of us.

March

Dear Principal of Jefferson Elementary:

As a follow up to our Executive Council meeting held last week, I would like to express our appreciation for allowing us to participate in the development and creation of the monthly parent bulletin. We understand the importance of positive family communication and want to establish a continuing theme of educational excellence and support by staff, students, parents, and the community.

As the Executive Council thought about this commitment we realized that we did not have a proper format or direction for this monthly newsletter. We want it to communicate current information, news and events that are in the near future, student highlights, staff acknowledgments, and parent notes. We realize that this newsletter has the potential to be the "signature" of Jefferson Elementary and want it to reflect all of the goals and aspirations that the school has to offer.

We need to meet. The Executive Council has a list of thoughts that we need to address in order that we can get this project off in the best manner possible. As you know, this council has high standards and is proud of its work and wants to be proud of our school.

Jefferson needs to be the best and communicate with its families in a way that makes us all proud!

Please give me a call to arrange a time for this meeting. We need to put our thoughts together and identify the directions, goals, and vision of Jefferson Elementary.

Sincerely,

Kim Attavery
Jefferson PTA
President

memo . . .

To: Principal of Jefferson High School

From: Curriculum Advisory Committee

Re: Curriculum Review

In our review of the strategic plan for our current school year, we have noted that there are many areas of pride and success for our staff, school, and community. Many of our school success indicators have met expectations and have become a positive direction for our entire school.

However, in a number of areas we realize that there has not been growth and that we need your support and direction. The following areas have been identified:

Strategic Goal Area #1: Student Education

- 9th grade student achievement scores for total reading, mathematics, and language have not met their targets for each of their quartiles.

- 9th grade English language learner students did not meet their level of fluency targets.

- Gifted and Talented education program has not conducted transition meetings for students who were promoted from the 8th to 9th grade.

Strategic Goal Area #2: Professional Practice

- Collaboration between Jefferson Elementary and Jefferson High School has not demonstrated successful communication or articulation of curriculum goals and needs.

- District initiated staff development to increase collaboration among 8th and 9th grade teachers has not been completed following invitations from the high school team.

As curriculum leaders for Jefferson High School we are concerned that our communication and level of participation with our feeder elementary school, Jefferson Elementary, has not been welcome and more collaborative. We seek common interests and goals for all students in our community.

We request your support and leadership to bridge this gap. We have scheduled a meeting on April 16th at 3:15 pm. Let us know if this day and time will be convenient.

memo...

Jefferson Elementary School
SITE Council

March 21

Thank you for your letter. We enjoyed the opportunity to talk about how we can improve the communications among parents, staff, and our high school programs.

We realize that we need to improve and become more consistent with how our community views us. At first the Site Council was defensive and wondered why the high school is not communicating with us, but then we asked ourselves how we can improve and be a part of the solution.

The Jefferson School Site Council has a major responsibility and role in school improvement. In this regard we are wondering if there is something we can do to improve how we are viewed in our community.

In this regard, we will begin discussions in the following area:

• Principal to meet with entire faculty to discuss and brainstorm schoolwide goals.

Based on the information about this school presented through the scenario and all the documents taken together how should the principal respond to these two questions?

1. How should the principal of Jefferson Elementary prepare to address the administrative team regarding the Superintendent's directive to promote student success?

2. Just as the understanding and analysis of goals are an important element of success, student performance data is an essential component of working toward these goals. How would a principal use this data to promote effective instructional practice and student success?

PRINCIPAL A   rudimentary response

The Jefferson Elementary School Principal is feeling positive about his first year. Staffing schedules that include library, computer lab, motor development, music, yard supervision, and the after-school extended day clinics are continuing to offer good monitoring of students and have reduced the number of conflicts on the playground. Teacher and substitute assignments during the first two trimesters met expectations and resulted in few scheduling conflicts or changes for students.

Textbook and material orders were delayed, however, with staff sharing and adjustments in unit presentation (particularly with science and history), the back order delays did not interrupt student instruction.

Staff meetings were without comment and, based on a review of faculty meeting minutes, the issues appear to have been met with satisfaction. The review of minutes highlighted the following areas: materials and ordering procedures, parent pick-up and drop-off locations, Penmanship Fair, Back-To-School Night, spirit and activity days, copy and reproduction schedules, need for faculty volunteers for afterschool events, and student safety. The principal was very proud of his communication with teachers. His Principal Advisory Council was very active and provided leadership in a variety of areas. The Council provided assistance with the allocation of the annual discretionary funds to staff ($250.00 for each teacher), review of duty assignments, review of faculty meeting agendas, purchase of risograph equipment, and the selection of staff members for advisory councils and curriculum representation. These school leaders were the most experienced and respected teachers in the school, and the principal acknowledged their support and admiration for his leadership.

The Jefferson Elementary principal is passionate about his new position and is proud of his ten to twelve-hour days. He feels empowered that he is able to support his teachers' instructional programs and facilitate their needs as their recommendations are presented through his advisory or curriculum councils. His monthly parent bulletins have recognized exemplary student projects and supported positive citizenship practices within the school and community, reminded the community of noteworthy activities that they should attend, and used the bulletin as a communications tool about safety, energy conservation, study tips, and the need for volunteers in the library and computer lab.

(Note: He wonders why the parent teacher organization wants to publish future editions. He is pleased about their support and feels they are accepting responsibility to help the school.)

Upon receipt of the Superintendent's memorandum (Document 1) the Jefferson principal is looking forward to presenting his vision of what his school values and how he provides the leadership to represent those values. In preparing for this presentation to the administrative team, the principal believes that his major role is to support and facilitate instruction. To accomplish these goals, his beliefs are that he should:

- be the leader of the school's instructional program, and it is his role to facilitate its success in whatever manner is necessary

- ensure and be the faculty's advocate to obtain the materials, equipment, and supplies necessary for them to do their jobs (grant writing, parent donations, facilitate pizza nights)

- coordinate procedures and processes to make the teacher's job easier

- represent the school and be a communicator of policy, curriculum, and beliefs

- supervise and ensure the safety of all students and be a consistent communicator of schoolwide rules

In preparing for the anticipated meeting, the Jefferson principal identifies the following areas of importance for this meeting and plans to assemble a summary report of his findings, develop a needs statement, and, ultimately, a VISION statement for his school.

Parent Survey

This survey will provide important data from parents on how they view specific areas of the curriculum, how they rate current services, and any comments they may have about Jefferson Elementary.

Staff Survey

This survey will provide staff input on the satisfaction teachers, instructional assistants, and support staff have about specific curriculum areas, levels of material support, areas of recommended improvement, and planning.

Program Quality Review

An independent program evaluation was conducted two years ago with specific emphasis on reading, mathematics, and writing. This review is a summary of commendations and recommendations based on the evaluation.

Coordinated Compliance Review

This self-review was conducted a year ago on federal and state compliance issues for specific programs such as: Title I, English Language Learners, Tobacco and Drug, Safe Schools, School Improvement, and Coordinated Programs.

The Jefferson Principal will assemble and highlight the data from the parent and staff surveys, Program Quality Review, and Compliance Review. This summary will be presented to the Principal's Advisory Committee for ratification. This ratification will provide for schoolwide support and understanding of the proposal. This information will be charted and presented at the Administrative Team meeting.

The Jefferson Elementary principal is eager to present these findings as they will represent information from parents, staff, and curriculum areas. The information will reflect current findings and lead a path for future planning. The principal views this vision as a cornerstone for his school that will guide his leadership for at least a three-year period.

PRINCIPAL B accomplished response

Begin with the end in mind

Does Jefferson Elementary believe that the education of every student to acquire knowledge, skills, and values to become successful adults is of primary importance?

Does Jefferson Elementary foster a climate of continuous improvement?

Does Jefferson Elementary build its commitment to high standards of learning for all students?

Does Jefferson Elementary facilitate the development of successful instructional practices to improve instruction?

Does Jefferson Elementary have a strategic plan that focuses on student learning that draws upon relevant achievement and demographic data to inform instruction?

Does the staff at Jefferson Elementary collaborate and believe in the development of a community of learners and leaders?

Does the community at Jefferson Elementary involve itself in the realization of the schoolwide vision?

A definitive "Yes!" is the response the school leader at Jefferson Elementary would give to these questions that he believes aptly characterize his school. Every moment of every day he is modeling and promoting this attitude of direction, purpose, and commitment. He is governed by the belief that every student will achieve success and that every teacher will facilitate the success. The community will embrace the school as an educational leader and commit all of its resources to the vision that learning is the priority!

The Jefferson Elementary leader knows his school community. This community, broadly defined, includes: students, parents, teachers, support staff, administrative team, governing board, advisory councils, groups and individuals who support Jefferson and those who do not, business partners, and those individuals who know little or nothing about Jefferson. The principal at Jefferson uses every opportunity to convey his values and beliefs that student success is the highest educational priority. This is done with specific acknowledgments in every parent bulletin, every staff bulletin, every special memorandum, and with every item that is published at the school. The vision must be acknowledged and spoken in the same breath as, "Jefferson Elementary… the school that believes in the success of every student." The vision will be articulated in a manner that extends beyond this thought, as it will include what the vision is and how it will be integrated throughout the school program. The vision will be embedded in all educational plans. The vision will become a part of the school decision-making process at every level. Staff, parents, and even students will be asking the same question, "How will/does this improve learning and student success?"

The school leader at Jefferson Elementary is confident. He is a risk-taker and encourages all of the stakeholders in the Jefferson community to reflect, think, and test the vision. He will create a variety of venues to discuss the vision. Monthly refreshment socials or breakfast meetings with parents — including parent clubs, Title I parents, parents with diverse ethnicities, and/or Gifted and Talented parents — are excellent opportunities to communicate individual ideas about student success. Venues such as site council, open forums, service club presentations, and senior citizen meetings are to be included as part of his plan. The school leader will welcome the difficult challenges of discussing and promulgating the school's vision in order for it to be embraced and understood by all stakeholders. This is a continuous cycle with no discernible beginning or end.

The school leader at Jefferson Elementary continually collects data from a variety of sources. It has been his mission to know and understand the successes and needs of every student at the school. This data-collection process occurs each trimester (November, February, and April) with principal-teacher meetings. During these leadership conferences teachers review the following materials with the principal:

- summary results of multiple measures (reading-math-writing)

- most recent standardized test scores (achievement and language proficiency)

- evaluation of progress of second language learners as compared to English only learners

- learning plans for students in special education

- review of teaching practices that support instructional success

- portfolio of student work samples

- attendance report

- current intervention modifications (such as tutoring, after-school program, reading and/or math clinics, homework clubs, parent-student reading partnerships, computer lab for writing skills)

- recommendations for individual students (such as an intervention plan and/or screening/assessment, or referral)

A major purpose of these meetings is to collaborate with and empower teachers. These meetings emphasize student data, and, through modeling and collaboration, teachers are taught to use data to inform their instruction. It is during these conferences that the leader at Jefferson communicates a focus of success for all students and recognizes the teacher as a major stakeholder in this process. These professional collaboration sessions will determine areas of professional need, topics for staff development, material acquisition, areas of curriculum strength, and areas in need of improvement.

During these meetings the principal can collaborate with the teacher and learn about his/her process of analyzing instructional improvement. It is at these meetings that the school leader and teacher can, together, analyze how specific teaching practices lead to student learning and, ultimately, success.

Encouraging all stakeholders to be introspective and reflective about what they need is critical to student success. A schoolwide team that is collaborative and shares the process of improvement will support schoolwide goals. Regularly scheduled collegial sharing meetings are held three times each month. It is important to note that these meetings are voluntary, held after school on Thursdays, last no longer than 45 minutes, and have no published agenda. The guiding focus of these meetings is that all discussion is specific to student instruction and beneficial to all staff members. Typical meeting foci: successful strategies for the English language learner; establishing successful practices for the teacher and parent relationship; developing writing rubrics; using technology to develop a student assessment database; articulation (Jefferson Elementary and Jefferson High); developing staff collegiality; successful teaching ideas; using the Internet for student research; successful writing traits; alternative strategies for the reluctant learner in math; and integration of science into the curriculum.

The principal believes that the vision of Jefferson Elementary is committed to student learning and continued growth. The vision is and will continue to be developed by the entire Jefferson community and monitored through a strategic plan that allows for specific achievement using demographic data reflective of each student and his/her family. The principal's goal is to delegate responsibility at Jefferson and develop a community of leaders.

The pages that follow outline the "Keys for Improved Performance." Specifically, they note:

> a) the differences in the performance of rudimentary Principal A and accomplished Principal B;

> b) the potential consequences of the continued performance of Principal A at the rudimentary level;

> c) strategies and suggestions on how to move from one level of performance to another level.

Again, these pages specifically relate to the case outlined herein and the two focus questions:

> 1. How should the principal of Jefferson Elementary prepare to address the administrative team regarding the Superintendent's directive to promote student success?

> 2. Just as the understanding and analysis of goals are an important element of success, student performance data is an essential component of working toward these goals. How would a principal use this data to promote effective instructional practice and student success?

KEYS FOR IMPROVED PERFORMANCE

DIFFERENCES IN PRINCIPAL PERFORMANCE

PRINCIPAL A
rudimentary response

PRINCIPAL B
accomplished response

Belief that his role is to support teachers and staff in their instruction.	Belief that his role is to promote excellent instruction, growth, and student success.
His effectiveness is due to efficient scheduling and consistent discipline.	His effectiveness is due to communicating vision, allowing for input, analyzing student achievement and demographic data.
Effectiveness supported by efficient staff meetings as evaluated by participants with no comment or controversy.	Challenges values and promotes discussion and dialogue on beliefs and vision. This principal seeks to stimulate positive and critical discussion to stimulate improvement.
Focus on day-to-day activities and events: schedules, ordering, duty assignments, reports, etc. in order to assist teachers in focusing on instruction.	Focus on improved student instruction. Model analysis of student data, seek ways to improve instruction, communicate with parents, collegial sharing with staff, identify staff development focus.
Belief that he is working at capacity as twelve-hour days are full and parent support is positive.	Goals are to develop leadership in others, delegate responsibility, create shared commitment of high standards for all.
Parent and staff surveys will give information to help develop vision.	School leader must arrive with passionate belief that the priority is student success. The vision is to be developed through dialogue, using relevant sources of information from within and outside of school.
School communication is provided by Principal Advisory Committee, comprised of leaders with senior status in the school community.	Communication is required to be broad based and include representatives from all constituency groups.

Potential Consequences of the Performance of Principal A

School organization will stagnate. Instructional growth will not occur. Currently, focus is on day-to-day practices that have little to no impact on student growth. Leadership focus is on coordination and processes that work without issues.

Staff meeting does not model improvement efforts for classroom. Focus is on day-to-day operations that include scheduling, ordering, and events.

Principal Advisory Committee is dangerous as it reflects individuals who most likely have the most seniority and the least need to change. This group has the potential to maintain the status quo and not seek improvement. This group may be the "I've done it that way before, and it doesn't work" group. They can give a false sense of success. They may or may not have support from parents, staff, and administration.

Parent bulletin most likely reflects efforts of "good" students and events that are going to be scheduled. There is not a focus on what values the school maintains, little or no direction for improvement, nor discussion of the vision.

Response to Superintendent is well intended but is not on target. Use of parent survey will provide points-of-view from a constituency that has little or no formal knowledge of the improvement process. Parents tend to react based on how content their child seems to be, the amount of homework, reports on report cards and parent conferences. Parent surveys reflect parent and student contentment and do not necessarily identify specific areas for school improvement.

Program Quality Review (PQR) offers school an objective evaluation into its school program and delivery process. It standardizes special programs and offers quality criteria. This does have the potential to reinforce school practices that are in need of change. The PQR is more content- than process-oriented. It will not likely be an impetus to change practices.

Coordinated Compliance Review (CCR), similar to the PQR, is an audit process that has been identified from outside of the school where compliance issues need to be evaluated. The CCR provides for audit checks required by law in many federal and state programs. Self-review proceeds an independent audit where outcomes are either compliant or non-compliant. Areas of non-compliance can be viewed as "their problems and not mine," and not an impetus to create ambitious changes within the organization.

VISION at Jefferson Elementary will not be understood by the school constituency. It is reflective of past reports, past practices, and a narrow group of staff. It has the grim future of being framed and placed in the foyer of the school office, never to be looked upon again. The school may dust it off every so often, when convenient, but it will not be used for improvement or to be an impetus for change.

PRINCIPAL A
rudimentary response

TO

PRINCIPAL B
accomplished response

HOW DO YOU MOVE FROM RUDIMENTARY PRINCIPAL A TO ACCOMPLISHED PRINCIPAL B?

- Read research.

- Learn from experts:

  - *RESULTS; The Key to Continuous School Improvement* (Schmoker, 1996)

  - *Leading with Soul* (Deal, 1995)

  - "School as a Community of Leaders" (Barth, *Building a Professional Culture in Schools*, Lieberman, 1988)

- Look among your colleagues and choose the very best principal leader. Learn all you can from that person. Then go on from there to another mentor. It will be a most rewarding journey.

- Embrace *A Framework for School Leaders: Linking the ISLLC Standards to Practice* (Hessel and Holloway, 2002). Wonderful text. Great thoughts and proven ideas by practicing administrators.

- Reflect on other steps one could take to move from rudimentary to accomplished. Add them to this list.

Notes

 CASE STUDY

Lincoln High School
9–12 Urban High School

As you read this case, consider these two questions:

1. What actions must the principal take to evaluate the progress toward achieving the vision of the school?

2. What creative tactics might the principal develop to overcome barriers in achieving the vision?

Lincoln High School is the oldest high school in the county. Most of the school's 2000 students have parents who had attended LHS, graduated, and stayed in the area to work and raise their families. When a large chemical plant moved to the area in the mid 1960's and set up shop with a pledge to be a community-based company, families came to the area in droves for the jobs and promised prosperity. Those who were already living in President City were delighted with the growth predicted for the community as the new industry offered a good financial package for employees, college tuition reimbursement, medical benefits, and assisted mortgages. Housing developments and apartment complexes quickly dotted the community creating a need for additional elementary schools, a middle school and several additions on the small high school. The midsize community of the 60's now took on the characteristics of a burgeoning city. Many other businesses moved into the area and before long, it was the fastest growing city in the state.

Through two decades, population growth continued, but the prosperity did not. By the late 80's, the chemical plant had closed its doors and moved, leaving thousands of President City citizens without jobs or benefits and holding large mortgages. It was not realistic to expect employees to move with the company. This led to the closing of local businesses as well, leaving the economics of the city to a variety of franchises that offered minimum wage jobs to the population. The city council had tried many ways for the community to rebuild, including attempts to lure shopping mall projects to the area. Large department stores responded but it was too little too late. The unemployment rate is still the highest in the state.

The schools have suffered tremendously. The rapid and poorly planned growth of the area over a twenty-year period forced the construction of additional elementary schools, a middle school and additions on the secondary school, Lincoln High. The taxes are high in President City and the schools that were built and modernized in the 70's are expensive to maintain. The taxpayers are under a financial burden with no assistance in sight.

The principal of LHS recently retired after a 37-year career at the school. Although he enjoyed the prosperity of the 70's and 80's, he did little in the 90's to promote the school's growth. Surprisingly, the community supported this. Since so many of the community members had graduated from Lincoln themselves, they had expected their children to enjoy the same education that they did. In their estimation, Lincoln was a good school and besides, change is expensive. They elected the same Board of Education members year after year because they worked hard to keep expenses down in the financially strapped community.

The staff is comprised of a number of new, young teachers since many Lincoln High teachers have recently retired after a long tenure at the school. Many of these veteran teachers believed that growing violence and student unrest and the rise in discipline issues were all new issues that they were unprepared to handle. The change in the school's academic achievements over the 30-year period was obvious as well. The once-growing school with unlimited financial resources to foster successful academic and co-curricular and extra-curricular programs was now stagnant and falling rapidly behind other schools in the area.

However, the school community does pride itself on long-standing traditions and strong community support, at least in theory, if not in finances. The community wants the best for its students and recognizes that now is the time to make changes before it is too late. The community recognizes the need to bring the school up to 21st-century standards and it is hoping that the arrival of the new principal will be the first step to bring the school back into the competitive standard that it once enjoyed as one of the leading high schools in the state.

DOCUMENT 1: MISSION STATEMENT

Mission Statement
Lincoln High School

The mission of Lincoln High School is the pursuit of excellence. Our school will expect our students to achieve success in public education by providing for all students the knowledge, skills, and scholarly environment to become competent, self-assured, and lifelong learners in their world.

Our students will become successful, productive members of the community with a commitment to truth, honor, and duty. The support, responsibility, and involvement of the entire community is the cornerstone to this success.

𝔑𝔢𝔴𝔰𝔭𝔞𝔭𝔢𝔯

Dear Editor:

I am a sophomore at Lincoln High School. I am writing this letter on behalf of many students at my school. You can use my name, but please do not think that this is the opinion of one student because it is the opinion of many.

We know that there are some students who give our school and our town a bad name because of what they do. They also give us a bad name because of what they don't do. They do not represent who we are. We become angry and frustrated when you publish articles like the one on October 5th where you criticized our test scores, our attitudes and all that we don't do.

We wonder if anyone has taken the time to notice all that we do. It is hard to keep up with all schoolwork when we have to work, but we try. Many of us are involved in school activities and we try to have a social life too, something that is very hard to do when our town offers us almost nothing but a movie theater and a YMCA that has a pool that is almost never available to us.

The students of Lincoln High have a lot to offer to this community, but we need your support, not your criticism. The next time you publish an article about our school not educating us or how bad our school is, come and see us first. Spend a day at our school. Talk to us, don't just criticize us.

Sincerely,

Jessica Rogers
10th Grade
Lincoln High School

DOCUMENT 3: AN OFFICIAL CORRESPONDENCE FROM THE OFFICE OF THE COUNTY SUPERINTENDENT

OFFICIAL CORRESPONDENCE

Dear Fellow Educator:

Please be advised that due to the state department's freeze on state aid to all public schools, it will be necessary to place a spending freeze on all county schools on all items not directly related to instruction and student health and safety. All requested items would be subject to review.

Please pay particular attention to all of the following at your school:

- All class trips scheduled for the remainder of the year are cancelled.

- All computer upgrades are postponed until further notice.

- Staff development sessions and stipend speakers are cancelled.

- All building renovations and upgrades are postponed until state funding is restored.

- All new programs scheduled to begin in the coming school year are postponed.

- New athletic and extra-curricular uniform orders are on hold.

- Athletic equipment requisitions will be approved on an as needed basis provided supervisors present a detailed explanation of the necessity.

Thank you for your cooperation as we continue to educate our children through these challenging times.

Sincerely,

R. Roberts
County Superintendent

memo . . .

To: School Principal

From: Lincoln Public Schools Education Association (LPSEA)

RE: Concerns

Date: October 20

Please be advised that at the recent meeting of the LPSEA, several issues were aired by our members:

- Lack of cohesiveness among the student body.

- Little to no collaboration among the staff on academic issues.

- The lack of any connection between the elementary programs and high school expectations.

- Recent criticism by the community and media regarding what we do each day at Lincoln High School.

- More frequent incidents of violence among students.

It is the consensus of this organizations that steps need to be taken now and that educational issues be addressed, even amid spending cuts and budgetary restrictions, to redefine the goals and mission of the Lincoln Public Schools.

Staff members, both experienced and developing, need direction. Our students need direction. Traditions that had once been sacred to our school are dying. Our students are becoming unmotivated and we see episodes of fighting among students. High absenteeism and truancy are more frequent. We need to develop a focus for our school as well as new school goals that will define who we are and what we can set as achievable goals for our students as we educate them to prepare them for future academic and career endeavors.

...continued on next page

Our high school's community has changed dramatically in the past twenty years. The current depressed local economy has been hard for our students. Clearly this makes the mission statement and school goals as outlined in the student and staff handbooks — originally written at the school's opening in 1955 — outdated and non-applicable to today's student body.

We have included a postgraduate survey for the past five years compiled by our guidance department. Clearly our students need technology, vocational training and business skills, including speaking and writing, that will prepare them for postgraduate plans.

Additionally, we are extremely concerned regarding the recent budget cuts and spending freeze. We need a clear understanding on how this will impact our classrooms individually and our school as a whole.

There are so many good things happening here at Lincoln High School that we know you have taken the time to address with our students and staff and that does not go unnoticed and unappreciated. We understand the challenges that you face each day and we support you as you address the challenge of running a safe school.

We respectfully request a Round Table Faculty Meeting in lieu of a full staff meeting this month. We have a number of staff members who would like to meet with you to present their ideas and recommendations for positive change at Lincoln High.

Thank you for your continued support of what we do each day at Lincoln.

Based on the information about the school through the scenario and all the documents taken together, how should the principal respond to these two questions?

1. What actions must the principal take to evaluate the progress toward achieving the vision of the school?

2. What creative tactics might the principal develop to overcome barriers in achieving the vision?

PRINCIPAL A rudimentary response

It is likely that this principal was hired because she had vision and showed an enthusiastic and fresh approach. She believes that hard work and long hours and a true caring attitude about the students and the school will be the cornerstones to success. The new principal has plans and ideas that she is anxious to implement. After serving many years as assistant principal, she has a strong background in discipline and plans to incorporate some new disciplinary techniques and updates of school policy and procedures during the school year.

One of the first tasks she implements is a meeting with the staff. Her agenda includes the following items:

- Introduction of new disciplinary procedures.

- Incorporation of community service into student suspensions.

- Addition of midterms into the curriculum.

- Ideas for a school slogan/message that she will ask everyone to vote on.

- Elimination of student clubs and organizations that do not focus on service, leadership, character building, or academic improvement. More academically-oriented clubs will replace the ski, surf, and modeling clubs.

- Plans for parent coffee klatches that will invite parents to meet with the principal and selected staff members twice monthly to address concerns and answer questions.

- Specific directions to the staff for cutting spending.

- Explanation of her *open door* policy to meet with teachers and assist them with issues and concerns.

- Description of her monthly newsletter to parents. She plans to invite staff members to contribute articles each month outlining what is being done in a particular program or classroom to emphasize student achievement.

- Invitation to the staff to volunteer to be a part of a Principal Advisory Group that will keep her informed on issues and concerns within the building.

Her energy is contagious and clearly she wants the best for the school. She is ready for her meeting with the representatives of LPSEA. She has solutions to address some of their concerns and will inform them on how she plans to implement the necessary changes to solve them. She will promise to take their suggestions under consideration, but she feels confident that she understands what is best for the school.

Additionally, she has already rewritten the mission statement for the school. It was one of the first things that she did when she came to Lincoln High. She has had it placed in the Faculty Handbook as well as the newly designed Student Handbook that she has revised with the help of her secretary and assistant principals.

She has scheduled a meeting with student leaders, including the student who wrote the letter to the newspaper. She plans to form a student advisory council from selected students with the hope that they will come to the table with ideas from the student body that will help her guide the school into the 21st century. She has a plan and is jumping both feet into the school environment, making a strong effort to show her support for the students and the staff. However, what she has in enthusiasm and vision, she lacks in practical application.

PRINCIPAL B   accomplished response

This principal has the task of bringing together the educational community of teachers, students, parents, and town leaders to meet the changing needs of Lincoln High School as well as the needs of the community that sends its children there to be educated. No task is without challenges and roadblocks and this situation is no exception. Budget cuts, dissension, and frustrated staff members bring additional dimensions to the needs that must be addressed. The teachers and students appear ready to take on the challenge, but are asking the principal for direction. The community is *critical* and it will be the principal's goal to include them in the process of change. The most important role that the principal must recognize here is that she is the *facilitator* for positive change, and it cannot be done without everyone working towards the process.

The first order of business will be to organize a group of stakeholders, including parents, Board members, community leaders/business people, and students to review and possibly rewrite the school's mission statement to determine adequately and effectively where the school needs to be. Honor and duty are fine aspirations. However, it is clear that Lincoln must define goals that are more manageable and needs-based. With clear and understandable school goals that include character education, duty and honor may naturally fall into place.

The successful principal will *guide and direct* to be sure that the mission statement does not become merely a catch slogan (although a powerful and helpful one could evolve from the mission statement) and that first the goal is to meet the educational needs of the students. This should be done using surveys, graduation statistics, and standardized test scores to assess and evaluate the needs of the current as well as the anticipated student population.

There are some immediate responses and creative tactics that the principal may implement to begin the process of getting the school back on track while initiating change and leading the stakeholders. They may include but are not limited to some of the following:

- Start by working with a stakeholder committee that will be responsible for setting two or three goals that will focus on increasing student academic achievement in areas that are determined to be weak. This should tie into both state testing mandates and college entrance requirements.

- Meet with the supervisors of each department individually and collectively to develop an ongoing staff development plan that will utilize the skills and knowledge of the current staff.

- Work with the curriculum committee to develop new courses or rewrite current courses to be sure that they are in line with State Core Curriculum Standards and state testing.

- Develop a committee to research other successful school programs in similar areas and meet with stakeholders on the feasibility of adjusting and applying some of their successes to Lincoln High School in the areas of safety, student achievement, student motivation, and student pride.

- Arrange opportunities for staff members to do educational research and to visit these schools.

- Encourage teachers to share their experiences with fellow staff members and community committee members by presenting workshops or mini-conferences.

- Develop a flexible, working student committee that will liaison with the community, principal's office, and the teaching staff to keep lines of communication open.

- Encourage members of the community to work with the school in developing contests, competitions, and programs that will showcase student skills and accomplishments within the community. This could include public speaking, public relations, writing/essay contests, technology skills, and other public relation activities.

- Encourage students to enter contests and competitions (outside of the immediate area) and encourage local businesses to sponsor student travel to these programs.

- Develop a grant writing committee. Staff members can research and apply for grants that may offer financial benefits to school programs.

- Look for all areas of student successes and strengths — academic, athletic, extra-curricular, and community-minded — and initiate a program that will recognize achievements and give accolades to offer support and provide a sense of school pride.

- Focus on an area of the school that can highlight these achievements. A wall of pride may already be in place. Facilitate a way for the STUDENTS to modernize this area and give them ownership of it.

- Develop a group of student ambassadors taking care to recruit students from all interest and academic levels, not just the top students. The members of this group will serve as liaisons to other groups but will also have the responsibility of being goodwill ambassadors to the community and new students.

Parents can be guided into positive and proactive roles within the school community. The effective principal will allow parents to see that school involvement is as important in high school as it is in the elementary school. Support through booster clubs and fundraising efforts is helpful, and in many cases, financially necessary, but parents should see themselves as more than candy sellers, and should feel comfortable visiting the school more than once a year on a designated night. For parents to welcome this, they should have opportunities to become acquainted with and understand the principal's vision. They should be encouraged to develop their own ways to work towards helping the school to achieve that vision. Effective communication tailored to the parents through meetings, open houses, newsletters, phone calls, and email can be powerful tools to gain parental support and understanding.

The principal must be proactive and look for strengths in the community. She should use a variety of tactics to define and present ideas for other community members about soliciting their input and support. The principal needs to "get out there," and step outside the walls of the school. In every town, regardless of economic status, there are community members who would delight in someone asking them for their professional support or expertise. That is a novel switch from the constant request for financial support that many professionals, retirees, and hard working taxpayers will welcome.

Talk to parents; talk to the community; LISTEN to what they have to say. Often people are reluctant to present ideas or even their needs to the principal because they may assume that the principal knows more than they do or is in the position to know what is best. They may only relate to the principal that frightened them when they were in school. The principal's office has the false reputation of a bad place. It also has the reputation of a place to go when you have a problem, not a solution. Naturally, there are other individuals that believe they can run the school better than how it is operating now, and that the principal and Board of Education are making decisions that are ineffective. The principal needs to listen to all of these opinions, process and direct answers and problem solve.

Community programs, intergenerational opportunities, and service organizations provide students an opportunity to share a variety of experiences and activities, both in and out of school. These programs are frequently effective in bridging understanding of the vision of the school. These activities may create an eye-opening experience for the school and community and help to identify each other's needs. Innovative programs can be tailored to each community, but the principal must be sensitive to what is required. That is not an easy task for even the most experienced principal. Often the inclination of a school leader is to defend and preach philosophy rather than to listen. Validating the public's concern, right or wrong, good or bad, may be the very best tactic in gaining its support.

If the principal believes that she is learning each day just as much as the students, this is a principal who will be more successful in achieving the visions of the school. Kids and the communities that they live in change each year, each day and each moment. What works in one place may fail in another. The bulk of the principal's work must be done outside the main office. There are good people out there—smart kids, caring families, and community members that want the best for their kids, with or without the finances, and unlimited resources of ideas and programs. The principal who listens with a 'third ear' will be more successful than the principal that lectures. The principal who communicates in a variety of ways to reach the largest number of people will get results. The principal who is willing to take control by guiding others will be a true school leader.

The pages that follow outline the "Keys for Improved Performance."
Specifically, they note:

a) the differences in the performance of rudimentary
   Principal A and accomplished Principal B;

b) the potential consequences of the continued
   performance of Principal A at the rudimentary level;

c) strategies and suggestions on how to move from one
   level of performance to another level.

Again, these pages specifically relate to the case outlined herein and the
two focus questions:

1. What actions must the principal take to evaluate the
   progress toward achieving the vision of the school?

2. What creative tactics might the principal develop to
   overcome barriers in achieving the vision?

 KEYS FOR IMPROVED PERFORMANCE

DIFFERENCES IN PRINCIPAL PERFORMANCE

PRINCIPAL A	PRINCIPAL B
rudimentary response	accomplished response
Belief that the principal has the sole role of promoting change for school improvement.	Belief that the principal's role is that of facilitator of change through dialogue, research, fact-finding and cooperation of stakeholders.
Belief that strong discipline will effectively strengthen school safety and student achievement.	Understands that school goals in all areas of student performance need to be outlined and balanced for all students.
Belief that the principal is expected to solve all issues with minimal input from students and staff.	Belief that collaboration of all stakeholders to gather information and resources will allow the school community to develop ownership of stated goals and their achievement.
Belief that solutions to school concerns lie within the office of the principal.	Belief that guiding participants in the learning community is an effective tool to increase student learning and promote success.
	Understands that the best school resources for school development are within the staff.
	Belief that professional development opportunities, commitment from the broader community, and effective communication among all stakeholders are pivotal to school success.

Potential Consequences of the Performance of Principal A

The staff will be resistant. When plans for instructional programs are presented to teachers without research, there will be resistance. Decisions involving instruction, assessment, and school philosophy that are dictated without staff input will meet with resistance.

Students will be resistant to radical change. The students want to be heard, yet no one is listening. Decisions have been made by the principal that will impact their school life, yet no one has asked for their input. Even the school slogan suggestions are coming from one individual without collaboration or input from stakeholders.

The monthly newsletter will focus on what has been done, not what is in the works. It will simply be a public relations piece rather than true information. This community is looking to be progressive, not reflective.

The LPSEA meeting will be disastrous if she enters the meeting with only ready-made answers. She needs to prepare by collecting information on academic issues, budgetary concerns, and discipline issues. She must be ready for others' input rather than just declare her own.

PRINCIPAL A   **TO**   PRINCIPAL B

rudimentary response   accomplished response

HOW DO YOU MOVE FROM RUDIMENTARY PRINCIPAL A TO ACCOMPLISHED PRINCIPAL B?

Getting from Principal A to Principal B is possible if the new principal has trust in her own leadership ability and is willing to trust the process of guiding the school with the resources it holds. A principal must be an excellent communicator with the written and spoken word. A good principal will take the time to validate everyone and support their efforts by highlighting their strengths as well as supporting and strengthening their weaknesses.

Strong discipline is the key to student success. When she comes in like gangbusters announcing her plans for new rules and disciplinary procedures, she will certainly meet with resistance from both students and staff. For teachers, this is often a double-edged sword. They would like to see stronger discipline, but they might not appreciate added responsibility in providing this increased level of student management. Discipline is often viewed as something for the "front office" to handle. Students will resist as well since tough, global discipline has the hidden danger of hurting the good kids more than the ones who consistently make poor choices.

New principals, especially those who have spent many years as an assistant principal or disciplinarian, believe that strong discipline will get the school back on track. There is no question that clear and appropriate consequences for violation of policy is necessary to maintain the safety and control of the school environment. "Small consequences for small infractions, big consequences for big infractions" has been the statement given to incoming freshmen for years. Principal A can seek out peer leadership programs or peer mediation workshops and arrange for teachers and student leaders to attend. When students have a voice in how discipline will be applied in their school and are presented with options as well as consequences, they may be more responsive than resistant. There are many anti-violence programs and presentations that highlight positive role models and behavior that would be worth investigating. Studying school pride initiatives and finding one good for the school may be well-received.

Writing the mission statement and changing the curriculum without stakeholder input is a sure formula for failure. No matter how educated, scholarly or educationally experienced a school leader may be, any policy change or curriculum adjustment without committee input will practically guarantee resistance from stakeholders. Again, her resources are the key to acceptance. Teachers, students, and parents should be key participants when writing the school mission. Understanding that the mission statement is not her personal mission, but that of the school and community is critical. Most principals find that they are impressed with the enthusiasm of the stakeholders when it is clear that the vision for the school is one that is shared, not dictated. Here is a wonderful opportunity to LISTEN and share and collaborate.

Elimination of the student clubs that seem frivolous or not focused upon student achievement. One would try to avoid attending this meeting when this is announced to students! Principal A is missing the point if she believes that clubs that foster non-academic student interest have no place in the school. In an area that is already depressed and struggling, removal of programs that foster camaraderie among students with similar interests in a city that already offers little for its teens to do on weekends and "off time" is a sure fire way to lose support of students and community. This principal needs to look at the research and understand the needs of this community. This is where getting outside the office and talking to stakeholders to find out what is in the community for students is critical. The letter written by sophomore Jessica Rogers clearly stated that there is little offered for students by the community in the area of entertainment. The school can be the hub of the social life of the students and that is better than some alternatives. Looking to the community and the staff for assistance and support in this area would be a better direction. Re-create instead of eliminate. Improve instead of remove. This will help to foster much needed support.

An open door policy is terrific if the principal plans to achieve nothing during the course of the school day. "Do you have a minute?" usually means ten minutes and a "Do you have ten minutes?" usually means at least an hour. It is necessary to validate every student, staff and parental concern, however, the principal dropping everything for everyone who stops by does make for very unproductive fourteen-hour days. Principal A can schedule bi-monthly meetings for staff, Friday (or Saturday) morning coffee for parents, and student-liaison meetings for the students. Making sure that parents have a direct email address is helpful, as many parents may not have the time to socialize to get their message to the principal. Networking with other principals is key to finding creative ways to be accessible. Colleagues are willing and wonderful resources. Principal A should used them whenever possible.

Monthly newsletters to parents can be an excellent form of communication if writing is the principal's forte. In the newsletter, invite the parents to offer feedback through email or at a specific time when the principal is in the office to take calls. Inviting the staff to write for the newsletter is good. Inviting the students is even better.

A Principal Advisory Group can be effective *if* the principal is willing to listen. If the principal keeps the membership of the group flexible and includes all stakeholders, it may be productive. Include staff members, the student services staff, and students, as well as parents. Listen and suggest and guide, but take control. This is a group to advise, not take over.

A principal should try to avoid the adage, "If you want anything done, and done right, do it yourself." Principal A may find this to be the easier course of action at first, but eventually it will discourage those groups and individuals who may have been great allies. This principal may be facing a much more difficult challenge in pulling together a fractured and disenchanted staff and student body. At first, it is easier to dictate than facilitate. Telling people what needs to be done suggests power on the surface, but weakness in the area of guidance. Everyone is resistant to a dictatorial presentation, but everyone responds to motivation, trust, inspiration, and enthusiasm. One person's good idea may develop into a GREAT idea with the input and work of a group and good resources. A project may not develop exactly as the principal had envisioned, but it may actually turn out better. What the principal may perceive as failure may not be failure at all if the **process is successful**. What is learned for "next time" will enable growth for the staff, the students, and the principal and will be part of *her* process in moving from Principal A to Principal B.

This scenario presents a school that has issues and concerns, but it is a school that has a staff that is supportive and a student body that is far from being a lost cause. School leaders need to believe in the strength and resiliency of children. When Principal A studies and understands the student body at Lincoln High School and all school stakeholders, she will begin to guide the school in a direction that will meet the needs of the students and get the school back on track to academic achievement, community respect, and support. Students are every school's biggest strength and natural resource. Employing that powerful source of energy and growth is the true power of the principal's office in the effort to improve a school, implement positive change, and educate students.

CHAPTER 3 SUMMARY

The rudimentary principals presented in this chapter have made errors in their leadership of the schools — not irreversible errors — but errors, nonetheless, in ascribing to the belief that they must do everything. Each neglects to delegate, verbalize, and listen to what is needed for their schools. The vision each presents does not convey a common mission to the stakeholders. They take the stance that it is easier to "do it yourself" rather that articulate to others what is necessary. With inexperience, there is a fear of disagreement or challenge of a decision. Accomplished principals have learned that developing and articulating the vision is a growth process that does not happen in the first week or month. They understand that every stakeholder has a voice and that voice is communicated through behavior, actions, and achievement.

A school leader today faces challenges and daily issues that our predecessors never had to even consider. Without a **strong vision** as a guide, school leaders in the 21st century will find the task of educating today's students daunting. The ability to create, articulate, and implement a school vision is more important than ever. School leaders today must be excellent communicators and original thinkers. They need to be sharply in-tune with their students, their community, the media, and most importantly, *themselves*, to best understand and implement what is necessary for the success of the school and the students who depend on them each day.

Both students and teachers respond best when they understand and know what is expected of them. The principal must model this each day in action and word. Trust and clear understanding of what school leaders will do when a situation arises that will impact their daily lives, academic or otherwise, is crucial to developing a collaborative group of stakeholders. A strong vision for the total school program should be at the core of all activity and planning for the school. Continued articulation and implementation of the vision and achievement of all students within the programs that have been developed and implemented by the stakeholders is the best accolade for school leaders in the 21st century.

STANDARD 2: THE CULTURE OF TEACHING AND LEARNING

The focus of the cases in Chapter 4 is on ISLLC Standard 2: The Culture of Teaching and Learning. Chapter 4 introduces you to issues of concern at Washington Elementary School, a Pre-K–6 rural school and Adams High, a 9–12 suburban high school.

As you read through this chapter and each subsequent chapter, you will find each case structured in a specific way.

First, you will be introduced to a specific Standard and to the case study scenario and its accompanying documents. Secondly, you will be given two focus questions to keep in mind as you read the case and as you analyze the two fictitious principals' responses: one principal at the rudimentary level, the second at the accomplished level.

As a reader, you will consider the core of the ISLLC standard and then apply this understanding to the rudimentary and accomplished principals' responses. We also invite you to consider other factors that could be built into each principal's response.

STANDARD 2

A SCHOOL ADMINISTRATOR IS AN EDUCATIONAL LEADER WHO PROMOTES THE SUCCESS OF ALL STUDENTS BY ADVOCATING, NURTURING, AND SUSTAINING A SCHOOL CULTURE AND INSTRUCTIONAL PROGRAM CONDUCIVE TO STUDENT LEARNING AND STAFF PROFESSIONAL GROWTH (CCSSO, 1996, P.12).

COMPONENT TWO **A**   Valuing Students and Staff

COMPONENT TWO **B**   Developing and Sustaining the Culture

COMPONENT TWO **C**   Ensuring an Inclusive Culture

COMPONENT TWO **D**   Monitoring and Evaluating the Culture

In every school there exists a unique and special community of professionals whose beliefs and values evolve over time to form the culture of the school. Effective leaders continually advocate, nurture, and sustain this culture. Above all else, this culture must revolve around student learning because teaching and learning are why schools exist. Student learning is the underlying purpose for all that takes place in a school.

An examination of an effective school gives evidence to the continual care given each and every student and staff member in the school. All aspects of the school community are embraced in the educational endeavor, including parents and community members. The students and teachers feel comfortable and at ease in their surroundings and are challenged each day to perform to high expectations. Parents are informed and aware of what these expectations are. Students and teachers alike know the beliefs and values held in the school. Successes are celebrated throughout the year. Teachers show their commitment to the students; students feel it each day. The principal shows his/her commitment to teachers by understanding, promoting, and recognizing how their efforts support student achievement. Valuing each other (students and staff alike) shows very clearly as a part of the culture of the school. When students, parents, and teachers, new to a school and community, are welcomed on their first day, they become acclimated to the school culture, and are on their way to becoming an integral part of the school by learning and acquiring the beliefs and values of the school.

Because the school exists for student learning, an important task is to keep that focus in the forefront. As part of that focus, there must be the belief that we have high expectations for all students to be successful. It is imperative that teachers hold high expectations for students and themselves at all times. The principal, as instructional leader, must ensure that high expectations are maintained and regularly assessed. Staff are encouraged to learn new strategies and try new teaching methodologies to assure that the needs of a diverse student population are being met. As a key element to sustaining a culture of mutual respect and responsibility, all stakeholders should be involved in the process. The principal has an ongoing obligation to work with all stakeholders to monitor and evaluate the school's belief system and vision and measure it against classroom practices. Barriers to student success should be identified and removed to ensure a comprehensive instructional program for all. It is only through continually assessing what is happening in the school that improvements can be assured. The culture of an effective school does not stagnate. It grows and changes as members of the school community continually evaluate it against the underlying mission of the school.

The following case studies focus on important components of the culture of teaching and learning. Student success is first and foremost and this is achieved through collaboration of stakeholders, nurturing a positive school culture that focuses on a comprehensive instructional program and staff professional growth.

 CASE STUDY

Washington Elementary
Pre-K–6 Rural Elementary School

As you read this case, consider these two questions:

1. What steps must the principal take to gain a better understanding of the needs of students, parents, and members of the larger community and how should this information be used to bring about changes in the school climate and culture for learning?

2. What kinds of resources and strategies should the principal consider to bring about needed changes in the school?

You are the newly assigned principal of Washington Elementary School, a Pre-K–6 grade school in a rural community, whose population consists of a small group of strawberry farmers, migrant workers who migrate to the area to plant and harvest strawberries, and year-around workers for the near-by phosphate plant. Washington Elementary School is comprised of children of migrant workers who typically arrive in September/October and depending on the yield of strawberries, move in March/April; White children of farmers and blue collar workers who live within the town of Milton, population 4000; and African American children of families who live in the larger town of Centerville, thirty minutes from the school.

You, the principal, are new to this part of Allen County, although you have been employed by Allen County Schools in an inner city school on the other side of the county. Washington Elementary School is considered to be a country school. The school enjoys the reputation of being a friendly school, where care and consideration for students' well being is the focus. The state's new testing guidelines have placed a greater emphasis than ever before on accountability of schools for academic gains. The testing results of Washington Elementary students, received during the previous summer, show the school made a grade of D, one of five elementary schools that made very low grades of D or F.

The Board of Education is very concerned with these failing grades, and is putting pressure on the schools to submit plans for improvement. The plans are due to the area director no later than September of this coming school year.

Upon arriving at the school during the summer, you are presented with the results of the previous year's testing. The Director of Elementary Education calls a meeting of principals of D and F schools. You are told that, as principal of a failing school, it is your job to come up with a plan for moving your school from a D to a C. You are told that support from central district personnel will be available to provide some assistance.

You develop plans to carry out the District's directive by planning a series of meetings with school personnel. Your secretary informs you that personnel were very unhappy with the many meetings called by the previous principal during the last school year to talk about new state testing guidelines for testing. The secretary shows you the memo sent by the district representative of the Classroom Teachers Association last February. The previous principal complied with demands by eliminating all but a few staff meetings. He sent memos instead, which in the secretary's viewpoint, were pretty much ignored.

As principal, you come into contact with some of the staff members when they stop by during the summer, and you note their disparagement of the testing results. Their comments often include:

Those tests are too hard.

Most of our students cannot handle the format of the test. The test asks them to explain their answers.

We might make progress in math; reading and writing are real problems.

We get no help from the parents of our students.

We as teachers have not been prepared enough for these tests.

Excerpt from Student Handbook, page 63a

Reporting Student Progress

- The progress report (report card) is an evaluation of the student's achievement in comparison to grade placement, progress against benchmarks, and instructional level.

- Progress reports that are issued each grading period can be interpreted by the teacher at a conference.

- Progress reports are only a part of the reporting system. Informational brochures shall be sent home at the end of the first nine weeks. Parent-teacher conferences and samples of work sent home throughout the year are designed to keep parents informed of their child's progress.

- Regular conferences between teacher and parent are an important part of the school's reporting system. Conference times are scheduled each year. The teacher shall send written invitations which should be answered promptly for efficient scheduling.

- Parents may also schedule conferences by contacting the school for an appointment. Conference times vary according to individual school schedules.

Washington Elementary

Demographics

Washington Elementary serves Pre-K through sixth grade students in the Allen County School District.

The school is located in the rural town of Milton, population 4000, surrounded by strawberry fields and orange groves.

The Hispanic population is composed largely of families whose primary language is Spanish. Many of the parents are themselves illiterate or have limited education, but are very supportive of the educational system. The majority of the Hispanic students are children of migrant workers. This is a highly transient population.

The African-American population is bussed from the town of Centerville, approximately thirty minutes from the school.

The white students are the children of strawberry farmers and blue collar workers who are employed in the phosphate plant nearby.

The school population is as follows:

62% Hispanic (5% growth in last 5 years)

33% White

5% African-American

Achievement Data

Washington Elementary — Previous School Year

School Grade - D

Reading

Criteria (to earn C)	Student Achievement	Meet Criteria
60% Level 2 or above	50% Level 2 and above	no

Mathematics

Criteria (to earn C)	Student Achievement	Meet Criteria
60% Level 2 or above	62% Level 2 and above	yes

Writing

Criteria (to earn C)	Student Achievement	Meet Criteria
50% Level 3 or above	49%	no

memo...

Allen County
Classroom Teachers Association

TO: J.A. Brown, Principal, Washington Elementary School

FROM: J. Lipscomb, District representative, Classroom Teachers
              Association (CTA), Allen County

RE: Faculty Meetings

DATE: February 20

We have received many staff complaints concerning the number and length of faculty meetings held at your school. Please be reminded of our teacher contract, section 3.7 which states:

> "Faculty meetings and in-service education shall be no longer
> than a total of 50 minutes per week beyond the normal workday,
> except for school accreditations. No more than one faculty
> meeting per week shall occur beyond the normal workday."

I request that you call to arrange a meeting with your CTA school representative, K. White, yourself, and a union representative who will be assigned to this matter. Please call me to schedule this meeting.

Minutes from School Board meeting

June 30

Superintendent of Schools, J.R. Smith, presented the test results of the previous school year state testing. Five elementary schools, two middle schools, and one high school fell below level in their school grading, receiving D or F scores.

The five elementary schools are as follows:

Elm Elementary School–F

Broad Elementary School–D

Washington Elementary School–D

T.J. Brown Elementary School–F

J.F. Kennedy Elementary School–D

Middle Schools:

Lincoln Middle–F

Graham Middle–D

High School:

Middleton High–D

The Board discussed the importance of investigating the issues that have contributed to the low scores at the eight schools, the need for these schools to show how they will improve, and the need to provide assistance as soon as possible to bring up the failing grades.

Based on the information about this school presented through the scenario and the documents, how should the principal respond to these two questions?

1. What steps must the principal take to gain a better understanding of the needs of students, parents and members of the larger community and how should this information be used to bring about changes in the school climate and culture for learning?

2. What kinds of resources and strategies should the principal consider to bring about needed changes in the school?

PRINCIPAL A rudimentary response

The principal gathers information available about his new school: the last three years' test data, including this year's test results, and staff development that took place within the last three years.

As the principal goes through test data, he notes the below average test scores earned by over 50% of the children tested within the past three years. He sees writing scores have been improving slowly over the last three years, although the school's writing grade from the state did not meet criteria above a D. Math scores have fluctuated in the last three years, but have generally been higher than reading and writing grades.

The participation of the faculty in staff development opportunities has been infrequent. A few teachers have attended two or three sessions a year, but other personnel attended only once, and in some cases none. The two professional study days set aside by the county office for staff development were poorly attended by a portion of the staff, with many teachers taking personal time on the dates of the trainings. The principal concludes that the staff is sorely in need of training and he must make sure it happens.

The principal believes that teachers will need to make great gains, especially in reading, this year to raise the school grade. He makes plans to call in district advisors to work with his teachers on reading strategies. Since the state tests in reading are given to fourth graders, he plans to arrange for professional development for his fourth grade reading teachers as soon as possible. Writing professional development will also be necessary for fourth grade teachers, as it is the fourth grade students who take the state writing test. Since math criteria have been met, he will forego math in-service for the year.

When the staff arrives for pre-planning before the school year begins, the principal explains the state grading of the schools, believing that the entire staff may not have internalized the importance of the grades the previous year. He explains the grade received by Washington Elementary in depth, pointing out the weak areas and the gains the school needs to make to change its grade to a C the next year. He tells them of his meeting with the Area Director, and the need for everyone to work hard to get the school off the failing list of schools. The principal gives out the dates set aside for fourth grade teacher in-service, letting them know they will be excused early to attend these sessions. He asks if any other teachers would like to go to the sessions, letting them know he will do his best to schedule them. He is disappointed when no teachers accept his offer.

Teachers are given copies of their previous school year state and national test results. They will be required to identify the skills on which their previous year's students scored in the below average category. They are asked to develop new strategies to teach these skills and to document this in their lesson plans. Many teachers complain that they are not given enough planning time to do this. The principal sets aside faculty meeting time each week, strictly adhering to faculty meeting timelines as stated in the Classroom Teachers Association Manual.

As the school year begins, the principal observes teachers in their classrooms. He sees well-managed classrooms but notes much busywork for some students, work that is nothing like the higher-level work required on state testing. When questioned about this, teachers indicate that many of the students cannot do that kind of work unless a teacher is working with them. There does not seem to be enough time and personnel to meet each child's needs. The principal expresses concern to district personnel who suggest the inauguration of a tutoring program for those students working below level in reading, math and/or writing to give them more time on task. The principal is able to gain monetary assistance from the district for the tutoring program. When he introduces the program to staff, he has difficulty getting buy-in for the program. Some teachers question him on what would be taught and what materials would be used. He relates that the district will provide the materials. Five teachers are hired to tutor after school. The program is then offered to a portion of the eligible below-level students, as many as can be accommodated by the five teachers. The principal is disappointed that more teachers have not signed up to tutor.

The principal believes that parents of the Washington Elementary students need to be informed about state testing and schedules a meeting to go over testing information. The meeting is attended by approximately 50 parents. He is later told that many parents attend church on the Wednesday night he scheduled for meeting. The principal is disappointed by the small number, but is encouraged by the interest of the people who come. He asks for parent input and hears from some parents that it is difficult to meet with the teachers when they see their child is having a problem. When conferences are requested in the middle of the day it is difficult for them to take off work to come.

Taking information from the parents, and recalling that teachers say parent input is low, the principal calls a meeting of staff members to discuss parent conferences. He is surprised by a teacher who suggests evening conferences, a procedure that the teacher knew to be in place at another school in the district. The principal gathers information about evening conferences, checking with the Classroom Teachers Association manual and informs staff. The majority of staff members question how much difference evening conferences will make. The principal tells them they will schedule evening conferences for the second half of the school year and then compare day with evening conference attendance.

The principal sees that he has made some progress but does not feel supported by the majority of staff members. It seems that a few teachers seem to sway others to object to new ideas. He anticipates that the next year will be another up-hill battle to get staff to work together to improve learning for students.

PRINCIPAL B accomplished response

The principal gathers information about his new school:

- the last ten years of testing data, looking for trends in scores

- records of staff development received by staff, recording the type and frequency, and staff members who participated

- demographic data on the student population for the last ten years

- teacher evaluation records for the past five years, noting especially the comment sections by previous evaluators

- records of last school year's recognitions, whether to students or staff (his secretary and teachers are queried about recollections of last year's accomplishments)

- student discipline records

In an effort to become acquainted with the community surrounding the school, the principal calls upon the pastors of two nearby churches, and also the church in the area of Centerville where some of the Washington Elementary students live. He concludes that the churches play an important role in the lives of many of his students and their families.

He contacts the school social worker and meets with her to discuss Washington Elementary families and the experiences she has had in working with them. He realizes she will be a great asset to him as he attempts to become acquainted with his students and their parents. He invites the PTA Executive Board to meet with him to introduce himself and his belief system and to gain knowledge of their priorities and perspectives on the school.

The principal visits the fire department chief two blocks away, and introduces himself to the sheriff's deputy at the near-by sheriff's substation. He is pleased to be invited to join the Milton Community Council, a new organization that will focus on the needs of the Milton community. The principal plans to attend as many meetings as possible to gain insight about the community. He also would like to reassure them of the worth of Washington Elementary, as the school grade of D had already been published in the newspaper. He sees the Council as a way to form close ties between the school and the community.

In contemplating the information he has gathered, the principal determines that staff will be feeling disheartened by the school grade and will need to rally together to address the academic achievement concerns of the school. He hosts a pre-planning welcome celebration at which he highlights last year's accomplishments and presents the school's vision and mission statements for review. Consensus at the opening celebration shows the vision and mission has great meaning and value to staff and is still appropriate. The vision and mission are posted in all classrooms, and throughout the school building and campus. Reference is made to them over and over again by the principal throughout the school year so they are internalized and serve as reminders of the beliefs and values of the school.

The principal, emphasizing the pluses and minuses of Washington Elementary's scores in recent years and the previous year's scores, presents the state testing guidelines. The principal reminds all members that every staff member, including the principal, has a responsibility to prepare the children to have the knowledge to be successful on the state tests. Each grade level team is asked to brainstorm suggestions for working with their students in reading, writing, and math. The principal meets separately with each grade-level team monthly to listen to their ideas. He makes suggestions to district personnel who might be able to give some assistance and is pleased to hear positive responses to the brainstorming sessions. He makes it a priority to visit classrooms daily, pointing out positive happenings in each class. He especially notes when he sees a teacher trying out a strategy talked about in one of the monthly meetings. He suggests materials that might assist a teacher in presenting lessons in a different way. He highlights higher level questioning techniques and problem solving activities as necessary for raising the expectations for Washington Elementary students. Students are praised for making academic gains during the morning announcements, pep rallies, assemblies, and at other venues.

When teachers express the feeling that some students do not have enough time on task, he asks for solutions. One suggestion is for after-school tutoring. Consensus is reached on attempting to begin a tutoring program for students falling behind their classmates. The principal asks and receives help from the district to fund a tutoring program. A task force of eight teachers who develop criteria for students attending the tutoring program initiates the program. It is discovered that all students needing tutoring cannot be served after school. As a result, school personnel begin to hold small in-school groups to give more one-on-one help. A number of students bussed in from Centerville show a need for tutoring but transportation is a problem. A staff member living in Centerville suggests that tutoring sessions could be held in conjunction with an after-school program beginning in a Centerville church. The principal and teacher make arrangements to begin the tutoring program.

Within the first month of school, the principal sets a date for a parent meeting, seeking input from grade-level team leaders for an agenda. To attract more parents, the team leaders plan for the school student chorus to sing as part of the program and the PTA offers desserts and drinks for the meeting. The principal explains the testing program and key teachers on different grade-levels ask parents for specific support, suggesting how children can be helped at home. The school social worker serves as translator for the meeting, ensuring that all parents understand what is being said even if their understanding of the English language is minimal. During the session, a parent survey is distributed in English and Spanish for parents to complete, asking for their concerns and suggestions for improvement. The PTA works with team leaders to plan ongoing, monthly informational meetings for parents.

The principal schedules monthly staff meetings, carefully preparing an agenda to make the most efficient use of time to share information and ideas. A time is set aside in each meeting to highlight student and teacher accomplishments. Staff members begin to inform the principal of good things they are seeing around campus. More and more good news initiated by teachers is shared during meetings.

As the year continues, the principal makes note of the key staff members who seem to enjoy the esteem of their colleagues. He calls on these people to spearhead task forces for various projects, knowing that the more reluctant teachers will be encouraged to try something new if led by someone they admire. He enrolls four key teachers, plus himself, in a leadership-training institute. The teachers return from the session with many new ideas, and they report enthusiastically to the faculty on their experiences and encourage other teachers to try some new teaching strategies learned. The principal is especially interested in the leadership team's ideas about starting school study groups the next year, which will become staff development opportunities. The leadership team will spearhead the program, gaining consensus from staff before going forward to implement the program. The principal sees study groups as an opportunity for teachers to choose areas for self-improvement and thus they will be more likely to be relevant to the needs of the students they teach.

Parent survey results disclose that parents find it difficult to stay informed about their child's work. These results are discussed at one of the monthly grade level meetings as an obstacle to student achievement. Information is shared at the meeting that a nearby school utilizes evening conferences in place of daytime conferences and this process is explained to the principal and staff. The staff decides to have evening conferences during the second half of the school year on a trial basis. During this time, the attendance rates for daytime and evening conferences will be compared.

As the school year comes to a close, the principal plans a celebration for all staff members to commemorate the progress made during the year. He plans to highlight the work of each task force and celebrate the successes of various programs that were begun to further academic achievement for Washington Elementary students. Staff members volunteer to prepare ribbons of achievement for parents, teachers, and students who made significant contributions during the year. A teacher climate survey will be distributed to all staff members. Information from this survey will enable the staff to continue to improve the culture at Washington Elementary School.

The principal looks forward to the next year as one that will enable staff to continue with the initiatives begun in his first year as principal at Washington Elementary. He is enthusiastic about the potential he has been able to tap from teachers and students, and is anxious to discover more in the years to come.

The pages that follow outline the "Keys for Improved Performance." Specifically, they note:

a) the differences in the performance of rudimentary Principal A and accomplished Principal B;

b) the potential consequences of the continued performance of Principal A at the rudimentary level;

c) strategies and suggestions on how to move from one level of performance to another level.

Again, these pages specifically relate to the case outlined herein and the two focus questions:

1. What steps must the principal take to gain a better understanding of the needs of students, parents, and members of the larger community and how should this information be used to bring about changes in the school climate and culture for learning?

2. What kinds of resources and strategies should the principal consider to bring about needed changes in the school?

KEYS FOR IMPROVED PERFORMANCE

DIFFERENCES IN PRINCIPAL PERFORMANCE

Upon being assigned to a new school, both Principal A and Principal B saw a need to gather background information about the school. The two principals collected the following information:

PRINCIPAL A
rudimentary response

Last three years of test data

Staff development records

PRINCIPAL B
accomplished response

Last ten years of test data

Staff development records

Staff evaluations — positive notes

Demographic data

Records of last year's accomplishments

Student discipline records

Principal A looked at three years of scores but failed to find a trend of upward movement of test scores, as found by Principal B over ten years of testing. In analyzing scores, Principal B also noted the rise in the Hispanic population within the past five years. The addition of youngsters whose primary language is Spanish could have an influence on test scores. Both principals also take into account that state testing includes a new format in testing, not familiar to teachers and students, especially in the first year of administration.

Principal A determined there would be a need for in-service for teachers and that staff might be reluctant to attend. He mandated training for teachers on the grade levels giving state tests. Other teachers did not ask to participate. In emphasizing in-service only for teachers giving tests, he is putting the burden for test preparation on one grade level. Other teachers may not take ownership for preparing their students academically and may see test results as, "It's not my fault."

Principal B, in noting records of poor attendance of teachers at professional development sessions, knew professional development would be needed, but chose to approach teachers in a different manner. Principal B chose to begin his tenure as principal with a celebration of the previous year's accomplishments, a re-affirmation of the school's vision and mission statements. Both of which were found to be appropriate and centered on student learning. Only after identifying strength areas did Principal B pinpoint areas for growth and improvement.

The underlying belief system expressed in the vision and mission statements was nurtured by posting the statements all around the school, but was especially nurtured by the principal as advocate for them. He used the language of the statements often to show his commitment to them, modeling these behaviors to the staff, students, parents, and community.

Principal B sought to engage staff members into taking ownership of the problem facing Washington Elementary (grade of D) by brainstorming with them on how they could make changes in their teaching to improve academic levels. It was important to have ongoing dialogue to deepen people's understanding of the issues to be addressed. One of the essential conditions for change is for comprehensive involvement. "Employees at all levels have to be engaged, have to be involved, and have to take ownership of the change" (Walsh, Saltes, & Wiman, March 2001). Principal B's teachers were involved on all grade levels to make positive changes and professional development was offered as needed. The principal utilized key teachers to bring new ideas (change) to the school to spread change gradually. The teachers themselves became catalysts for change, with Principal B encouraging and giving input all the way (Richardson, May 2001).

Principal B's overtures into the community served as an important first step to blending school and community. Principal B is able to utilize information gained by these visits to better plan for parent meetings and is able to extend into the community with tutoring. Membership in the Milton Community Council provides a forum for him to meld community/school issues.

Principal A understands the importance of informing parents about concerns of the school, but is less accomplished than Principal B because he has not obtained needed community information. Many more members of the community need to be involved in the workings and concerns of the school.

Both principals have tried to be solicitous of the timing of staff meetings, both realizing if meetings are called for frivolous reasons and do not have a clear agenda, staff members will believe their time is wasted. Principal B utilized a portion of staff meetings for celebrations, giving staff members something to anticipate at each meeting. He found reasons to celebrate people's efforts and showed support for teachers trying new endeavors. He validated their efforts to take a risk and learn new behaviors. The message he sent is one of high expectations for all personnel.

Principal A initiated a tutoring program at Washington Elementary. Principal A's program was funded by the district but with a "top-down" approach. The principal is not using his teachers to his advantage by engaging them in the planning stages of the program. To have ownership of the tutoring program, people need to be involved in its conception and the planning of the components of the program. Principal B involved a task force to investigate the program, and the momentum of the program encouraged additional features (small-group help during school hours and a tutoring partnership). More students are served in Principal B's program that was guided by these important stakeholders in students' academic success. The enthusiasm for the program has come from within the school community.

Teachers at Principal A's school questioned the suggestion of evening conferences at Washington Elementary. Again, although a teacher brought up the idea for evening conferences, staff was negative about it and reluctant to go ahead with evening conferences. Principal A used good judgment in having a trial period but had to contend with negative attitudes. The outcome of the survey on daytime versus evening conferences may be skewed by teachers' less than enthusiastic attitudes.

Principal B garnered a positive attitude toward evening conferences by providing parent survey results which supported differing conference times and getting consensus from staff to try a new procedure.

The end of the year finds both principals contemplating the next year. Principal A feels he has not gained full support of his faculty. The climate in the school continues to radiate doubt and reluctance to change. New programs have been initiated but do not seem to be supported by all staff members. Principal A has reason to be concerned about this. Principal A hopes that state tests will show improvements but knows his school has a long way to go to become an effective school that is focused on student learning.

Principal B is also contemplating the next year. He has presented a climate survey to his staff so he will be able to assess the school's climate and to seek ways to improve it. He has approved and nurtured new programs with the support of his staff. He has key teachers in place who inspire their colleagues to work toward the vision and mission of the school. Whatever the results of the state testing, he knows his staff has worked to improve student learning and feels that gains will be made because of the efforts of his teachers.

Potential Consequences of the Performance of Principal A

During his first year at Washington Elementary School, Principal A has made his staff aware of low test scores and the need to improve. He has put much of the burden of raising test scores on the fourth grade teachers, whose students take the state tests. Since he has not emphasized professional development for the other grade-level teachers, the students coming up to the "testing grade" will not have had the benefit of enhanced learning provided by teachers who have received additional strategy training. *All* staff in the school need to be aware of and alert to needed teaching strategies that new research says will enhance learning. Strategies in all academic areas (not only reading) need to be studied and enhanced. The potential for higher test scores in all academic areas in the years to come is **low** if *all* staff are not working together to prepare students for enhanced learning in every academic area.

Principal A will continue to struggle to introduce new ideas and programs into Washington Elementary School until he builds a climate of true commitment for the school's vision and goals. He has not encouraged collaborative effort among staff members and thus he has difficulty getting staff to initiate ideas and "buy into" alternative ways of promoting teaching and learning in the school. His school will remain at risk for failing grades until he breaks through the wall of resistance to change that seems to be commonplace at the school and builds a structure of caring and belonging among staff, students, and parents.

PRINCIPAL A
rudimentary response

TO

PRINCIPAL B
accomplished response

HOW DO YOU MOVE FROM RUDIMENTARY PRINCIPAL A TO ACCOMPLISHED PRINCIPAL B?

Principal A is operating the principalship as an authoritative figure who is trying to be a catalyst for change but has not fully involved his staff members to facilitate the change along with him. His entire staff must share common beliefs (vision and mission) and talk about them often. They must believe they can achieve what they set out to do. They must develop ownership of the problem to be addressed. Positive change and high performance can only happen when all stakeholders (teachers, students, parents) are a part of the preparation and execution of the plan. Principal A needs to involve the community in school life. He must ask for input from all stakeholders and then know he needs to ask for commitment from them. Celebrations of good ideas, projects, and awards must be a regular part of school and community life. Culture is built upon the notion that, "We are special; we can achieve what we set out to do." All stakeholders need to develop a pride in the organization and its accomplishments.

Principal A can evolve into Principal B with thoughtful planning, and the appreciation and utilization of the community of people around him who will bring enthusiasm and motivation to the task of promoting student learning at Washington Elementary.

CASE STUDY 4

Adams High School
9–12 Suburban High School

In the following case study, the principals are confronted with four issues: declining test scores, professional development, concerns expressed by the Business Council to the Superintendent, and establishing a culture of success for all students. Principal A and B are varied in their approaches to addressing the key issues with potentially varied results and ramifications.

As you read this case study, consider these two questions:

1. What kinds of data should the principal use to gain a better understanding of student achievement and how should these data be reported to the faculty and the community?

2. What steps should the principal take to ensure that all students benefit from a challenging academic program?

When Adams High School (AHS) opened in the early 70's many community members and educators called it the "Country Club" because, with the exception of a very small population of bussed-in students, the resident students were from upper class backgrounds. The campus is safe, clean and orderly with very little ethnic or socioeconomic-related problems. The school has had a reputation for academic excellence, innovative course offerings and extra-curricular achievements. The facility is approximately 25 years old and has been well-maintained with any site improvements largely due to the support given by its affluent families. The staff is composed of older teachers who opened the school, and due to some retiring, there has recently been an influx of younger teachers; many of whom were graduates of AHS. The school serves grades 9–12. For most of the early years the school served mostly affluent white students who went on to attend four-year colleges. Most of the families of those students were prominent business owners and professionals. Recently, there has been a sudden influx of minority students of lower socioeconomic backgrounds entering AHS. In order to provide additional support to their families, many of the students are employed after school on a part-time basis. After graduation some go on to attend junior college, start a family, or go into the labor market. There has been a noticeable lack of enrollment in the advanced classes by these students. Even so, these minority students are active participants in extra-curricular activities, which contribute to the public's positive image of the school.

While the school has maintained a reputation of excellence over the years, there has been an increasing decline in positive test results for specific groups within the school. The data show that there are minority students from lower socioeconomic backgrounds who are not performing at the same level as the rest of the student body. There is a growing concern in the affluent community that the increase in the number of impoverished students is affecting test scores and changing the school's culture, affecting the type and level of classes being offered. They have voiced concerns about the curriculum possibly being watered down and have demanded that advanced classes be increased and the teacher-student ratio be lowered so their children will remain competitive in increasingly rigorous college entrance standards. In recent years, some colleges have reported that the basic skills scores of AHS students on entrance exams have declined to the point that many students are forced to take remedial college entrance level courses and an increased number have dropped out and gone to a junior college instead.

It is widely known that the input from the wealthy families and business community usually results in action on the part of the administration. Despite efforts by the school's administration to diversify the parent support organizations and to bring the underrepresented families into the culture of the school, the parent groups are still made up of the more vocal and powerful affluent families with little or no involvement from the minority families. This cycle is demonstrating a duality in the school's culture where affluent students are achieving and lower socioeconomic students are underachieving.

Another dichotomy that exists within the school is that the experienced staff members have been successful in their teaching strategies and are reluctant to change even through district-provided staff development. They feel that the younger/newer staff members who are striving to be more innovative in their approach with the changing student population will eventually come to realize that not all students are going to be successful regardless of how hard they try. The attitude of the veteran staff regarding professional development is that it is a necessary evil that goes with the job. The newer staff members are eager to do interesting professional development activities.

AHS has never dropped below an acceptable assessment score, but has never ranked as a high performing school. The teachers believe that the recent drop in achievement scores is a result of changing populations and is not a result from teaching practices that have been effective for many years. They believe that the caliber of student that is coming to AHS is lower than in the past, which has an impact on the achievement scores and report card grades. In their opinion, the students should be held responsible for doing the work and if they fail, it is a result of lack of performance and hard work and not teaching strategies.

Summary of Major Findings Based on Data

- Current assessment results show that Adams High School met its school growth target for the third year in a row, but still did not improve in all sub-groups.

- African-American and Hispanic sub-groups improved in grades 10, 11 and 12 but did not meet or exceed their target scores.

- White and Asian sub-groups improved in all grades and did meet or exceed their target scores.

- 90% of eligible students were tested.

- The attendance rate has declined each of the past three years. It was 92.8% three years ago, 91.4% two years ago, and 89.6% last year.

- Only 36% of the 9th graders tested on last year's High School Exit Exam passed reading.

- Only 27% of the 9th graders tested on last year's High School Exit Exam passed math.

- In reading, passing rates for sub-groups were as follows:

    Asian-57%
    African-American-19%
    Hispanic-23%
    White-49%

- In mathematics, passing rates for sub-groups were as follows:

    Asian-34%
    African-American-13%
    Hispanic-21%
    White-41%

memo...

Adams High School
From the Office of the Principal

To: Staff

From: Principal

Date: May 1

Subject: Survey Results

Two years ago our faculty responded to a staff survey prepared by Adams High School Instructional Council in preparation for our upcoming accreditation. The student survey was administered during the same time period. Both staff and students responded to many areas on the surveys that will be very helpful as we endeavor to improve our educational services to students and prepare for our accreditation visit.

The main area that we will need to address as a result of the surveys is:

- The apparent difference in student and staff perceptions of our instructional delivery system.

Question 4; Student Survey   67% felt they were bored in classes and not being challenged.

Question 7; Staff Survey   97% felt that they were doing a great job in teaching their subject matter.

Question 8; Staff Survey   95% felt that students were being appropriately challenged in classes.

Our Staff Development Day, scheduled for May 6, will address this topic. Please be prepared to closely examine to your teaching techniques, strategies, and curriculum.

Superintendent of Schools
Adams School District

Dear Superintendent:

We appreciate your focus on high academics and we in the Business Council plan to continue our support in making the work environment attractive to our graduating students. We are writing you to share information that we feel to be important to you and our community.

We recently sent a questionnaire to our membership soliciting information on factors in our community that contribute to a good business environment and requested candid suggestions on areas of improvement. Many of the respondents expressed concern about the caliber of job and college applicants and attributed the lack of qualified applicants to the educational system.

The Council has charged a committee to study this issue and bring back recommendations for action. We would appreciate any support that you can give by providing our committee access to school principals to obtain student achievement data, curriculum information, and school profile information. We will keep you informed on our Council's findings and plan to work cooperatively with you to implement our recommendations.

We know what a difficult job you have and we stand ready to be of assistance to you in bringing about your vision for well-educated students and to assure the Council of a well-trained work force in our growing community.

Sincerely,

James Jones
Executive Director

e-mail @

From: Superintendent of Schools
Date: August 4
To: All Principals
Subject: Adams Interschool Network

I have attached to this e-mail a copy of a memo that I received from the Business Council requesting access to principals to gather information on the issue of a well-prepared work force. It is important that we let our community know what we are doing to prepare our students. To assist you, the Testing Services Department will provide the Business Council with achievement data. You will receive copies of all information sent to the Council.

When the Council contacts you, please be prepared to share your school's mission statement, academic focus, and any other information you deem important for our community to know. It is key that you share what you are doing to prepare our students for success. Keep in mind when talking with them, that the Council's interest is centered in what we are doing to provide our community with a well-prepared work force.

Next week during my scheduled principals' meetings, please be prepared to share and discuss:

- Student achievement scores for the last three years

- Steps you are taking to assure that all students achieve

- Progress on achieving your school's vision

Keep up the good work for our students.

Based on the information about this school presented through the scenario and the documents, how should the principal respond to these two questions?

1. What kinds of data should the principal use to gain a better understanding of student achievement and how should these data be reported to the faculty and the community?

2. What steps should the principal take to ensure that all students benefit from a challenging academic program?

PRINCIPAL A rudimentary response

It is likely that because Principal A in this case study does not have a complete grasp of all aspects of the job, he may miss issues that have significance which may cause him to only deal with issues that directly impact his image as a principal. By overlooking or not understanding important issues presented in this case study such as diversity in the classes, the importance of developing staff to affect student learning, and involving stakeholders in decision making, there is potential to create more problems for himself and the school in the future.

Principal A is likely to take action quickly in preparation for the planned meeting with the Superintendent without regard to involving other staff members or community persons. His research efforts are limited to what he knows about test data, the curriculum, and student learning. The possibility exists that Principal A will focus on gathering information to demonstrate to the Superintendent that his leadership is having a positive effect on student learning. Because there may be little evidence of actions taken to address some important instructional needs prior to receiving the Superintendent's memo, his preparation may disregard addressing a core issue of program examination and improvement and instead center on self-preservation issues.

In an effort to have knowledge of classroom practices, Principal A identifies his most effective teachers and visits their classes to gain some insight about teaching practices and only refers to them in upcoming discussions with the Superintendent. Teachers who are not challenging students academically are not encouraged to take leadership roles in the plan for improvement because of the time involved in bringing them up to his perception of professional standards. It is unethical and unwise for the principal to ignore these teachers. To have an effective educational program, all staff should be engaged and involved in improvement efforts.

In this case study, the affluent parents have a significant impact on decision making in the area of curriculum planning and course offerings and have considerable influence in the overall culture of the school. Principal A does not nurture this parent leadership potential, and feels threatened by the fact that it is necessary to collaborate with them. He spends valuable energy and time employing strategies designed to gain power over them rather than make them partners. There may be times in the future when the lack of parental involvement will have a negative effect on State or Federal program reviews.

The issue of maintaining a focus on teaching and learning is a critical one because of the infusion of students who are not experiencing success in the educational focus of the school. Because the course offerings over the years have successfully addressed the educational needs of the affluent students, Principal A attempts to maintain the status quo and chooses the option of generating more remedial classes to accommodate the needs of the poverty students. Such a step could cause the school's populations to be segregated and will not encourage equitable, diverse enrollment in college level classes.

There are many issues in this case study that will no doubt be faced by most principals during their careers. Here are some that are common and worth discussing: declining test scores, professional development for teachers, pressures brought by the Business Council via the Superintendent, and the need for establishing a learning culture that will benefit all students. Whenever important issues arise, a principal should have an understanding of the issues and be able and willing to share information with stakeholder groups. Stakeholder groups typically look to the principal for understanding of issues related to the school and they have an expectation that the principal will take appropriate leadership in preventing and/or resolving issues.

Principal B, in addressing the issue of declining test scores, helps the staff gain an in-depth understanding of what the data is reporting about student achievement. The staff/student surveys reflected that the staff thinks they are doing a great teaching job and the students feel that they are bored. These conflicting findings directed discussion to teaching strategies. Principal B orchestrates the collection of data and reports these in such a way that all staff are now knowledgeable about student achievement data. Looking at disaggregated data in standardized tests is one of the most effective ways Principal B can develop a plan of action with the staff to improve student performance.

Principal B and the planning group plan a format for a professional development experience that is conducive to learning. This well-planned professional development session means the difference between an engaging learning experience and another non-productive meeting. Principal B remembers that an effective professional development session is one that makes sure staff members feel their time is being spent productively and has practical application for classroom use. Principal B establishes an appropriate format for a professional development venue by having the staff break into job-a-like units so that discussions are pertinent and focused. Groups report out to the large group so everyone feels a sense of responsibility and ownership. Staff members who usually do not participate are involved with their job-a-like peers. Principal B knows that making a professional development experience worthwhile to teachers is worth investing time and energy. The experienced Principal B ensures that teachers have "buy-in" to the professional development experience by giving them a key role in planning.

Over the years the make up of the school has changed which presents Principal B with an opportunity for some active curriculum discussions. The original course offerings were primarily designed to meet the needs of the affluent students. Now, however, Principal B can demonstrate a need for staff to encourage the growing population of students living below the poverty line to enroll in high-level course offerings. The total staff recognizes their obligation to ensure that all students feel success and are motivated to excel. Principal B knows collaboration with all stakeholders in addressing these issues is crucial.

In response to the memo sent from the Superintendent, Principal B immediately calls the school leadership group together and begins to develop a plan of action to address issues. It should be noted that this is not done in isolation with the site administrators, but is shared with school leadership groups and parent leadership groups. Principal B immediately develops a plan to gather and prepare information to respond to the Superintendent and the Business Council members. Principal B knows the importance of assembling test data and preparing to share it with the Superintendent along with the school's mission statement. Principal B accepts responsibility for leading this endeavor and preparing the response. Because of the delicate nature of the concern expressed to the Superintendent, Principal B is aware that a rationale must be developed that can address the successes of the school's mission and show what is being done to address overall student achievement.

The pages that follow outline the "Keys for Improved Performance." Specifically, they note:

a) the differences in the performance of rudimentary Principal A and accomplished Principal B;

b) the potential consequences of the continued performance of Principal A at the rudimentary level;

c) strategies and suggestions on how to move from one level of performance to another level.

Again, these pages specifically relate to the case outlined herein and the two focus questions:

1. What kinds of data should the principal use to gain a better understanding of student achievement and how should these data be reported to the faculty and the community?

2. What steps should the principal take to ensure that all students benefit from a challenging academic program?

 KEYS FOR IMPROVED PERFORMANCE

DIFFERENCES IN PRINCIPAL PERFORMANCE
DECLINING TEST SCORES

PRINCIPAL A	PRINCIPAL B
rudimentary response	accomplished response
Focus is on professional reputation not on student achievement results.	Approaches the concern openly with staff to get general "buy-in".
Actions that are taken are designed to give rationale for test results.	Recognizes the problem and takes action to ensure understanding of the problem and leadership needs.
Does not involve staff in addressing the concern.	Provides leadership in getting all stakeholders involved in addressing the concern.
Does not take action to comprehend test data.	Focuses on the benefits of examining disaggregated data to focus on needs.
Fails to anticipate the growing concern about the test scores.	Understands the link between test data and curriculum content.
Does not link the test data with curriculum content.	

DIFFERENCES IN PRINCIPAL PERFORMANCE

PROFESSIONAL DEVELOPMENT

PRINCIPAL A	PRINCIPAL B
rudimentary response	accomplished response

Looks to high-performing staff to critique professional development opportunities for staff.

Principal B makes the staff and community aware of the changing student body; finds effective ways to include diversity in the culture of the school; and presents opportunities for staff to keep abreast of the school's changing population.

Does little to involve the impoverished community in the culture of the school; lacks focus when adjusting the curriculum; and does not provide professional development activities to address the barriers to student success.

Develops a plan that includes all teachers in professional development that will ensure a more unified approach to teaching practice.

Offers staff opportunities for professional development to increase proficiency in teaching practice.

Gives staff a key role in planning and implementing professional development sessions.

Encourages staff to become familiar with backgrounds of all students, but allows some teachers to elect not to participate.

Establishes a job-a-like format that assures greater participation of all staff.

Assembles staff to review the mission statement and shares the Superintendent's/Business Council's concern.

Communicates to staff that professional development is an important element for student achievement.

Goes about professional development in the same manner that proved to be ineffective in the past.

DIFFERENCES IN PRINCIPAL PERFORMANCE

BUSINESS COUNCIL AND SUPERINTENDENT

PRINCIPAL A	PRINCIPAL B
rudimentary response	accomplished response

Gathers information for meeting with Superintendent without involving staff in the planning process.	Collects data to illustrate many aspects of the student body profile (attendance, achievement scores, parent educational background, mobility rates, course enrollment data, teacher grading practices).
Collects data that only deals with student achievement in academics without regard to other data that has an impact on student performance.	Brings key personnel together to discuss action plans to address student performance needs for the meeting with the Superintendent.

CREATING AND ESTABLISHING A LEARNING CULTURE THAT WILL BENEFIT ALL STUDENTS

PRINCIPAL A	PRINCIPAL B
rudimentary response	accomplished response

Lacks a focus to challenge all students to take high-level classes.	Works collaboratively with staff to implement a plan that will assure all students are enrolled in high-level courses.
Student survey indicates that all students are not being challenged in curriculum, yet Principal A seeks to include more lower level classes in the master schedule.	

Potential Consequences of the Performance of Principal A

- The issues of diversity may not be addressed and curriculum will be geared towards affluent students.

- There will be no "buy-in" from parents who are in poverty, which will result in lack of parent involvement.

- Principal A's ethics may be compromised because of the focus on self-preservation.

- The school vision may not be met.

- Principal A will lose support and respect as his performance is seen as weak and self-centered to staff and community.

- The curriculum may not address the needs of the impoverished population.

- Capable students will not be challenged.

- Teachers who could improve instruction under good leadership and staff development will not learn to become better teachers.

- When monitoring teams from the state or Federal levels visit the school, there will not be a cadre of parents to represent all populations.

- Principal A will not have a grasp of the individual talents of all teachers on staff.

- Most likely discrepancies in student achievement will continue.

- The lack of teacher "buy-in" will perpetuate the inequities among the diverse parent groups.

- The culture of the school will serve to isolate minority and poverty students.

PRINCIPAL A   TO   PRINCIPAL B

rudimentary response   accomplished response

HOW DO YOU MOVE FROM RUDIMENTARY PRINCIPAL A TO ACCOMPLISHED PRINCIPAL B?

- ▦ Attend local, regional, state, or national professional development opportunities.

- ▦ Shadow successful principals to gain knowledge and insight into successful practices.

- ▦ Develop an advisory council composed of key parents, students, staff, and community to discuss educational issues.

- ▦ Generate and participate in reading groups on current educational issues.

- ▦ Link up with a critical friend.

- ▦ Bring in district-level test coordinators to review and interpret test data with staff.

- ▦ Read material and attend sessions regarding innovative educational strategies and processes.

- ▦ Continue to nurture positive school culture through celebrations of excellence and achievements.

- ▦ Seek opportunities to involve parents, students, and community in the life of the school through such activities as career days, student exhibition days, student shadow days, teacher shadow days, mentoring programs, and other such activities.

- ▦ Reflect on other steps one could take to move from rudimentary to accomplished. Add them to this list.

CHAPTER 4 SUMMARY

The principals of the schools highlighted within this chapter are school leaders whose challenge is to promote the teaching and learning of all students in their schools. They are faced with the task of building a positive school culture where all students have the opportunity to learn.

To understand student needs is another task of each principal. He/she must ensure that his/her staff possesses this knowledge. One challenge for principal and staff is to develop ways to accommodate the diverse needs of the individual learners. As each principal and staff work to provide for all learners it is necessary to make sure that, through continual dialogue among staff, the instructional program is understood and promoted. The staff members need to develop the motivation to learn new strategies to carry out the program and to have the expectation that they can make the difference with their students. That expectation of increased learning needs to penetrate the thinking of students, their parents, and the community to ensure success of increased learning programs.

Successes marked by celebrations, symbols, and ceremonies begin with the principal and permeate the fabric of the school, ensuring a culture that promotes a caring staff and student body who all feel a sense of belonging in their school.

As staff initiate new strategies and programs, the important task of monitoring and evaluating is another responsibility of the principal. He/she, along with staff members, must constantly reflect on practices and continually research ways to improve the teaching and learning in the school.

STANDARD 3: THE MANAGEMENT OF LEARNING

The focus of the cases in Chapter 5 is on ISLLC Standard 3: The Management of Learning. Chapter 5 introduces you to issues of concern at Tyler Elementary School, a Pre-K-6 rural school, and Monroe High, a 9-12 urban high school.

As you read through this chapter and each subsequent chapter, you will find each case structured in a specific way.

First, you will be introduced to a specific Standard and to the case study scenario and its accompanying documents. Secondly, you will be given two focus questions to keep in mind as you read the case and as you analyze the two fictitious principals' responses: one principal at the rudimentary level, the second at the accomplished level.

As a reader, you will consider the core of the ISLLC standard and then apply this understanding to the rudimentary and accomplished principals' responses. We also invite you to consider other factors that could be built into each principal's response.

STANDARD 3

A SCHOOL ADMINISTRATOR IS AN EDUCATIONAL LEADER WHO PROMOTES THE SUCCESS OF ALL STUDENTS BY ENSURING MANAGEMENT OF THE ORGANIZATION, OPERATIONS, AND RESOURCES FOR A SAFE, EFFICIENT, AND EFFECTIVE LEARNING ENVIRONMENT (CCSO, 1996, P.14).

COMPONENT THREE A — Making Management Decisions to Ensure Successful Teaching and Learning

COMPONENT THREE B — Developing Procedures to Ensure Successful Teaching and Learning

COMPONENT THREE C — Allocating Resources to Ensure Successful Teaching and Learning

COMPONENT THREE D — Creating a Safe, Healthy Environment to Ensure Successful Teaching and Learning

Effective school leaders are individuals who can communicate to others a clear vision for success that focuses on teaching and learning techniques that will enable all students to master the academic skills, concepts, and knowledge necessary to become productive citizens and lifelong learners.

Effective school leaders are individuals who grow and cultivate collaborative cultures that reflect a decision-making model that engages stakeholders in a data-driven, decision-making process. Essential components of this culture include the establishment of a safe, caring, and supportive environment that recognizes the developmental needs of children as well as one that tolerates and welcomes wide ranges of diversity.

Effective school leaders are individuals who align their words and actions as they allocate resources to meet the instructional needs of students. Such a leader promotes the alignment of the school mission with the daily practices within the school. Resources include money, time, facilities, and personnel. The effective school leader maintains his/her focus on the school mission in the decision-making process and distribution of resources to ensure that teaching and learning is at the core.

Effective school leaders create an environment for teaching and learning that is safe and healthy. They understand that it is the responsibility of all stakeholders in the school community to work together to ensure that all students and staff feel safe and secure within the learning community. Effective school leaders understand that physical and emotional safety is critical to the success of all learners.

Most importantly, effective school leaders are individuals who inspire others to think critically and creatively and to take risks while solving problems — creating and implementing ongoing practices that build leadership capacity through a process of reflection and inquiry. They are people who stand firm in the belief that leadership is about learning that leads to constructive change.

 CASE STUDY

Tyler Elementary School
Pre-K–6 Rural School

As you read this case study, consider these two questions:

1. What are the critical barriers to teaching and learning that presently exist at Tyler Elementary School and what will be the future impact of these to the school over time?

2. What are some creative things the principal can do to address the issues immediately and in the future?

"Welcome to Tyler Elementary School, a New Standards School, where the... **extraordinary is routine**."

Tyler Elementary School, which includes Pre-K through sixth grade, has been open since 1991 and serves a community of five townships, encompassing 100 square miles. Although rural in nature, the economy of the school district is not agricultural. Many residents work outside the district in white-collar occupations located in several large urban centers. Tyler Elementary is one of three elementary schools, one middle school, and one high school in the district.

Tyler's staff of fifty-five full- and part-time professionals provides the educational program for 542 students. Supplemental programs include special education classes, gifted classes, Title I reading support, an after-school *Meet the Standards Club*, and a summer school program.

The educational program is based on the belief that all students can master the academic skills, concepts, and knowledge necessary to ensure their participation in our democratic society as life-long learners and productive citizens. Tyler's innovative and integrated curriculum was designed to align content, best instructional practices, and assessments of standards.

Tyler holds high expectations for all students. Tyler students celebrate high levels of academic success as evidenced by fourth grade performance on the state standardized exam (SSE) where 98% of the students met or achieved the standards with honors in all areas of reading and math.

Academic success for Tyler Elementary has not come without a price. In recent years, the school has experienced rapid growth as a result of extensive real estate development in the area. Student population increases have started to exceed the limits of the facilities, teaching supplies, and faculty. With resources being limited, an increase in the annual budget to support these areas in need appears highly unlikely.

Moreover, with the implementation of rigorous academic standards in a high-stakes testing environment, the district has turned to ability grouping as a means to better serve the instructional needs of its students. This *ability tracking* of students has, in turn, created a very complex master schedule already taxed beyond the limits of flexibility. As a result, recent documentation (listed below) indicates that class size has become a pressing issue at Tyler. Sadly, teachers and support staff have been reluctant to change instructional techniques or planning to address this new challenge.

History of Tracking Students at Tyler

During Tyler Elementary School's first six years of operation (1991–1997), the tracking of students into specific grouped classes did not occur except in learning support classes and several accelerated math classes. The principal at the time strongly believed that the tracking of students was not developmentally appropriate for elementary school children. As a result, all students were heterogeneously grouped into classes by grade level. It was not until the inception of a new math program in the fall of 1997 that wide-scale, homogeneous tracking occurred. It was believed that in the midst of the New Standards movement and the pressures of a high-stakes testing environment, the academic gains that a new math program could provide far outweighed developmental concerns.

In addition, during Tyler's first six years of operation, the Talented & Gifted Program (TAG) remained relatively unchanged. Starting out as a satellite program run by the county intermediate unit and then ultimately becoming a district-directed program in 1993, TAG was always a pullout program. On a six-day cycle, the identified gifted students were pulled from language arts classes in order to receive enrichment instruction. In 1999, the principal assigned a classroom teacher as the gifted coordinator. During this school year, this teacher provided gifted instruction on a "push-in" basis at each grade level. In the fall of 2000, the District's gifted committee made a recommendation that gifted instruction at each grade level be provided on a regular basis as a specific class. At Tyler, teachers were selected to teach gifted instruction to students during what ordinarily would have been their language arts block. These three classes were given the name Connections.

With the advent of the new gifted program at Tyler, there are now three separate and distinct academic tracks servicing students: (1) a gifted track serving 48 students; (2) a special education track serving 80 students; and (3) a regular education track serving everyone else.

Summary: Since the inception of Tyler Elementary School, the fundamental operating philosophy of how it serves students has changed from one that valued small, teamed communities of students heterogeneously grouped to meet the developmentally appropriate needs of students to one that values academically rigorous, new standards-driven, cross-teamed communities of students homogeneously grouped to succeed in a high-stakes testing environment.

This simple truth has had a profound impact on the school's master schedule and class size.

Impact of Tracking at Tyler

The placement of a class for gifted instruction (Connections) at each grade level added six single courses (i.e., singletons, courses that are offered only once in a master schedule to a specific number of students) to the schedule. As anyone who is familiar with the scheduling of schools knows, singleton classes greatly reduce scheduling flexibility and causes, in many cases, class size imbalance. This programmatic change coupled with the fact that 15 new students enrolled at Tyler at the start of the school year and the special education population increased by 23 students. The overall class size average at Tyler this year went from 23 students per class last year to 25 per class in this year.

Possible Solutions: Thinking Out of the Box

Since changing a time-proven, academically rigorous schedule or increasing staff are not options available for consideration at this time, the following two possible solutions are offered:

OPTION #1: Changing the entire Tyler Master Schedule (or changing how students and teachers are scheduled):

A stakeholders scheduling committee has been proposed at Tyler and has been charged with the responsibility of investigating alternative master schedules that could meet students' needs. To date, the staff has been reluctant to participate as members of the committee.

OPTION #2: Changing instructional strategies/techniques in the various classes to meet the increased class size demands. This change would involve an extensive staff development initiative involving a stakeholder's commitment from the faculty. To date, the staff has been reluctant to participate in discussions involving the planning of staff development initiatives to meet this pressing need.

The Tyler principal thinks...

The new principal has just encountered these problems. How can he formulate management decisions with an eye toward his personal and the district's vision for success, a focus on teaching and learning, an involvement of all the stakeholders involved in the issue, and a demonstration of ethical behavior?

The following documents may assist in his decision making.

𝕹𝖊𝖜𝖘𝖕𝖆𝖕𝖊𝖗

Tyler Planning Board and School District Unexpected Allies

Tyler Planning Board members and long-time open space advocates Howard Berger and Clarence Roth are experienced in-fighters when it comes to standing up to land developers who want to convert open space into large housing developments. Now they have an unexpected ally in the Tyler School District.

With enrollment at Tyler Elementary School already at or near capacity, there just isn't enough room in the school for the substantial increase in students that a new housing development would bring. In addition, the District budget won't support the new staff or supplies needed to accommodate a substantial enrollment increase. "We just don't have the resources to build new schools," stated Roy Joseph, Tyler School Board President.

During the past decade, the District has been the victim of its own success. Being a lighthouse, new standards district with exceptionally high State Standardized Exam scores (see SSE test data listed below), Tyler has become very attractive to families who want better schools for their children. As a result, new housing starts are up 25% throughout the District. And new houses mean over-crowded classrooms. Just this year alone, Tyler Elementary School has seen a significant increase in class size in twelve of its sixteen classes.

Without the resources to build new facilities, district administrators have looked to the teachers for creative solutions to the class size problem. "They've asked us to think creatively, out of the box," said Tyler Teachers' Association President, Frances Robbins. "Instead of building new schools, they want us to adapt our teaching strategies and techniques to meet the needs of the students. Why is it our job to get them off the hook?"

The newly appointed Tyler Elementary School Principal was more reserved, stating, "Change is a process, not an event. Working together, involving the stakeholders in a collaborative way, we can make a difference in the lives of children. I look at this situation as an opportunity for my staff to grow as educators."

We wish the principal well in his efforts.

DOCUMENT 2: STATE STANDARDIZED EXAM (SSE) SCORES

TYLER ELEMENTARY SCHOOL*

YEAR	READING				MATHEMATICS			
	School	District	State	Similar Band Schools	School	District	State	Similar Band Schools
Three Years Ago	1350	1310	1310	1330–80	1500	1380	1300	1300–70
Two Years Ago	1410	1360	1310	1340–80	1510	1400	1300	1310–80
One Year Ago	1470	1400	1310	1340–80	1530	1410	1300	1340–90
Last Year	1510	1430	1310	1350–90	1580	1440	1300	1360–1400

*Score reports range from 1000–1600. Scores of 1300 or above are indicators of top quartile scores.

memo . . .

TO: Tyler Elementary School Principal

RE: Curriculum Alignment/Differentiated Learning at Tyler Elementary

The purpose of the Tyler School District's *Data-Driven Staff Development Program* is to attain the district mission to enable all students to master academic skills, concepts, and knowledge. This year's State Standardized Exams (SSE) defined areas where Tyler students needed to improve and the focus for staff development efforts.

Based on the test results the district:

1. Provided training for all principals to enable them to work with leadership teams of faculty to analyze their assessment data and develop annual building goals.

2. Provided substitutes so teachers could visit other classrooms in the district to see examples of differentiated instruction.

3. Worked continually on changing the culture of the district to that of a learning community where everyone, staff and students both, are expected to achieve and be supported in reaching the high expectations in the district mission statement regardless of class size.

4. Worked continually on analyzing data as it relates to student performance.

It has come to my attention that there has been a significant increase in the pupil to teacher ratio at Tyler Elementary School. We do not anticipate the Board supporting additional staff to meet your personnel and supply needs at this time. In lieu of the facts listed above, what steps are you and your staff taking to differentiate instruction in these larger classes to ensure that all students are achieving the standards?

Please plan to meet with me in my office on Wednesday to discuss this matter.

Sincerely,

Marilyn Jones, Curriculum Coordinator

e-mail @

————-Original Message———-

From: Smith [mail to: smith@awl.net]
Sent: Tuesday, March 05, 8:09 AM
To: Tyler Elementary Principal

Subject: Class Size Problem

For your information, at its Executive Council meeting on February 26, the Tyler Elementary School PTO drafted a position paper regarding the class size issue at Tyler Elementary School. Enclosed is a draft of that position paper. We would welcome the opportunity to meet with you at your earliest convenience to discuss our collective concerns. You can reach me via e-mail or at 555–5555 anytime during the day.

Mary Smith

OFFICIAL CORRESPONDENCE

Tyler Elementary School PTO Position on Class Size

As parents dedicated to ensuring that ALL of our students master the academic skills, concepts, and knowledge necessary to become productive members of our society, we are concerned that the high numbers of students enrolled in many classes at Tyler Elementary School will have a negative impact on the education of our children.

Our district has earned the distinction of being recognized throughout the county and state for having outstanding student achievement, high SSE scores, and three Blue Ribbon schools. We celebrate these success each and every day.

Now, however, the blueprint for this success is being threatened. Twelve of the classes at Tyler Elementary School are seriously overcrowded. There are not enough books and supplies for every student in every class. Teachers are having difficulty coping with the challenges (and stress) that these new problems pose. Students already struggling to meet the standards will fall further behind. Most of these particular students already hold a precarious belief in themselves as learners.

This class size issue is also a cause for community concern, driving a further wedge between families and their local schools as questions are raised about the fairness of resource allocation (e.g., why one teacher or one school has more or fewer students).

We, the leaders of the Tyler Elementary School PTO, collectively urge that a community task force be formed so that these issues can be discussed openly and honestly. Working in concert, these stakeholders may be able to find solutions that will achieve lasting results to enable all of our students and teachers to perform in an environment conducive to learning. Our children and our community deserve no better or no less.

Respectfully,

Mary Smith
Tyler Elementary School PTO President

THE PROBLEMS

Based on the information about Tyler Elementary School presented through the scenario and the documents how should the principal respond to these two questions?

1. What are the critical barriers to teaching and learning that presently exist at Tyler Elementary School and what will be the future impact of these to the school over time?

2. What are some creative things the principal can do to address the issues immediately and in the future?

The newly hired principal finds himself in a very difficult situation. On one hand, he has to address the impact that overcrowded classrooms has on his staff's ability to teach and the students' ability to learn knowing that resources are extremely limited. On the other hand, he has to counter the emerging **political negativism** that exists between management and staff regarding possible solutions to the problem.

Sorting out possible solutions poses a unique challenge. Despite the critical barriers to teaching and learning at Tyler, issues over which he has little control, the principal is still expected to "deliver the goods"—high test scores in the fall. He is also expected to support, encourage, and lead disillusioned students, parents, and staff knowing that additional resource allocations are out of the question. A quick fix or stopgap solution is not going to drop into his lap. He needs a plan for action, one that cannot include new buildings, additional staff, or increased funding.

Listed below, you will find two different responses to the stated scenario: Response A describes how a rudimentary/novice principal reacts to the issues, while Response B chronicles the reaction of an accomplished/experienced principal.

PRINCIPAL A rudimentary response

Principal A has arrived from a school district that was demographically very different from Tyler: a large, urban community with over 1,200 students in each elementary school. The decision-making model employed by that district was top-down and rule bound, focused on administratively-centered agendas rather than what was in the best interests of children. It is from this experiential perspective that the principal approaches his class-size dilemma. The following response attempts to show that many rudimentary administrative reactions to educational issues really mask resistance to effective change. As a result, Principal A drafts the following memo to staff that he disseminates at the next regularly scheduled faculty meeting of Tyler Elementary School.

**Tyler Elementary School
Office of the Principal**

March 18

TO: All Faculty

RE: Curriculum Alignment / Differentiated Learning at Tyler Elementary

I am in receipt of correspondence from the Curriculum Coordinator of the Tyler School District which states in part:

> "It has come to my attention that there has been a significant increase in the pupil to teacher ratio at Tyler Elementary School. We do not anticipate the Board supporting additional staff to meet your personnel and supply needs at this time. In lieu of the facts listed above, what steps are you and your staff taking to differentiate instruction in these larger classes to ensure that all students are achieving the standards?"

As some of you may already know, in differentiated instruction, teachers plan varied approaches to curriculum content, process, and product in anticipation of, and response to, student differences in readiness, interest, and learning needs (Solitario, 1999). Some of you may actually believe in differentiation as an effective instructional tool to bring all students up to standards. The challenge that lies before us is to put this new educational theory into practice.

Concomitant with this end, I have invited a nationally recognized consultant in differentiated instruction, Ronald Wessel, from the State Education Department (SED) to provide in-service training for our staff during the next regularly scheduled staff development day on March 28th. With the information gained from this workshop, I expect each Team to submit to me in writing a "Differentiated Instruction Plan" for each class by the last day of school in June. Each plan should contain an outline of the process through which the team's teachers will differentiate teaching and learning for the students and a list of the specific strategies to be used.

In addition, between now and the end of the year, I expect each teacher to design, deliver, and submit a copy to me of one lesson plan reflecting a differentiated lesson. You may use the principles found in your differentiated instruction handout (to be disseminated to staff at the in-service session) as a guide.

I will be sharing your plans with both Dr. Barnett and Dr. Jones.

Thank you.

Within hours of receiving this memo, Frances Robbins, President of the Tyler Education Association (TEA), approached the principal with a typed list of questions / concerns. Assuming that this encounter would be confrontational in nature, Principal A reacted very defensively. He was indecisive and unsure when challenged as to why the stakeholders were not involved in the decision-making process. He attempted to defer responsibility for the problem to the Superintendent and School Board. Was it not their fault that the budget didn't support new facilities and staff? The meeting concluded poorly, with little resolved, feelings hurt, trust destroyed. The principal's honeymoon was over.

News of this confrontation quickly spread throughout the faculty. Both pro- and anti-differentiation cliques of staff could be seen huddled in the hallways and the faculty rooms discussing what now was known as *The Memo*. It was inevitable that students would soon overhear some of the negative comments exchanged among staff members. Within days, parents began calling the principal to inquire about the dissension that was escalating in the building. Frustrated, the principal responded in the only way that his training and experience would dictate — with intimidation. Was he not the Principal of Tyler Elementary School? Wasn't he the instructional leader? Didn't he have the right to make decisions regarding the instructional program? He considered the staff's reaction to be divisive and insubordinate. He threatened to write anyone up who was not in compliance with his wishes.

As evidenced by the memo and information listed above, Principal A has not involved his staff in the decision-making process. His differentiation memo divided staff and was not based on data or research. He was indecisive when challenged and resorted to intimidation when things started falling apart.

Principal A, as the school leader, has not made accomplished management decisions with an eye toward a vision for success, a focus on teaching and learning, an involvement of all stakeholders, and by demonstrating ethical behavior. His performance is rudimentary at best.

Being an accomplished and experienced principal, Principal B contacts the individual members of Tyler Elementary School's Building Leadership Team (BLT) in order to convene a meeting to discuss the issues raised above.

Upon his arrival at Tyler the month before, the principal endeavored to facilitate, along with staff, a growing collaborative culture at Tyler that reflects a decision-making model that engages the stakeholders in a data-driven process. Concomitant with this end, a building-level committee structure was established to address identified need areas. Included in the infrastructure of this decision-making model was the BLT, which was made up of staff and parents, and community members.

After several meetings, the Tyler Elementary School BLT submitted the following Class Size Action Plan to the Superintendent for approval.

TYLER CLASS SIZE PLAN
SUBMITTED BY TYLER ELEMENTARY SCHOOL'S BUILDING LEADERSHIP TEAM

Strategy: We will partner with parents, staff, administrators, and community members to implement programmatic and curricular responses to the increased class sizes of twelve Tyler Elementary School classes that do not include increased resource allocations (e.g., supplies staff, etc.).

Specific Result: Write a Class Size Action Plan for Tyler Elementary School that meets the strategies listed.

#	ACTION STEP	Assigned To:	Starting Date:	Completion Date:
1	The Building Leadership Team (BLT) of Tyler Elementary School will establish a Class Size Task Force Team of community stakeholders that will: ■ Hold town meetings/public forums throughout the district to solicit community input on the class size issue and to inform citizens of the district's plans to address the problem. ■ Conduct a district-wide survey to solicit community input on the class size issue to be shared at a future BOE meeting. ■ Conduct, in conjunction with the central office administration, an attendance study designed to collect data that will identify the projected enrollment of Tyler Elementary School. ■ Discuss (along with the Resource Management and Fiscal Responsibility Committees of the Board) the future budget implications identified by the enrollment study.	BLT	March	June
2	The BLT, in partnership with staff, will create a Tyler Elementary School Scheduling Committee whose primary focus will be to find/create alternatives to the current master schedule through visitation/partnership with outside experts and other school districts.	BLT	March	June

TYLER CLASS SIZE PLAN (continued)
SUBMITTED BY TYLER ELEMENTARY SCHOOL'S BUILDING LEADERSHIP TEAM

#	ACTION STEP	Assigned To:	Starting Date:	Completion Date:
3	The BLT, in partnership with staff, will create a Professional Development Committee whose primary focus will be to address the emerging class size issue through the following instructional/curricular responses: ■ Provide release time and training in New Standards and Technology applications for all staff as well as time for collaborative work on differentiated lessons. ■ Working with your respective colleagues, establish year-end performance benchmarks for each student by mid-April. These benchmarks **must** be measurable. Please communicate these benchmark targets to parents and the BLT as soon as they are determined. ■ Again, working with your respective staffs, create a building *Meet the Standards Instructional Strategy Plan* that should, in a step-by-step manner, plan and monitor differentiated instructional strategies geared toward getting all of our students to the pre-determined benchmark targets by the end of the school year. ■ As building administrators, it will be your responsibility to monitor the effectiveness of this initiative. You will be expected to report out on your building's progress each month at the administrative cabinet meeting. ■ During the last week of school, please forward the numbers / names of students who have not met these pre-determined benchmarks. Lists of students recommended for special tutoring, retention, and summer school attendance should also be forwarded.	BLT	March	June

...continued on next page

TYLER CLASS SIZE PLAN (continued)
SUBMITTED BY TYLER ELEMENTARY SCHOOL'S BUILDING LEADERSHIP TEAM

#	ACTION STEP	Assigned To:	Starting Date:	Completion Date:
4	The BLT, in partnership with the public relations office, will create a class size Web page with links for parents, teachers, and community members designed to inform, educate, and involve its visitors as it relates to Tyler's efforts to resolve education-related issues.	BLT	March	June
5	The BLT, in partnership with the central office, will endeavor to hire grant writers whose specific task is to secure funding to alleviate problems caused by increased class size in the Tyler School District.	BLT	March	June
6	The BLT, in conjunction with the local Chamber of Commerce, will mutually explore ways that alternative means of funding can be solicited from local businesses.	BLT	March	June
7	The Tyler Elementary School Principal will be charged with the responsibility of keeping the School Board, Superintendent, and committee facilitators appraised of the status of this plan, and to make a final report to the School Board of Directors by the end of the year.	Principal	March	June
8	The stakeholders, as needed, will make adjustments and revisions to this plan.	BLT	March	June

As evidenced by the action plan listed above, the principal has involved his staff in what William J. Cook in *Strategic Planning* (1999) calls "total-gain decision making," where all decisions are:

- consistent with the organization's stated beliefs and mission; and

- made in the best interests of the student.

The principal, as the school leader, has made accomplished management decisions with an eye toward a vision for success, a focus on teaching and learning, an involvement of all stakeholders, and by demonstrating ethical behavior.

The pages that follow outline the "Keys for Improved Performance." Specifically, they note:

a) the differences in the performance of rudimentary Principal A and accomplished Principal B;

b) the potential consequences of the continued performance of Principal A at the rudimentary level;

c) strategies and suggestions on how to move from one level of performance to another level.

Again, these pages specifically relate to the case outlined herein and the two focus questions:

1. What are the critical barriers to teaching and learning that presently exist in Tyler Elementary School and what will be the future impact of these to the school over time?

2. What are some creative things the principal can do to address the issues immediately and in the future?

 KEYS FOR IMPROVED PERFORMANCE

DIFFERENCES IN PRINCIPAL PERFORMANCE

PRINCIPAL A	PRINCIPAL B
rudimentary response	accomplished response
Use of resources is not tied to vision.	Allocation of resources is linked to values delineated in the vision of the school.
Resources are not linked to specific learning goals.	Creative avenues are accessed to obtain resources needed to support teaching and learning.
Little access is given to stakeholders in decision-making process.	All stakeholders are engaged in the ongoing decisions related to resource management.
There is little evidence to suggest that the leader engages stakeholders in creating a positive environment for teaching and learning.	Positive collaborations are established within the school and community to create a positive and safe learning environment.

Potential Consequences of the Performance of Principal A:

Use of resources is not tied to vision. The Rudimentary Principal's inexperience comes to bear here. Faced with the uncertainty that a new position in a new district brings, he has imposed procedures that may have been successful in his previous district, but would not be successful in Tyler. He has also reacted emotionally when confronted by the Association. If the principal is committed to fulfilling the mission of the school, he must listen to the needs of all stakeholders before imposing his mandates on the very people who are expected to do the bulk of the work in solving the problem (e.g., planning for differentiated instruction).

Resources are not linked to specific learning goals. Bringing in a national consultant to in-service staff without consulting the very staff on those instructional goals that needed to be addressed builds a considerable amount of mistrust among all stakeholders.

Little access is given in decision making to all stakeholders. The Rudimentary Principal's decision to impose procedures on an uninvolved staff creates unnecessary dissension among the constituent groups in the school. This is never an optimal situation for a new principal attempting to build lines of communication.

There is little evidence to suggest that the leader engages stakeholders in creating a positive environment for teaching and learning. As evidenced by the supporting documentation listed below, the Rudimentary Principal has not involved his staff in the decision-making process. Instead, he has resorted to a dictatorial management style that has defeated any chance that the staff could work collaboratively in a solution to this problem.

 **TO**

PRINCIPAL A
rudimentary response

PRINCIPAL B
accomplished response

HOW DO YOU MOVE FROM RUDIMENTARY PRINCIPAL A TO ACCOMPLISHED PRINCIPAL B?

- Nurturing and sustaining a school culture and instructional program conducive to student learning and staff professional growth;

- Articulating and providing stewardship for a vision of learning shared by the school community;

- Managing the organization to promote an effective learning environment;

- Knowing how to collaborate with families and community members to mobilize community resources; and

- Acting with integrity and fairness to influence each school's larger political, social, and cultural context.

Concomitant with this end in mind, the inexperienced, unproven Rudimentary Principal/Leader can also move from the rudimentary to the accomplished level through personal and professional growth and development that is focused on the **Four E's**:

Education

The accomplished school leader is a life-long learner who places significant emphasis on his/her own professional development. This attribute includes, but is not limited to, attendance at graduate courses, conferences, and workshops. In addition, the effective principal seeks out other accomplished leaders with whom a collaborative relationship is formed.

Experience

The accomplished school leader usually has served as a successful assistant principal, has been mentored by an accomplished school leader, and has shown competencies in key leadership roles at both the building and district levels.

Expectations

The accomplished school principal is a proven innovator and is instrumental in developing and leading initiatives that increase and then maintain leadership capacity in the building and district. In addition, the accomplished leader is fluent in current educational research as it relates to curriculum, instruction, and assessment.

Empowerment

The accomplished school principal is collaborative by nature in creating and implementing ongoing practices that sustain the energy and commitment of a staff who are actively engaged in setting and reaching high expectations for student achievement.

Monroe High School
9–12 Urban School

As you read this case study, consider these two questions:

1. What steps should the principal take to prioritize the allocation of available resources to address the learning and safety issues in the school?

2. What must the principal do to address the concerns of the parents and the faculty and have each group understand their separate issues?

Monroe High School is a public school, grades 9–12, located in an urban setting within a large Midwestern city. It has long been recognized as a school of excellence and until recently has maintained this tradition for many decades. The primary goals of Monroe High School are to provide a learning environment that enables students to thrive and succeed in a public school that reflects the values of the larger community. The high school implements plans, procedures, and policies to ensure that all students and staff work and learn in a safe and secure environment. In the past five years, Monroe High School has undergone significant change that is characteristic of many high schools across the country. The changes have two themes: severe budget considerations that impact student learning and a heightened need for student and staff safety within the school community. The changes include the following:

Budget constraints impact on teaching and learning:

- Recent state and national test scores are dropping at Monroe High

- Staff and parents are asking for smaller class sizes

- Changes in student population (diversity is rising)

- Crowded classrooms/student numbers rising

- Administration moving toward a ninth grade neighborhood plan to reduce class size and promote meaningful relationships between students and staff

- Growing number of students needing remedial support

School safety issues:

- Significant increase in student enrollment

- Increased number of students who neither speak nor read English

- A predominately white population is now becoming diverse

- Policy of open enrollment

- Larger school facilities and expanded external resources such as student parking

- Exterior doors and access to the high school have increased with building expansions

- New programs for students with learning disabilities, behavior problems, and social challenges

- Increased incidents of on campus vandalism

- Increased anonymity and inability to distinguish between members of the school community and strangers accessing school property

In the 1970's the educational community realized by feeding hungry children breakfast that student performance could be improved. School safety may become the "breakfast" issue of the next decade. Monroe High School strives to maintain its culture of excellence during significant budget cuts while also insuring the safety of its staff and students by maintaining a secure learning environment for everyone. Many significant social changes have occurred at Monroe High School and in the community-at-large. Monroe believes that it is possible to maintain community values and a tradition of excellence only by insuring the safety of all staff and students.

Currently Monroe High School is facing severe budget issues that have had a negative impact on classroom instruction. Parents are concerned about the large (+32) class size in the core subjects with little time given for individual help for students. In particular, the ninth grade students are alienated and intimidated by the sheer size of the high school. In addition there has been a rise in reports of vandalism in the ninth grade that must be addressed.

There are two recent events that have triggered conflict. One day during the start of the current school year, three young males, two of whom had been recently expelled from Monroe High School, broke into the school and started a fire in the media center. Though the fire was contained by the sprinkler system, the entire media center, including the computers was destroyed. That facility was out of service for over three months. The damage to the center and equipment was approximately $500,000. Though the vandalism might not have been preventable without 24/7 monitoring of video cameras and around-the-clock police protection, the underlying issue remains alienation. Parents are now anxious about ongoing incidents of vandalism and theft at the school.

The second event was triggered by a newspaper announcement that only three students received National Merit® Scholarship Finalist distinction at Monroe High School. Over the years there have been a minimum of ten students receiving this distinction annually. For the past three years this number has continued to fall. Teachers place the blame on larger class sizes and the changing profile of the students at Monroe High School. A small group of teachers and administration are pursuing a differentiated program for ninth graders at Monroe that will reduce the isolation and increase the rigor of curriculum and accountability for all ninth grade students. The other teachers at Monroe fear that this program will cause a disparity within the entire school community. Ninth grade teachers will have low (20–25) class size and resources needed to ensure a quality program. Other staff members will have class sizes of over forty students with limited resources. They fear that this new model will create multiple new tensions in the school community of tenth through twelfth graders that will result in lower academic expectations for all students and lower accountability that will result in a higher number of vandalism reports at Monroe High School.

Recently, tension has continued to mount between the parent community, staff, and administration. A letter from a high school parent admonishes the administration for allowing repeated reports of victimization that have affected her ninth grade student. Monthly reports indicate that reports of student vandalism are rising. The School Board is currently considering further budget cuts that will again impact class size at the high school. Amid all of these issues, the high school staff council has expressed anger over the possibility of the ninth grade model at the expense of all other programs.

The principal at Monroe High School is caught between the desire to pursue a new model for ninth graders that will have a potential long-term impact on student learning and help to lower the incident reports, and the need for equity throughout the school community that ensures high standards and safety for all students.

letter

November 12

Principal
Monroe High School
11 School Avenue
Monroe, MN

Dear Madam,

I was distressed to learn of the recent vandalism to the Monroe High School media center last weekend. In my last letter to you I expressed concern about the school climate and the ongoing intimidation my daughter has felt in the hallways at your school. The media center is but one more example of the lack of discipline at this school. I, for one, and I speak for many, many of my neighbors am outraged! Where is the concern for student safety within your walls? I wonder if I should even send my child to school. I worry each day that she will come home with yet another backpack, radio or CD player stolen. Or worse, that she will feel intimidated by the bullies that run rampant in your hallways.

My child is afraid of reprisals if I sign this letter. Please act immediately.

Sincerely,

A Concerned Ninth Grade Parent

Monroe High School Monthly Vandalism Report

Incident Report — Last Year and Current School Year

Type of Incident	Last School Year	Sept. This Year	Oct. This Year	Nov This Year	Dec This Year	Jan This Year	Feb This Year	Total to Date
Theft from students	49	9	11	8	9	15	12	64
Damage to school property	7	3	2	4	2	2	0	13
Assaults	5	2	4	1	2	1	1	11
Arson	0	0	0	2	0	0	0	2

Note: Last school year shows a 77% rise in theft over the previous year. In addition, during the same time period there was a 54% increase in damage to school property.

DOCUMENT 3: BUDGET INFORMATION/ISSUES/PROBLEMS

In the last four years the school operating budget at the high school has been cut by $40,000. The School Board is being asked to again look to the high school for budget cutting measures. Left with nowhere else to turn the issue of class size has returned to the conversation.

The following excerpts from the School Board minutes reflect the current budget cutting measures:

"…with the current budget crisis in our school district and in our state the School Board is left with decisions to make that negatively impact students, learning and our core instructional program. It is not our intent to single out one group of students to bear the pain of these decisions. In fact, over the past four years the budget cuts have impacted all learners from early childhood programs through twelfth grade and beyond. In this current round of budget trimming we will focus on all levels of instruction."

"…At the high school level the cost containment measures will include the following:

- Increased fees for parking permits from $200 to $400 annually. Carpooling will be a condition of issuing the permit. A minimum of three passengers must ride in each car.

- Bus transportation will be provided only for those students living more than two miles from the school. A $350 fee will be charged for each student annually choosing to ride the bus.

- The current seven period day will be reduced to six periods. This will impact the number of classes offered during the course of the high school experience. This will result in the loss of 21 teaching positions that will raise class sizes in all core subjects to 36+.

- There will be fees assessed to all co-curricular programs that will offset expenses incurred.

While it is not the intent of the School Board to cause our students and families any hardships the cost containment measures above will aid us in establishing a budget for next school year that is within our current constrictions.

There will be a Town Hall meeting on April 15 at 7:00 p.m. in the small auditorium at MHS to discuss the current budget plans."

Concerns from the English Department about money going to increased security instead of to instructional programs/materials.

The reassignment of paraprofessional support to the large common areas of the school was a volatile decision that impacts student learning. The following letter was written to the principal shortly after the reassignment.

December 1

Dear Principal:

It is with great disbelief that our department was informed on Monday that our highly skilled paraprofessional support was removed from our Advanced Placement and regular classes to perform menial supervision tasks in the lunchroom and hallways at the front of our school. Our mission statement reads:

"Monroe High School strives to provide a supportive but challenging environment to enable EACH student to develop skills, knowledge and attitudes realizing his or her fullest potential. With the help of the home, Monroe High School fosters the development of integrity, self-esteem and physical and mental well-being to equip students to adapt and respond to change and grow as responsible citizens of their global community."

We obviously are not operating with this vision written together just two short years ago! We have now turned into a closely guarded school that reacts to misbehavior rather than focusing on teaching and learning. While each of us believes that safety is important it is a sad state of affairs when precious dollars designed to "provide a supportive but challenging environment to enable EACH student to develop skills, knowledge and attitudes" are reassigned to surveillance of our students. We plan to share our beliefs and this letter with the school board at the next televised meeting.

-The English Department at Monroe High School

THE PROBLEMS

Based on the information about her school presented through the scenario and the documents, how should the principal respond to these two questions?

1. What steps should the principal take to prioritize the allocation of available resources to address the learning and safety issues in the school?

2. What must the principal do to address the concerns of the parents and the faculty and have each group understand their separate issues?

The new principal at Monroe High School spends the fall of her first year out in the public. She is visible during the school day, visiting with students and staff. Her goal for her first year is to continue current practice with little change. She shares the existing vision statement with her staff at the Back-to-School all-staff meeting. Throughout the fall she is able to find dollars in the budget to support the requests of teachers for supplemental supplies and books. By late October she is feeling very good about the year. When the vandalism of the media center occurs in early November she is shaken. With her administrative team she sets up new, stricter procedures for the students that are posted throughout the building. Support staff is re-assigned from classroom and hallway support to monitor student behavior throughout the day in the common areas (lunchroom, front of school, media center) and into the evening during co-curricular activities. Classroom teachers are assigned hall duty between classes and asked to make do without individual student assistance given previously by the classroom paraprofessionals during their instruction. Monthly reports since September attribute the highest number of vandalism reports to ninth graders.

In early January the principal is approached by a small group of teachers with the idea for the ninth grade neighborhood system. As a past ninth grade teacher herself, the principal is acutely aware of the needs of this age level and the isolation that they feel from the upperclassmen. She gives the teachers approval to continue developing a model. By early spring the teachers present her with a comprehensive model with an additional cost of $60,000 for teachers and materials. The principal takes the proposal to the Superintendent for approval. She is very excited to make the presentation. She believes that the teachers have developed a model for ninth graders that will make a difference in their learning and lower discipline issues for them, as well. The project will require additional district support that the principal argues will be well worth the investment. The Superintendent gives his support of the project.

Upon hearing the news of the new ninth grade neighborhood model the high school staff is incredulous. This is the first that many of them had heard of the planning. For the past few months they have been struggling with the increased supervision responsibilities and the lack of para support in their classes. For the past three years they have experienced escalating class sizes. This proposal will again require them to add more students to their classes. They argue that if there is more funding available during the current budget shortfall, why can't it be used to lower everyone's classes, not just one grade level. At a staff meeting faculty members wonder what happened to the school's mission statement that reads in part, "Monroe High School strives to provide a supportive but challenging environment to enable each student to develop skills, knowledge and attitudes realizing his or her fullest potential." The principal prepares a Microsoft PowerPoint® presentation on the merits of the ninth grade model to share with staff at the next meeting. A parent meeting is scheduled for incoming ninth grade parents. The same slide presentation will be shared with them.

PRINCIPAL B accomplished response

The accomplished veteran principal was assigned to Monroe High School on July 1st. She spends the summer meeting with stakeholder groups of certified and non-certified staff members, parents, students, and executive staff members to learn about the culture and history of this school community. The principal meets with school staff and parents that were instrumental in designing the current mission statement to better understand the underlying values embedded in the words chosen. She meets with the administrative council to determine the allocation of resources for the coming year, reviewing the past five years of budget sheets and building recommendations. In addition, she meets with the safety committee, on site, and the local police department to review the health and safety challenges facing this school community.

The accomplished principal invites all staff, School Board members, and community members to join her in a "Visioning for the Future" event at the high school. She holds the meeting during workshop week in August. At the meeting she reaffirms the words of the mission statement as being a call to action for the coming years under her leadership. She shares her findings of her work over the past two months. She celebrates with them the history of academic success this school has enjoyed and the many successes of the past. She challenges them to decide if the best years at Monroe High School are behind them or ahead of them. She invites all those present to share their hopes and dreams for Monroe High School. She acknowledges the challenges facing them. In the coming year the priority will be to address the negative impact of budget reductions over the past three years on instruction and the increased cases of vandalism on the school property. The recorded notes will become one of the documents used to write the blueprints for working together in the years ahead.

The school year begins smoothly. The feeling in the community is one of optimism. Staff, students, and parents appreciate their opportunities to share their personal stories and experiences with the new principal. They feel they are vested members of the design for the current school year and the future. The principal continues to work in collaboration with students, staff, and parents to understand the complexity of the school culture and current challenges facing them. She establishes two new collaboratives with the high school community. The first is the Focus on Excellence Committee that is comprised of students, staff, School Board members, parents, and school district administration. They are charged to develop a template for excellence at MHS. This committee will review all requests for budget reductions that affect learning and enhancement ideas. The second committee is the Safety on Our Campus Committee. The composition of this committee is similar to the Excellence Committee with the addition of a police liaison from the local police department. This committee is charged to ensure that the entire school campus is a safe and healthy place to be at all times of day and night. New initiatives to support this endeavor will be organized and supported by this group. Both new committees select chairpersons and set their meeting times for the year. The chairs from both committees will also serve on the administrative council that meets monthly. The committee's membership represents each grade level and department.

In November the vandalism to the media center catches everyone by surprise. After the initial work by the site crisis committee the event is channeled back to both the Excellence and Safety committees for recommendations. The feedback in the form of two committee recommendations strongly suggests two changes at the high school to be initiated immediately from each committee. The Safety Committee first recommends the reallocation of four of the forty members of the paraprofessional staff currently assigned to classroom and hallway duty to before and after school supervision during co-curricular activities. The remainder of the paraprofessional staff will work with classroom teachers to ensure that the hallways are safe for all students. There is a high value placed on the role of the paraprofessional during class time to individualize instruction for students.

The second recommendation is to develop a plan to personalize the school, as it grows larger, to decrease the anonymity prevalent at this time. With the rapid growth in numbers and diversity, the students don't know their classmates nor do teachers know their students. The safety committee will pursue a grant to access a bar-coded identification system that will be available to the entire school community. After careful consideration of the vandalism reports and the review of the compelling data collected regarding the overall lower number of students excelling at MHS, the Excellence Committee recommends the creation of two study groups. The first will examine the need for a different ninth grade model that will address the isolation students report as they enter MHS. This model will focus on academic rigor in a safe and welcoming environment. The study group will report back to the Excellence Committee in late March. The second study group will focus on the use of existing dollars to determine creative ways to use limited dollars to increase student learning. This group will work in collaboration with the community outreach group at the district office to build a partnership with a local business to support the school endeavor. This group is given the same March deadline.

The principal receives the reports from both groups and prepares to present her findings to the Superintendent in early April. She is encouraged with the progress both groups have made. In addition to their work together they have kept the entire MHS staff apprised of their ongoing efforts at the bi-weekly staff meetings and through newsletters. In addition, they have involved staff, parents, and students in small focus groups twice during the process. At the April meeting the principal asks the committee chairs to share their findings.

The Excellence Committee is proud to share that the MHS staff supports a one-year pilot of a ninth grade model of neighborhoods to increase student rigor and accountability and decrease anonymity at their school. The Safety Committee chair reports that Monroe is the recipient of a $60,000 grant from the state to pilot an identification program designed to decrease the isolation felt by students and staff in a large high school. The program will include:

- ID cards with student/staff photo to distinguish between members of the school and visitors on school property

- Improved security at all access points to the school and school property

- An assessment of the school safety programs and policies that are consistent with the best research on school safety preparedness

- Focus groups at the middle school to learn of safety concerns that students and staff have regarding the migration of students to the high school

- Focus groups of students and staff at the high school to expand awareness of safety issues

The goal of the program, and a challenge for all high schools, is to create a climate where anonymity is reduced, where students continue to feel supported, and where they feel they can receive help and guidance during stressful times. Realistically, there will always be students who will not ask for help or will not know how to ask. These students need to be identified and sought out. Help needs to be available for each student within the school setting. The big events, like the vandalism of the media center, will never be 100% preventable. The goal of this pilot is to reduce the likelihood of such a thing happening.

At the April School Board meeting representatives of the high school staff, students, and parents attend demonstrating their support for the proposals from both committees. The principal welcomes each to the meeting by name.

The pages that follow outline the "Keys for Improved Performance." Specifically, they note:

a) the differences in the performance of rudimentary Principal A and accomplished Principal B;

b) the potential consequences of the continued performance of Principal A at the rudimentary level;

c) strategies and suggestions on how to move from one level of performance to another level.

Again, these pages specifically relate to the case outlined herein and the two focus questions:

1. What steps should the principal take to prioritize the allocation of available resources to address the learning and safety issues in the school?

2. What must the principal do to address the concerns of the parents and the faculty and have each group understand their separate issues?

 KEYS FOR IMPROVED PERFORMANCE

DIFFERENCES IN PRINCIPAL PERFORMANCE

PRINCIPAL A
rudimentary response

Use of resources is not tied to vision.

Resources are not linked to specific learning goals.

Little access is given to stakeholders in decision-making process.

There is little evidence that the leader has accessed resources sufficiently to ensure that the school is a safe and healthy place to learn.

There is little evidence to suggest that the leader engaged stakeholders in creating a positive environment for teaching and learning.

PRINCIPAL B
accomplished response

Allocation of resources is linked to values delineated in vision of the school.

Creative avenues are accessed to obtain resources needed to support teaching and learning.

All stakeholders are engaged in the ongoing decisions related to resource management.

There is a clear commitment to creating a safe environment valuing learning.

Positive collaborations are established within the school and community to create a positive and safe learning environment.

Potential Consequences of the Performance of Principal A:

Use of resources is not tied to vision. Principal A is currently creating an environment of winners and losers at Monroe High School. The ninth grade team is set up to be a winner of added resources that are not being given to the other staff members. If the principal is committed to fulfilling the mission of the school, she must listen to the needs of all stakeholders, not just one group.

Resources are not linked to specific learning goals. Reallocation of resources to meet individual needs without the consensus of all stakeholders builds mistrust among all stakeholders.

Little access is given in decision making to all stakeholders. There are many constituent groups in a growing high school. Taking time to listen and learn about the school only through the lens of those different groups is a lethal mistake for any principal coming to a new building. Moving forward with a new structure like the ninth grade neighborhood model isolates everyone when there is a lack of communication and collaboration within the school.

There is little evidence that the leader has accessed resources sufficiently to ensure that the school is a safe and healthy place to learn. Budget cuts are common to many, if not most, school districts at this time. It is imperative that the principal looks beyond the traditional avenues of funding to ensure that the school continues to be academically focused and a safe and healthy place to learn.

There is little evidence to suggest that the leader engaged stakeholders in creating a positive environment for teaching and learning. Safety is a priority in our schools and our world today. Building partnerships with the local police departments and other community groups eager to share this common vision of safety is imperative. The limited resources within a school district are not always adequate to meet the challenges of our current communities and schools.

173

PRINCIPAL A TO PRINCIPAL B

rudimentary response   accomplished response

HOW DO YOU MOVE FROM RUDIMENTARY PRINCIPAL A TO ACCOMPLISHED PRINCIPAL B?

Principal A can move toward the level of Principal B by stepping back from her decision-making process in order to learn more about the community and the school. It takes time to build the bridges needed to assure that all stakeholders are part of the solutions needed to make our schools a safe place focused on teaching and learning. By investing time in understanding the rich history of the school, the principal will grow in understanding of who the stakeholders are and how to engage them in meaningful dialogue. Bringing groups together to make decisions that affect the school community is essential to ensure that everyone is valued. It is important for Principal A to engage staff, parents, students, and community in the necessary work of the change process prior to making presentations to the Superintendent and School Board. True power comes from building capacity for change within the entire school community. Finally, engaging the community in the schools is critical in these times of limited dollars. Working in collaboration with community groups may ensure the ongoing focus on safety within a rich and diverse learning community.

CHAPTER 5 SUMMARY

In this era of New Standards, empowerment, restructuring, and school-based management, the principal emerges as a key participant in the enhancement of education for our children. Leading is skilled and complicated work, and it is our belief that leaders are made—not born. These assumptions advance the ideas that are essential if we are to develop sustainable, self-renewing schools that are receptive to change.

Effective school leaders are individuals who can communicate to others a clear vision for success that focuses on teaching and learning techniques that will enable all students to master the academic skills, concepts, and knowledge necessary to become productive citizens. They are individuals who grow and cultivate collaborative cultures that reflect a decision-making model that engages stakeholders in a data-driven, decision-making process. They align their words and actions as they allocate resources to meet the instructional needs of students. And they create a safe and healthy environment for teaching and learning. *Most importantly, they are people who stand firm in the belief that leadership is about learning that leads to constructive change.*

STANDARD 4: RELATIONSHIPS WITH THE BROADER COMMUNITY TO FOSTER LEARNING

The focus of the cases in Chapter 6 is on ISLLC Standard 4: Relationships with the Broader Community to Foster Learning. Chapter 6 introduces you to issues of concern at Wilson Middle School, a 6–8 urban school, and Taft High, a 9–12 urban high school.

As you read through this chapter and each subsequent chapter, you will find each case structured in a specific way.

First, you will be introduced to a specific Standard and to the case study scenario and its accompanying documents. Secondly, you will be given two focus questions to keep in mind as you read the case and as you analyze the two fictitious principals' responses: one principal at the rudimentary level, the second at the accomplished level.

As a reader, you will consider the core of the ISLLC standard and then apply this understanding to the rudimentary and accomplished principals' responses. We also invite you to consider other factors that could be built into each principal's response.

A SCHOOL ADMINISTRATOR IS AN EDUCATIONAL LEADER WHO PROMOTES THE SUCCESS OF ALL STUDENTS BY COLLABORATING WITH FAMILIES AND COMMUNITY MEMBERS, RESPONDING TO DIVERSE COMMUNITY INTERESTS AND NEEDS, AND MOBILIZING COMMUNITY RESOURCES (CCSSO, 1996, P.16).

COMPONENT FOUR **A**   Understanding Community Needs

COMPONENT FOUR **B**   Involving Members of the Community

COMPONENT FOUR **C**   Providing Opportunities for the Community
                          and School to Serve Each Other

COMPONENT FOUR **D**   Understanding and Valuing Diversity

Today's educational leader promotes the success of all students by collaborating with families and community members, responds to diverse community interests and needs, and mobilizes community resources. The significance of ISLLC Standard Four is the importance of administrators making informed decisions in collaboration with staff members and other stakeholders such as students, parents, and community leaders. This collaborative relationship is underscored in the four components that define Standard Four. They are:

Understanding Community Needs

Involving Members of the Community

Providing Opportunities for the Community and
School to Serve Each Other

Understanding and Valuing Diversity

The accomplished school leader understands that:

- Business, civic, and religious leaders can be natural allies who are available to support the school during critical times and situations.

- Public engagement involves two-way communication between the school and the larger community.

- Strong connections with the community create an environment where community groups feel free to approach the principal (and do).

- Opportunities for the school and community to serve each other must exist.

- Critical thinking and intercultural collaboration skills among stakeholders must be developed to effectively engage the various school communities.

- Fundamental understanding of issues of diversity, multiculturalism, and pluralism, both on campus and throughout the community, must be prerequisite.

- Diverse voices are valued in the decision-making process.

- Theoretical and philosophical frameworks for understanding identity and culture are necessary.

- Multiculturalism maximizes educational opportunities.

■ Only through a nurturing school community that validates stakeholders' support, will enhanced teaching and learning flourish.

■ Trust and openness, framed on a conceptual foundation of each constituency working with and helping one another, sharing resources, expertise, skills, and mutual respect will improve student learning.

Standard Four calls for the vision of the school to reflect the diversity of the community with an expectation of high standards of excellence for all students regardless of race, ethnicity, socioeconomic class, or gender. Classroom instructional and enrichment activities and programs celebrate the diversity of the community that is supported, encouraged, and motivated by the effective school leader. The respect for diversity permeates the value system of the school and is the cultural fabric of the institution. The effective school leader understands and continuously promotes respect for diversity, equity for all students, and outreach programs to enable the stakeholders to be represented in shared decision-making activities in the school.

The case studies that follow will require the reader to put Standard Four into actual practice; to reflect upon one's present belief system and practice in reviewing relationships within the whole school community. Perhaps self-reflection will lead the reader to seriously review one's concept of openness to community, trust of community, and a comprehensive assessment of enhancing student success as a result of collaborating with families and community members, responding to diverse community interests and needs, and mobilizing community resources (CCSSO, 1996, pp. 16–17).

CASE STUDY  7

Wilson Middle School
6–8 Urban School

As you read this case study, consider these two questions:

1. What are some of the factors that have created this animosity of the community toward the school and what are some steps the principal might take to address this feeling?

2. How might the teaching and learning program benefit from better community relations, both directly and indirectly?

Of the ten middle schools in Community School District 10, Wilson Middle School is the most popular school of choice for families. Wilson is recognized for its gifted program, minor behavioral issues, and an excellent, experienced staff. Parents are active and have high expectations for the school and its students. The school district has recently reorganized the middle school and has created small thematic schools. Although these types of schools have received significant funding through federal funds and magnet grants, Wilson Middle School is not a recipient of these funding sources. As a result, this limits the principal's ability to create and expand student programs and activities. A parent leadership team exists in the school, but has not been very active in the past. The school has an effective Parent-Teacher Association. Most parent requests made to the principal usually reflect the interests and desires of the more vocal and aggressive parents who are well-known in the school community. The principal is in the second year of this assignment.

The newly appointed Superintendent has received a mandate from the local Board of Education to:

- reform the failing and under-enrolled middle schools

- increase parent and community awareness and support of the district middle schools

- increase student performance in the middle schools as measured by standardized test results

- increase the school day hours to provide greater opportunities for students to be in school after the normal dismissal hour

The Superintendent has been given additional district funding by the Board of Education to be allocated to the low performing and under-enrolled schools as a way to increase their success and popularity. Wilson Middle School is excluded from the additional budget allocations based upon its record of success and student and parent popularity.

Wilson Middle School Fact Sheet

1. Wilson Middle School (grades 6–8) is one of ten middle schools in Community School District 10.

2. Upon leaving the fifth grade, students in District 10 have a choice of applying to any middle school in the geographic zone for the district and are admitted based upon each middle school's acceptance criteria.

3. Wilson Middle School has the largest student enrollment of any middle school in the district (1178 students) and has the largest number of staff members. Its present enrollment has greatly exceeded the capacity of the building. However, eight of the remaining middle schools in the district are under-enrolled with student populations of 525 or less.

4. Students who attend Wilson Middle School can be accepted into one of three core educational programs:

   • Gifted—Admission is competitive and determined by standardized reading and math scores.

   • Creative Arts—Admission is determined by talent auditions and interviews. The program consists of music, art, drama, photography, dance, and media.

   • Special Needs—This program serves learning and emotionally challenged students who have been identified through a screening and assessment process.

5. There are financial concerns in the school and in the district: and Wilson Middle School does not qualify for Federal Title I assistance or any state or city grants.

6. Wilson Middle School has a budget based on $5750 per pupil while the average per pupil expense in the other district middle schools is augmented by special funding by the local Board of Education and is now about $9800 per pupil.

7. Almost 47% of the students attending Wilson Middle School receive free or a reduced price lunch based on their socioeconomic status.

8. Wilson Middle School has existing parent organizations. These parents, however, have not been very active in supporting teaching and learning opportunities, either financially or in other ways.

OFFICIAL CORRESPONDENCE

Parent-Teacher Association
Wilson Middle School

December

Dear Principal,

Last night, the Executive Board of the Wilson PTA met in my house. Most comments about the school were positive; however, several parents expressed concerns that the school needs to develop more diverse as well as additional after-school programs for students so that the children can take full advantage of the wonderful opportunities that exist in our school. At a recent meeting, you brought to our attention that budgetary constraints were the primary reason for not being able to create programs. You informed us that the Superintendent has asked middle school principals to begin to plan for such activities, but our school does not qualify nor receive the additional funding given to the other district middle schools.

One sixth grade parent stated that her child wanted to participate in the basketball program, but after several unsuccessful attempts to join in with seventh and eighth graders, he finally stopped going to the program. Several other parents shared stories that the creative arts teachers only invited their art, music, drama, dance and photography students to participate in their programs and no additional students were welcome at this time. Besides the educational advantage of participating in these programs, some working parents strongly expressed an interest in extended school day programs because they did not want their children on the streets, unsupervised for several hours before they arrive home.

...continued on next page

The Executive Board passed a resolution requesting that you re-examine our after school programs and activities. It was agreed that a greater variety of activities should be offered to include enrichment, acceleration and tutorial programs; more staff participation in these programs; and no child denied access to any program. We realize that there are obstacles that you must overcome, but the need for an exciting and creative schedule of programs is needed.

A subcommittee has been formed, with Mrs. Clarke being the chairperson. Please expect a call from her within the next several days to plan for a meeting to discuss this concern.

Thank you,

Mr. Gonzales
Co-President, PTA

letter

November

Dear Principal:

I am a parent of a special needs sixth grader who is in the mainstream program. She is a good student, who is passing every subject and behaves in school. She enjoys coming to school every day. She is motivated to be successful, likes her teachers and is happy to be a student in your school.

Yesterday, she tried to enroll in the Show Chorus Music program. I believe that she has a good voice, as she is a member of our church youth choir. The music teacher told her that only his talent singers could participate in the program. She told me that these students come from the gifted program. I was shocked and angry to hear this from my daughter.

Is this true? Several parents have told me that their children were not allowed to participate in other after school programs. Their children were given the same reason that only students in the talent programs could participate, mainly because these programs are not funded for additional times during the week. Is it possible that a public school can discriminate against children like this? It appears to me that you have created elitist programs for some children but not for every child!

Also, other schools have programs like homework help, tutorial, research and library. Why don't you have programs like this in your school? Wilson Middle School's reputation is that it is the best school in the district. When we took a tour of your school last year, you stated that there were after school programs; you failed to tell us that they were only for some students. I want my child to be a participant, not an outsider!

Please call me to discuss this matter.

Sincerely,

Mrs. Klaus
cc: Superintendent of the School District

DOCUMENT 4: PUPIL PERFORMANCE DATA

Wilson Middle School
Community School District 10

Daily Attendance Statistics:
Daily attendance rate: 93.6%

Results in the State English Language Arts Assessment

Number and Percent of Students at Each Performance Level by Category

Year	Category Tested	Number #	Level 1 %	Level 1 #	Level 2 %	Level 2 #	Level 3 %	Level 3 #	Level 4 %	Level 4 #	Level 3 + 4 %
Current Year	General Education	1007	71	7.1	392	38.9	443	44.0	101	10.0	544	54.0
	Special Education	112	62	55.4	45	40.2	5	4.5	0	0.0	5	4.5
	All Students	1119	133	11.9	437	39.1	448	40.0	101	9.0	549	49.1
Last Year	General Education	985	30	3.0	298	30.3	512	52.0	145	14.7	657	66.7
	Special Education	83	48	57.8	27	32.5	8	9.6	0	0.0	8	9.6
	All Students	1068	78	7.3	325	30.4	520	48.7	145	13.6	665	62.3

Level 4 Students exceed the learning standards for English Language Arts. Their performance shows superior understanding of written and oral text.

Level 3 Students meet the learning standards. Their performance shows thorough understanding of written and oral text.

Level 2 Students show partial achievement of the standards. Their performance shows partial understanding of written and oral text.

Level 1 Students do not meet the standards. Their performance shows minimal understanding of written and oral text.

Results in the State Mathematics Assessment

Number and percent of Students at Each Performance Level by Category

Year	Category Tested	Number #	Level 1 %	Level 1 #	Level 2 %	Level 2 #	Level 3 %	Level 3 #	Level 4 %	Level 4 #	Level 3 + 4 %
Current Year	General Education	985	173	17.6	353	35.8	325	33.0	134	13.6	459	46.6
	Special Education	120	89	74.2	27	22.5	3	2.5	1	0.8	4	3.3
	All Students	1105	262	23.7	380	34.4	328	29.7	135	12.2	463	41.9
Last Year	General Education	981	169	17.2	348	35.5	345	35.2	119	12.1	464	47.3
	Special Education	90	71	78.9	15	16.7	3	3.3	1	1.1	4	4.4
	All Students	1071	240	22.4	363	33.9	348	32.5	120	11.2	468	43.7

Level 4 Students exceed the learning standards for mathematics. Their performance shows superior understanding of the key math ideas.

Level 3 Students meet the learning standards. Their performance shows thorough understanding of key math ideas.

Level 2 Students show partial achievement of the standards. Their performance shows partial understanding of key math ideas.

Level 1 Students do not meet the standards. Their performance shows minimal understanding of key math ideas.

Based on the information about this school presented through the scenario and the documents, how should the principal respond to these questions?

1. What are some of the factors that have created this animosity of the community toward the school and what are some steps the principal might take to address this feeling?

2. How might the teaching and learning program benefit from better community relations, both directly and indirectly?

A Rudimentary Principal:

1. Fails to recognize the specific needs and desires of the parent community (e.g., extending the school day and the request for a more comprehensive and rich extended school day program for all students).

   - The Rudimentary Principal, in an attempt to resolve the issue as quickly as possible and to demonstrate control and leadership, makes unilateral decisions based on what his or her perception is of being best for the students.

   - The Rudimentary Principal may permit some parents to voice opinion, but only those that initiate these discussions.

   - The Rudimentary Principal, typically, fails to act on the opinions of parents.

   - The Rudimentary Principal might allow some other members of the administrative team to participate in making decisions, but does not provide any decision-making role for community stakeholders.

2. Allows existing financial restraints to drive the decision-making process and fails to exercise leadership in responding to the lack of resources.

   - The Rudimentary Principal allows the current economic and or political status to control the decision-making process.

   - The Rudimentary Principal relies on past practice and does not consider the potential of exploring alternate, creative funding sources.

   - The Rudimentary Principal acknowledges the concern of the Parent-Teacher Association and may attempt to pressure the Superintendent and Board of Education for additional funding.

3. Fails to use the interests and abilities of the parents and members of the larger community in seeking new sources of funding to provide a comprehensive educational program.

   - The Rudimentary Principal does not motivate stakeholders to think of creative funding alternatives.

   - Principal A covertly suggests that parents form pressure groups to lobby local and state politicians in an attempt to force the Board of Education to change its funding policies.

   - The Rudimentary Principal might suggest to parents that they send their children to community agencies (e.g., YMCA) without formally facilitating a collaborate venture between the agencies and the school.

4. Disregards issues of fairness and sensitivity by allowing some groups of students to be excluded from educational opportunities enjoyed by others.

> - The Rudimentary Principal defends the use of past selection practices as the criteria to admit students to after-school programs.
>
> - The Rudimentary Principal attributes the community perception that gifted students are the recipients of special treatment to jealousy and the complaints of a limited, vocal minority.
>
> - The Rudimentary Principal does not consider the needs of the school's diverse population to ensure inclusion of the various student groups as a priority. This principal views fairness as adhering to out-dated selection rules.

5. Lacks a vision for the establishment of an effective, comprehensive school organization that meets needs of the middle school students.

> - The Rudimentary Principal sets expectations differently for different groups of students and does not establish a program that will allow all students to be held to the same high standards.
>
> - The Rudimentary Principal only values learning that occurs in the traditional classroom setting and does not create learning opportunities beyond the classroom.

6. Is not sensitive to the needs of the parents, who rely on the school to address many of their issues.

> - The Rudimentary Principal demonstrates a lack of leadership in soliciting community support and acting as a resource person to the parent community.
>
> - The Rudimentary Principal simply acts or fails to act because of limited expressions of concerns from the parents. There is no effort to survey the community to ascertain its desire to maintain after-school programs or why they consider these activities to be important to their children and their families.

7. Does not use pupil performance data to inform the decision-making process.

> ▪ The Rudimentary Principal uses student data superficially, perhaps to simply reinforce the fact that the school is overcrowded.
>
> ▪ Principal A fails to use student performance data to target the needs of individual pupils and support their improvement and may use the excuse that the data is irrelevant or outdated.
>
> ▪ The Rudimentary Principal does not rely on data to ensure that all students have equal access to all programs.
>
> ▪ Principal A fails to understand the value of student performance data to analyze and address the interests of multi-talented students in several creative arts areas.

8. Does not enlist the support of the Superintendent in bringing about change.

> ▪ The Rudimentary Principal cannot meet the expectations of the Superintendent for expanding after-school programs and fails to either look for creative solutions or to consult with the Superintendent to reach some type of resolution.
>
> ▪ Principal A fails to use student performance data to present an educationally sound proposal to the Superintendent in responding to the issue.
>
> ▪ The Rudimentary Principal does not wish to disturb the Superintendent by alerting him/her to the concerns and interests of the school's parent community towards after-school programs.
>
> ▪ The Rudimentary Principal does not act as an advisor to the Superintendent (e.g., raising the issue of equity and equal access to existing programs).

9. Fails to collaborate with the school staff in responding to this issue.

> ▪ The Rudimentary Principal acts in isolation and does not engage the staff in activities designed to identify sources of assistance and support in resolving the issue (e.g., potential grant writers who could secure funding).
>
> ▪ Principal A does not recognize the talents and strengths of the staff and does not take the initiative to access their interests and skills.
>
> ▪ Principal A might survey the staff simply to get opinions to support or defend his/her past actions.

An Accomplished Principal:

1. Finds ways to continually identify and analyze the needs and desires of the parent and larger community.

> ■ Principal B will develop a strategy or action plan to survey community needs with respect to broader, more inclusive after-school programs.
>
> ■ The Accomplished Principal will seek community input as part of the research to support these after-school activities.
>
> ■ The Accomplished Principal will establish ongoing, two-way channels of communication to continually monitor the needs of the parents of the larger community.
>
> ■ Principal B considers concerns expressed by any individual as a possible sign that deeper and broader problems might exist and becomes active in thoroughly exploring these issues.

2. Uses the vision of the school as a foundation and catalyst to identify the needs within the school community.

> ■ The Accomplished Principal is committed to establishing and promoting high standards for all students.
>
> ■ Principal B promotes parent partnerships to enhance the teaching and learning process by not only involving parents as school volunteers, but to become part of the decision-making process.
>
> ■ The Accomplished Principal is aware of the educational principles that support the necessity for including a comprehensive, inclusive, and extended after-school program for middle school students.
>
> ■ Principal B is able to articulate and communicate to the school and larger community the educational necessity for after-school programs for promoting the success of all middle school students.
>
> ■ The Accomplished Principal possesses an understanding of adolescent behavior and is able to articulate sound educational and behavioral reasons that underscore the problems and issues faced by adolescents who are not productively engaged in meaningful activities beyond the normal school day.

> - Principal B shares the belief and research that supports the need for students to have opportunities to participate in a structured, organized, well-planned and enriched environment beyond the normal school hours.
>
> - Principal B uses the school vision to create programs that are diverse and serve individual needs, have fair staff and student selection procedures and guidelines for participation, and ensure safe and protective learning environments.

3. Uses student performance data and other measures of success as an integral part of the process to plan and organize school instruction.

> - Principal B will gather all appropriate sources of data needed to make appropriate decisions. These data will include, among others, socioeconomic status reports, attendance information, and reports of pupil academic progress over time and disaggregated by grade level, race and ethnicity, gender, program placement, and other critical categories.
>
> - Principal B will enlist the support of others, for instance faculty and parents, to become a task force that will seek sources of data and participate in the analysis of this information. In creating this task force, Principal B will ensure student confidentiality and adhere to all legal and ethical guidelines in sharing data about individual pupils with others.
>
> - Principal B will use student performance data to measure and monitor student progress to establish levels of achievement and set standards of performance.
>
> - The Accomplished Principal will use these data to make judgments for appropriate instructional interventions that will assist students to move to a higher level of achievement.
>
> - Principal B will use student data to develop instructional strategies that will inform decisions on after-school program planning designed to meet the needs of each student and each group of students.

4. Understands that issues of student inequity in access to school programs must be addressed promptly and effectively.

> ■ The Accomplished Principal is always alert to issues of fairness and equity among all students and staff.
>
> ■ Principal B continually monitors equal access to educational programs through observations, input from the school community, and a variety of sources of data.
>
> ■ Principal B continually demonstrates a clear and convincing appreciation for sensitivity by all to the needs and values of the diverse school community.
>
> ■ The Accomplished Principal will support opinions and conclusions surrounding this issue based on data. These data will be used to identify the actual existence and nature of the problem and be useful in addressing the scope of inequity.
>
> ■ Principal B will demonstrate that the belief system of the school is that all students will have equal access to school activities and programs.

5. Will work with the faculty and staff to review processes used to place students in school programs.

> ■ The Accomplished Principal will collaborate with representatives from the larger school community to review current processes for determining student participation in after-school programs.
>
> ■ Principal B will use this collaborative team to make recommendations for a process that will ensure equity and fairness in the selection process.
>
> ■ Principal B will create guidelines that will allow the review team to communicate its progress to the student/parent community for review and comment.
>
> ■ Principal B will take measures to assure that programs will be in compliance with these revised established guidelines and develop a system for sustained, ongoing review.

6. Will enlist the support of the school and larger community in seeking sources of financial support for the school programs.

- Principal B will enlist the support and assistance of representative members of the school and larger community in reviewing ways to reallocate existing resources to better support after-school programs.

- Principal B will create a task force made of staff, parents, and community members to devise creative ways to acquire the funding needed to support a new, expanded, and enriching after-school program.

- Principal B facilitates a collaborative effort to address both immediate and long-term funding support by exploring the possibility of creating financially self-sustaining after-school programs and other innovative options.

- The Accomplished Principal will collaborate with community representatives to secure financial assistance and funding from outside sources.

- Principal B will assure that all appropriate stakeholders become part of a shared decision-making process that will create funding opportunities and guidelines.

- The Accomplished Principal uses community representatives to identify individuals who have talents and experience in obtaining funding through grant writing and by developing proposals.

- Principal B organizes staff members, as well as parents, to research, write and submit proposals to organizations and sponsors who might offer support for after-school programs.

- The Accomplished Principal will solicit the support of the school community to recruit appropriate adult volunteers to be part of the extended after-school program. These adult volunteers will comply with all local and staff requirements designed for the safe and effective operation of the school.

7. Uses the political process in appropriate ways to marshal support for school programs within and beyond the school community.

> - Principal B understands the political process and uses that knowledge in appropriate ways to enlist the support of a variety of community and school leaders to assist the school to acquire supplemental sources of funding.
>
> - Principal B will enlist the support of parent leadership groups in involving local community leaders in school activities.
>
> - Principal B will marshal school staff and parents in creating sustained channels of communication with local leaders, designed to share ideas and identify needs.
>
> - The Accomplished Principal will continually demonstrate to others a clear and convincing focus on nurturing school links with members of the broader community whose organizations can support student learning.

8. Will view the Superintendent as an ally and resource in addressing the issues of equity of district budgeting.

> - Principal B will share with the Superintendent appropriate data to support a cause of equity in funding across all schools and programs.
>
> - The Accomplished Principal will keep the Superintendent informed of public opinion and the concerns of staff, students, parents, and the larger community.
>
> - The Accomplished Principal will not only present issues to the Superintendent in a clear and concise way, but will offer the Superintendent possible strategies to resolve or address these issues.
>
> - The Accomplished Principal will assist the Superintendent in securing the support of parent and community groups.

9. Will involve parents and community members in developing supportive relationships with community agencies and resources.

> ■ The Accomplished Principal will enlist the assistance of representatives of the school and community in identifying local agencies that might support opportunities for after-school programs beyond the walls of the school (e.g., the YMCA, library, or museum).
>
> ■ Principal B will collaborate with community representatives in developing opportunities for local agencies to sponsor or conduct appropriate after-school activities within the school.
>
> ■ The Accomplished Principal will work with parents and community representatives to seek out opportunities for scholarships and matching funds from these agencies to support the after-school program.
>
> ■ Principal B will collaborate with parent and community groups to develop a sustained communication process that links the school to the local agencies.
>
> ■ Principal B will provide the parents and community representatives with data to assist them in identifying specific needs to be addressed by the proposed agency.
>
> ■ Principal B will assure that any agency involvement with students provides a safe, protective, nurturing environment for the students and for the staff.

The pages that follow outline the "Keys for Improved Performance." Specifically, they note:

a) the differences in the performance of rudimentary Principal A and accomplished Principal B;

b) the potential consequences of the continued performance of Principal A at the rudimentary level;

c) strategies and suggestions on how to move from one level of performance to another level.

Again, these pages specifically relate to the case outlined herein and the two focus questions:

1. What are some of the factors that have created this animosity of the community toward the school and what are some steps the principal might take to address this feeling?

2. How might the teaching and learning program benefit from better community relations, both directly and indirectly?

 KEYS FOR IMPROVED PERFORMANCE

To improve, the rudimentary principal responding to this case study must take some immediate and long-term action. Principal A should:

- communicate and take actions that reflect the school's vision

- collaborate with community members to create a vision that promotes the success of all students

- understand community needs and respect diversity

- align the principal's action plans and strategies with the vision

- model what is pertinent to the school vision

To implement these actions, the principal must meet with parents and invite them to become part of the school leadership. This can create a school culture that endorses and supports shared decision making and one that values and respects input and contributions of students and staff.

Additionally, Principal A must become a risk-taker and model progressive educational planning. This can be accomplished by:

- establishing high standards for all members of the school community

- creating school programs and activities that reflect these high standards

- reviewing academic and organizational structures on a continual basis

- modifying, altering, and adding to educational programs when the need arises

Principal A can achieve some of this by relying on members of the school community to collaborate in the development, planning, and implementation of new programs and redesigning existing programs.

Principal A needs to become an instructional leader. This can happen through:

- the use of research-based decision making about curriculum design and programs that nurture, support, and facilitate the learning process

- the appropriate interpretation of data that provides evidence and documentation to support new programs and/or modifies existing programs

- the employment of the skills and abilities of members of the school community

- the engagement of data- and evidence-gathering devices (e.g., surveys) to ascertain needs and desires of the school community

- the demonstrated openness, appreciation, and trust for community input and involvement

Principal A must be willing to reach out for assistance to create and achieve the vision for the school. This can be accomplished by inviting community engagement: to gather, interpret, and disseminate school-related information, standardized testing results, and other pertinent data. This collaborative effort allows the principal to facilitate effective communication between the school and the entire community and ensures that this information is shared with all stakeholders in appropriate and meaningful ways.

Principal A must become proactive rather than reactive. This can be done by:

- addressing issues and concerns honestly

- sharing information and demystifying the school operations

- respecting, nurturing, and supporting sensitivity, fairness, and equity among all the diverse stakeholders

- advocating programs and activities that are available for all students and that meet the educational needs of all individuals and groups

- developing a belief system in the school community that is founded in democratic ideals and the respect for divergent points-of-view

The principal must ensure that the culture of the school reflects these high ideals and expectations for all stakeholders. This happens when the principal creates an open dialogue with the whole-school community. This dialogue must be grounded in the sustained use of measured, respectful language and professional behavior. The principal, whenever possible, must show foresight in anticipating and identifying problems, concerns, issues at their earliest stages and addressing them before any crisis occurs. The principal must develop school leadership roles among the stakeholders that are supported, endorsed and respected. And, finally, the principal must work to replace an atmosphere of defensiveness with one of understanding built upon planning and collaborative decision making.

Principal A must become knowledgeable about all the programs in the school. With this understanding the principal establishes:

- expectations for programs, guidelines, directions

- guidelines for appropriate staffing and school community participation in activities

- benchmarks to meet standards and personal observations of all programs as part of the evaluation process

- channels of communication so that expectations are clearly presented to all stakeholders in a variety of formats and venues and which allow stakeholders to provide feedback

Principal A can begin to accomplish this by establishing rubrics for assessing the performance of programs. Using these guidelines the principal can then engage in planned, sustained observations of all programs. This data-gathering process will provide evidence the principal can then share with staff, students, parents, and community. Further, the principal can use this new information about program performance to provide targeted professional development opportunities for the staff to increase and enhance student instruction. Lastly, this evidence allows the principal to document performance and set new goals for continued, sustained success.

Principal A must allocate resources in service of teaching and learning and seek creative ways to finance needed programs and activities. To do this, the principal:

- finds ways to secure resources by seeking assistance from competent colleagues, reading literature, or through professional development

- explores possible budget modifications or the reallocation of resources to support new programs

- considers fundraising part of the job and solicits the assistance of staff and community individuals

- submits grant proposals throughout the year

- creates a fundraising and grant writing committee to write and submit proposals

- gathers data to support and inform budget proposals

To accomplish these tasks, Principal A must collaborate with staff and parents to seek creative ways to reallocate resources and secure additional funding. By facilitating the work of these stakeholders, the principal can establish new contacts for outside sources of financial support and become better able to solicit ongoing support for the school.

Principal A must gain a clearer understanding of the political forces that impact the school. This can be accomplished by:

- introducing the school community and its programs to local community and political leaders

- inviting leaders to the school to attend special functions

- arranging for these leaders to speak before school groups, such as at Parent-Teacher Association meetings

- facilitating the visits of community leaders to classes, assemblies, and other similar events

The principal must create strategies for how these community leaders can assist the school community in promoting greater student success. Part of this implementation process can be facilitated when the principal solicits the assistance of individuals in the parent community who have influence and/or have experience in political action.

Principal A must communicate and share concerns with the district Superintendent. This must begin immediately, with the principal:

- describing for the Superintendent the concerns and issues of the broader school community

- asking for the Superintendent's advice and support in addressing sensitive and critical issues

- preparing for discussions with the Superintendent with supporting data and documentation to facilitate ongoing collaboration with community members

- demonstrating a positive attitude toward and respect for the Superintendent

- sharing concerns with the Superintendent honestly and professionally

- providing the Superintendent several options for resolving or addressing issues

- becoming a facilitating link or conduit between the Superintendent and the school community

Principal A must prepare for meeting with the Superintendent by collecting relevant data to support his/her position. In addition, the principal must be forthright in offering specific examples of staff and community concerns that impact student achievement. Besides coming to the Superintendent with this evidence, the principal must be prepared to present suggestions and recommendations. Finally, the principal must facilitate a strong collaborative relationship between the Superintendent and the school community. The focus of the discussions between the principal and Superintendent and any ultimate decisions must be centered on teaching and learning and promoting the success of all students.

Principal A must be aware of the services available in the community that support teaching and learning. This is done by:

- preparing a detailed list of community agencies and organizations that exist to provide assistance to the school

- introducing the school community to these organizations

- inviting community representatives into the school

- facilitating school community involvement in these organizations as part of activities such as volunteer outreach activities

The principal effectively organizes the school to bring community agencies and organizations into the school to support teaching and learning. At the same time the principal enables school community members to support these organizations.

Principal A must model the desire to work collaboratively with community members. Demonstrating this spirit of cooperation is accomplished by:

- exhibiting openness and a sense of fairness

- sharing and exchanging appropriate information about the school and community

- respecting the diversity that exists in the community

- tolerating and accepting divergent points-of-view

- creating formal and informal partnerships in service of a healthy, sustained relationship with stakeholders

The principal can accomplish each of these tasks by creating effective channels of communication and by inspiring actions by the school community and the larger community that exhibit a common goal of supporting success for all students.

The rudimentary principal in Case Study 7 can begin the path to the accomplished level by examining each of these foregoing suggestions for improvement. By taking these immediate and longer-term actions our principal can begin to approach the accomplished level.

As you read this case study, consider these two questions:

1. What should the principal consider in preparing a short-term plan of action that would ensure the successful implementation of the Career Academy concept and the other issues presented in this case study? How should the principal organize the steps in the strategic effort to improve the school's climate and restructure the school? Who should the principal enlist in responding to these issues?

2. The principal has a mandate to bring order and organization to the operation of the school and transform the school's culture from one of chaos to one of improved learning. Describe specific progress benchmarks and the processes applied for ongoing analysis of results.

On a Thursday afternoon in July, the associate superintendent assigns a new principal to Taft High and asks that he report to his new assignment the following Monday. The administrative team at the school consists of the principal, three assistant principals, one disciplinarian, and one instructional coordinator. The only administrator being replaced, however, is the principal. Taft High is a large urban high school with a student population of approximately 1500 students. Taft High has a rich history dating back to its opening in 1926. From the time the school opened through 1958, the student body was predominately white. However, that population began to change in 1959 to include students from very diverse backgrounds. In the early 1970's to the present the student enrollment has become 100% African American. The school is now racially isolated from the larger community. As a result, the school receives little support from the alumni because, historically, these former students have not sustained a close connection with the school.

For the past few years Taft High has been plagued with discipline, attendance, and achievement problems. Some of its challenges have become major stories on the evening news. The school Superintendent, with the support of the Board of Education, has ordered a reorganization of the school starting with the removal of the principal and the restructuring of the school into smaller, more manageable units based on the Career Academy concept. The charge for the new principal is to implement the Career Academy concept as quickly as possible, bring the school under control, eliminate the daily negative press coverage, improve the school climate, and change the culture from chaos to one where learning is paramount. The Superintendent and the Board of Education believe that there will be a marked improvement in school climate and ultimately student achievement when this large bureaucratic school is transformed into smaller learning communities. They believe that this new organization will dismantle the existing barriers and bureaucratic structures that hamper student success in favor of the development of small nurturing learning communities or schools-within-a-school.

The school is a large, comprehensive high school whose attendance area now has one of the highest crime rates in the city. As a result, there has been an exodus of middle class families that were closely connected to and supported the school. The median income for a family of four in the community that surrounds Taft is below the poverty level. The respect and support parents and community once held for the academic and other school programs have totally eroded. Parents, the community, and students feel the school is unsafe. The perception of the community is that because of its large student enrollment the administration cannot control the students, the pupils have poor attendance, are at-risk of dropping out and are not succeeding academically. It is believed that students are being neglected and are disconnected from the school. The prevailing belief is that the climate and culture of Taft is one of chaos.

Taft High has much latent potential even though this may not be manifested in the data. There is a pool of talented students and many dedicated, competent teachers and staff who appear to have just given up due to frustration. There are many successful and noted community leaders and celebrities that are alumni of Taft. The new principal has been given the autonomy to be as creative as he likes, but the bottom line is: restore order and create an environment where teachers can teach and students can learn.

Taft High School

School Fact Sheet

- Approximately 90% of the students receive free or reduced-price lunches.

- The school is a large four-story structure of approximately one million square feet, encompassing the entire length and width of a city block.

- The school has a veteran teaching staff with an average length of service of 26.5 years.

- One third of the students receive services from special education.

- The largest department in the school is special education with 34 teachers.

- Approximately 24% of Taft students drop out each year, with the majority occurring during the freshman year.

- The student attendance rate is between 65–73%, and Taft has become one of the lowest academic performing schools in the district.

- The climate of the school has deteriorated to the point where teachers lock themselves in their classrooms and interact with students and colleagues as little as possible.

- The majority of the school's social and extra-curricular activities have been banned.

- Teachers, students, and parents feel isolated and totally disconnected from the school.

- Based on a constant barrage of negative media attention, the community's perception of the school is that Taft is academically deficient and unsafe for students.

- Taft High has recently been plagued by gang violence. The school, literally, is out of control and, as a result, the principal has just been replaced.

memo...

Office of the Principal

To: Taft Faculty and Staff
From: The Principal
Date: September 27
Re: School Reorganization

As you know, we have been given an opportunity to restructure our school into small, nurturing learning communities. A model that we will implement next school year is the Career Academy, a school-within-a-school. This memo contains some of the highlights of my discussions with the Superintendent regarding Career Academies, schools-within-a-school.

Developed over 28 years ago in Philadelphia, the concept of Career Academies has been quite predominant around the country as school districts grapple with large high schools, high dropout rates, declining academic test scores, and stagnant teacher morale.

Career Academies are schools-within-schools that recognize the strength of a large high school lies within its diverse course offerings and extracurricular activities. The smaller units capitalize on that diversity while providing nurturing environments that are safe, caring, and instructionally challenging. A team of teachers works with a group of students for a span of years in core academic subjects and those related to the career focus. Students select the remainder of courses from a variety of school options. Each Career Academy has a specific career focus with a sequentially developed plan of instruction and experiential activities. Classroom instruction is supplemented with experience in the workplace such as visits to employers, internships, and professional mentors.

There are different ways that communities structure their Career Academies. One effective way has been to link Career Academies with the economic development plans of an area or region so that young people are realistically pursuing goals that have a potential future. Examples of Career Academies from around the country include:

transportation/energy	aviation/aerospace	medical/healthcare services
business/finance	hospitality/tourism	law/criminal justice
graphic arts/design	marketing/public relations	JROTC/leadership

Nationally, there are a variety of models for Career Academies. Typically there are between 60–150 students in an academy, ranging in grades 9–12 or 10–12. Block scheduling is an organizational approach that provides needed flexibility. Academic courses are the centerpiece of each academy with a strong focus on integrated curricula.

Across the country, Career Academies have succeeded in increasing student achievement and lowering dropout rates. The academic achievement is influenced by four key elements: (a) students immersed in learning that is focused and cohesive in its approach; (b) the nurturing and watchful eye of staff members remaining with the students for the duration of high school; (c) a large school divided into manageable, identifiable units; and (d) the interest, attention, and resources from business, college, and community organizations.

This subject of reorganization, understandably, produces tension and anxiety. As principal, it is my responsibility to provide you with as much information as I possibly can. I am scheduling a meeting in the school auditorium, Thursday, 3:15 p.m. so that you can learn more about this initiative.

I look forward to this opportunity to meet with you. While the session is not mandatory, it would be helpful for everyone to attend as I attempt to implement this new program.

memo...

Office of the Principal

To: Superintendent of Schools
From: Principal, Taft High
Date: September 15
Re: Restructuring Taft High School:

This memo is to inform you of our vision for the Career Academy model we will implement next school year.

Taft High School's objectives for Career Academies include:

- creating a school-within-a-school environment in which the diverse course options of a large high school are interwoven with specific career-focused classes and experiences

- providing a cadre of core teachers who remain with academy students over the course of their high school experience, providing a nurturing environment

- immersing students in applying their instruction within a pragmatic context assisting them to see the relevance of what they are learning and enhancing their self-esteem

- enhancing the awareness of a particular career field and the many types of jobs and college training found within that area

- balancing negative peer influences by regularly exposing young people to constructive adult peer groups within college and corporate environments

- supporting students who come from disadvantaged backgrounds by helping them gain access to the formal and valuable channels of being connected to jobs/college

- providing experiential activities such as shadowing, internships, focused research, and college exposure in a specific career field

- designating an avenue for industry, labor, and community associations to commit human, financial, and technical resources to a specific school-within-a-school

Career Academies depend on a cluster of teachers who teach core subjects and the related career focus. Extensive professional development is provided to the teachers in the career focus area and teachers work collegially through coordinated planning times.

Very often, persons from the career area who are professionals or college instructors join them in the classroom. Teachers teach their academy classes followed by regularly assigned classes for the remainder of the day. Career Academies do not generally require the assignment of extra teachers. If a staff member is added, that person is generally a program coordinator or liaison.

I will keep you updated as we move through the implementation process.

DOCUMENT 4: SCHOOL REPORT CARD

Taft High School — School Report Card

Taft High School *School of Opportunity* *Enrollment*	1500
Free & Reduced Lunch	90.0%
Attendance Rates	73.0%
Parent Conference Rate	20.0%
Special Education Rate	34.0%
Graduation Rate	45.1%
ESL Rate	NA
Students per Teacher Rate	28
Student per Administrator Rate	500
Low Income Students	98.3%
College Admission Testing Applicants	14.8%
Dropout Rate	24.0%

State Assessment Results

	Com. Arts			Science			Mathematics			Social Studies		
	Year 1	Year 2	Year 3	Year 1	Year 2	Year 3	Year 1	Year 2	Year 3	Year 1	Year 2	Year 3
Advanced/proficient (white)	6	1		2	1	4			5		1	1
Nearing proficiency (light blue)		16	12					8			2 20	4 9
Progressing/step 1 (medium blue)	94	83	88	98	99	96	89 11	92	95	90 10	77	86

- The top level on the state assessment ("advanced and proficient"). On the charts, these two levels are combined and shown in white area. The number represents the percentage.

- The middle level on the state assessment ("nearing proficiency"). On the charts, this level is shown in light blue. The number represents the percentage.

- The bottom two levels on the state assessment ("progressing and step 1"). On the charts, these two levels are combined and shown in medium blue. The number represents the percentage.

Based on the information about this school presented through the scenario and the documents, how should the principal respond to these two questions?

1. What should the principal consider in preparing a short-term plan of action that would ensure the successful implementation of the Career Academy concept and the other issues presented in this case study? How should the principal organize the steps in the strategic effort to improve the school's climate and restructure the school? Who should the principal enlist in responding to these issues?

2. The principal has a mandate to bring order and organization to the operation of the school and transform the school's culture from one of chaos to one of improved learning. Describe specific progress benchmarks and the processes applied for ongoing analysis of results.

PRINCIPAL A rudimentary response

A Rudimentary Principal:

1. Leads the staff in the implementation of the Career Academy concept.

> ■ The Rudimentary Principal views this as an opportunity to demonstrate leadership skills and directs the staff in assigning them roles and teaching responsibilities.
>
> ■ Principal A will not involve the staff in the decision-making process because it is believed that they have been ineffective in the past and that they must have confidence in his professional expertise and guidance.
>
> ■ The Rudimentary Principal will isolate the staff from the community and parents to protect them from external distractions so they can focus on the new work.
>
> ■ The Rudimentary Principal will convince the staff that Career Academies will be effective in bringing about change because of the literature that describes their effectiveness in other urban areas around the country.
>
> ■ The Rudimentary Principal will present a prepared plan of action at his orientation presentation to the staff.
>
> ■ Principal A will reassign leadership roles in the building to signal changes in staffing that will come.
>
> ■ The Rudimentary Principal is willing to take full responsibility for the success of this new program and, as a result, limits the decision-making process to only a few trusted colleagues.

2. Isolates parents and community members from the implementation process.

> ■ The Rudimentary Principal will not involve parents in the implementation process because the parents are viewed as uncaring and ineffective in supporting the academic achievement of their children.
>
> ■ Principal A will not involve parents or community members because the concept of the Career Academy is so new to them they will not understand how the program will work and their involvement will only slow down the process.
>
> ■ Principal A decides it is important for the safety of all to limit parent and community member access to the school building.

> ■ The Rudimentary Principal views the community and the school as two distinct entities and does not feel it necessary for members of the community to become involved in internal professional school matters.

> ■ In an effort to provide support for the implementation process, Principal A creates an expert Leadership Advisory Team. The team is composed of the principal's former professor of school leadership, a political leader from the area in which the principal lives, and two members of the Board of Education of the school district the principal's children attend.

> ■ A communication plan is put into place by the principal to keep the parents informed of the progress in this school reform initiative. The plan consists of a monthly newsletter to the parents, written by the principal and delivered home by the students.

3. Prevents community business leaders from becoming involved in the process.

> ■ Principal A does not invite local community and business leaders to become part of the implementation process because of a past history of their poor or nonexistent relationships with the school.

> ■ Principal A decides it is best to wait until the Career Academy program is fully developed before sharing it with business leaders to prevent any misunderstanding or interference.

4. Decides not to include community agencies and resources in the development of the concept.

> ■ The Rudimentary Principal lacks confidence in local agencies and community outreach programs and does not enlist their support.

> ■ The Rudimentary Principal focuses only on business opportunities for the students and the new program and excludes other possible sources of assistance.

5. Excludes the media from the planning process.

> ■ The Rudimentary Principal controls negative media comment by deciding not to share any reorganization plans with the media.

> ■ Principal A establishes strict guidelines that greatly limit teacher-media communication.

> ■ Because of recent news coverage of incidents of school violence, Principal A will not talk directly with the media and refers all calls to a member of the district central office.

6. Does not seek student involvement.

> ■ Principal A limits student involvement in any implementation discussions.
>
> ■ The Rudimentary Principal uses student academic performance data to support the development of a strict, new discipline code.
>
> ■ The Rudimentary Principal prepares to assign students to career paths based on the need to maintain a balanced teaching load and maximum use of all rooms.
>
> ■ Principal A establishes the same standard of high expectations for all students, regardless of individual need or aspiration.

PRINCIPAL B accomplished response

The Accomplished Principal:

1. Engages the staff in the implementation process.

> ■ The Accomplished Principal educates the local school community to expect shared leadership and representation by multiple persons of authority within the school and larger community.
>
> ■ Principal B uses the concept of distributive leadership to build capacity and understands that the range of administrative responsibilities within large bureaucratic schools is too great for one person to assume.
>
> ■ The Accomplished Principal provides support to teachers so they can become creative problem solvers and assists them to realize that they have specialized skills that will be needed to revitalize the education of both staff and students.
>
> ■ The Accomplished Principal engages the whole-school community in the reform process and stands in support of teachers.
>
> ■ The Accomplished Principal will create effective classroom observation processes, surveys, and other strategies to collect evidence on individual teacher performance and strengths and use those data to inform decisions on teacher assignment and professional development initiatives.

- Principal B involves the entire school faculty in school planning and identifying the types of data that will be needed to monitor implementation targets and benchmarks.

- Principal B involves relevant stakeholders to develop plans for both short- and long-term objectives and develops a systemic process to accomplish and monitor the tasks.

- The Accomplished Principal understands the best way to improve schools is to enhance the dignity, autonomy, and professional status of educators.

2. Promotes parent and community input in the decision-making process.

- For Taft High to show improvement, the Accomplished Principal establishes a culture that is permeated by a common vision, collaborative partnerships, and broad-based meaningful participation by parents.

- Principal B understands that collaboration does not occur simply by putting groups of individuals together. The process requires continual reinforcement, outreach, and coaching.

- The Accomplished Principal understands the importance of healthy relationships between the school and larger community and uses the teachers and students to build these relationships.

- The Accomplished Principal builds positive relationships by seeking to understand the concerns of parents and community members through sustained communication, surveys, and other methods.

- Principal B involves key people from parent and community groups in the design and implementation of the change process.

- Principal B creates an environment and culture in the school that respects parents, welcomes them into the school, and is sensitive to their diverse backgrounds. The school provides parents dignity and respect accorded to adults in the community caring for youth.

- Principal B does not wait passively for parents and community organizations to become involved, instead, the principal finds ways to actively encourage and promote parent and community involvement.

- The Accomplished Principal will create channels of communication between the school and the community that promotes sustained, two-way discourse in a variety of venues and through a variety of sources (e.g., direct conversation, print, telephone, or electronic).

3. Establishes strong, sustained links to local businesses and agencies.

  ■ The Accomplished Principal will facilitate the creation of an implementation plan that involves the participation by representatives of community agencies, industries, small companies and shops, vocational trainers, and college professors.

  ■ Principal B will promote a Career Academy plan that will provide opportunities for business and agency leaders to be partners with Taft High to ensure that students will participate in activities that will improve the surrounding and larger communities.

  ■ The Accomplished Principal will create a communication process that will allow a sustained, meaningful dialogue between the school and these business leaders.

  ■ The Accomplished Principal will provide opportunities for the staff to become active in community events and organizations.

4. Enlists the support of the media to create a positive image of the school.

  ■ The Accomplished Principal has the ability to enlist the support of others both inside and outside the school to effect meaningful change. One way of doing this is to establish positive relationships with the press and provide these sources with information about school accomplishments and reform measures.

  ■ Principal B will share with the media, at the direction of the Superintendent, background information about the Career Academy concept and how it will benefit the students and the community.

  ■ Principal B will use this improved image of the school to sustain ongoing relationships with vital business and community leaders.

5. Relies on student participation in the implementation process.

  ■ The Accomplished Principal builds positive relationships with the students and uses this as a key to improving student achievement.

  ■ The Accomplished Principal creates expectations for behavior and performance that are fair and provides consequences that are based on equity and designed to promote a positive learning atmosphere.

  ■ Principal B enlists the involvement of students in developing strategies for managing student behavior.

- The Accomplished Principal involves students in the planning of the Career Academy program and uses multiple sources of student data to inform decision making designed to meet the needs of the students and the community.

- Principal B will ensure that an effective school organization and climate promotes the success of all students.

- Principal B will demonstrate a professional behavior that is associated with achievement in student learning.

- Principal B will work with the staff, students, and community to provide an educational program for students that invites parental support, but one that is not dependent on parental assistance for the success of the student.

- The Accomplished Principal uses community and parent data to create a realistic educational program for students that reflects the status of the home (e.g., few two-resident parents and a non-working mother).

- Principal B will continually monitor data on student performance and use this information in the community and the school to support the reform initiatives.

A LOOK AHEAD

The pages that follow outline the "Keys for Improved Performance." Specifically, they note:

a) the differences in the performance of rudimentary Principal A and accomplished Principal B;

b) the potential consequences of the continued performance of Principal A at the rudimentary level;

c) strategies and suggestions on how to move from one level of performance to another level.

Again, these pages specifically relate to the case outlined herein and the two focus questions:

1. What should the principal consider in preparing a short-term plan of action that would ensure the successful implementation of the Career Academy concept and the other issues presented in this case study? How should the principal organize the steps in the strategic effort to improve the school's climate and restructure the school? Who should the principal enlist in responding to these issues?

2. The principal has a mandate to bring order and organization to the operation of the school and transform the school's culture from one of chaos to one of improved learning. Describe specific progress benchmarks and the processes applied for ongoing analysis of results.

To become effective, organizations must first begin by changing the skills, attitudes, and behaviors of the people within the organization. In this case, Principal A must:

- establish collaborative teams that can work to change behaviors and attitudes

- develop a collaborative school culture that encourages all stakeholders to trust each other

- share information, and work together in the best interest of the students

- commit to the creation of a collaborative culture that will make the school a comfortable place in which to work and learn for students as well as adults

- empower others to become successful in the school's restructuring effort

- demonstrate skill in building and mending relationships. The principal shows compassion and sensitivity, is able to put people at ease, and understands and respects cultural, religious, gender, socioeconomic, and racial differences

To accomplish this, Principal A must take full advantage of the rich backgrounds and abilities of all stakeholders. Principal A must demonstrate that honesty is rewarded and diversity valued by creating greater diversity in positions of influence and power and by seeking and encouraging different points-of-view. Team members should feel they have the knowledge and authority to make important decisions. They must, however, be prepared to take responsibility for the decisions they make.

To improve, the rudimentary principal needs to develop and convey a shared vision of high expectations as a support structure for children. This principal can accomplish this by:

- developing and acting on a set of firm, professional beliefs

- believing in a strong sense of academic mission and high expectations for all

- communicating this vision to all stakeholders

One example of how this can be accomplished is when the principal creates a strong culture of reflective practice. The principal must value and use a variety of decision-making tools, such as student test scores and other measures that might include parent, student, and teacher satisfaction. All restructuring approaches should be determined based upon an analysis of results. It is essential that the principal evaluates the data and surveys staff, students, and parents to ascertain what has been effective and innovative in helping produce academic success.

Principal A must provide an environment where purposeful and organized conversations can take place. The focus for this principal must shift to include:

- collaboration in the building of a new vision for the school

- cooperation between the school and members of the larger community that is sustained over time

- communication with the larger community that is effective and ongoing

Principal A must discover a variety of ways to facilitate structured and purposeful collaborative vision-building. Ways to promote sustained community involvement in the school might evolve from a series of ongoing activities in the form of open-houses, town meetings, district mailings, newsletters, parent conferences, Web sites, school activities, and school meetings. Such communications with representatives from various sectors of the community discussing educational concerns are a few examples for structured conversation to occur.

Principal A must understand that leadership is not a characteristic that can be assigned; it is rather the result of performance. Principal A must believe that:

- a very basic level of leadership is not derived from the job position or as a result of completing education administration requirements

- accomplished leaders demonstrate a style that encourages risk-taking and values ethical practices

- high performing leaders outperform their colleagues as a result of setting goals for themselves

- effective leaders communicate the vision to all stakeholders

- outstanding leaders provide appropriate and ongoing recognition to others, while at the same time recognize their own contribution to problems, and acknowledge their own mistakes

It is not uncommon to find many programs started by school leaders that vanish within a year or two. For sustained change to occur, Principal A must empower others within the organization to provide leadership for continuous improvement. One danger in leadership is in concentrating all of the power, inspiration, and knowledge in one or even just a handful of people. To become an accomplished principal, Principal A must realize that leading is influencing and providing guidance in direction, course, action, and opinion. Further, Principal A must learn that a leader is not an autocrat, but a facilitator and one who appreciates the ideas of others and not a defender of the status quo. Principal A must understand what sets high performers apart from the rest is that they are effective at solving problems, rather than simply placing the blame on others or events. They never feel comfortable with the present level of performance. Instead, compelling internal goals motivate them and they are willing to take risks after investigating all possible consequences.

Principal A must understand the value of clear communication. To become an accomplished principal, Principal A must:

- realize that a major responsibility for the principal is to communicate effectively between the school and its constituencies

- consider both internal and external constituencies

- seek community support

- understand that the focus should not be on selling the school, but rather, communicating the school's mission and goals and steps needed to reach them

- know the value that is placed on openness and directness

- establish clear lines of communication regarding goals, performance, expectations, and feedback

To improve, the rudimentary principal must create an effective dialogue between and among all stakeholders. Two-way communication must be encouraged so that all individuals and groups can express their concerns and ideas about the objectives of the school. Schools should be proactive and not wait for a crisis or problem before establishing lines of communication with community stakeholders. Principal A must realize that if the negative rhetoric about school failure continues unabated, the community may soon irrationally conclude that attempts to fix the worst practices cannot be effective because past efforts have yielded no useful results. The principal must value the maxim, "Make friends before you need them." This is done by showing that the school is open and responsive, by strengthening community connections between the school and the community, and by being aware of community impressions and issues so the leader can respond proactively.

The principal and the administrative staff directly influence the morale in the building and the effectiveness and efficiency of its programs. The principal is the chief executive officer in the school and is responsible for the overall management of all functions. The responsibility to create an atmosphere within the school which fosters and maintains good staff morale is the duty of the principal.

Finally, to become an accomplished principal, Principal A must:

- maintain the ability to perceive the needs, concerns, and personal problems of others

- develop tact in dealing with others from diverse backgrounds

- be sensitive to the multitude of socioeconomic influences on the school, with the diversity of population, and community values that inspire patterns of performance

■ be able to reach logical conclusions based on quality decision-making skills founded on the evidence available

■ Provide opportunities for the members of the school community to become active participants in community events, organizations, and programs

To improve, it is incumbent on Principal A to acquire the sensitivity and skills that ensure that all school programs address cultural diversity. As instructional leader, the principal provides the leadership for the inclusion of culturally diverse and culturally sensitive curricula into the school's instructional programs.

Notes

STANDARD 5: INTEGRITY, FAIRNESS, AND ETHICS IN LEARNING

The focus of the cases in Chapter 7 is on ISLLC Standard 5: Integrity, Fairness, and Ethics in Learning. Chapter 7 introduces you to issues of concern at Roosevelt High, a suburban 9–12 high school and Jackson Middle School, a suburban 6–8 school.

As you read through this chapter and each subsequent chapter, you will find each case structured in a specific way.

First, you will be introduced to a specific Standard and to the case study scenario and its accompanying documents. Secondly, you will be given two focus questions to keep in mind as you read the case and as you analyze the two fictitious principals' responses: one principal at the rudimentary level, the second at the accomplished level.

As a reader, you will consider the core of the ISLLC standard and then apply this understanding to the rudimentary and accomplished principals' responses. We also invite you to consider other factors that could be built into each principal's response.

STANDARD 5

A SCHOOL ADMINISTRATOR IS AN EDUCATIONAL LEADER WHO PROMOTES THE SUCCESS OF ALL STUDENTS BY ACTING WITH INTEGRITY, WITH FAIRNESS, AND IN AN ETHICAL MANNER (CCSSO, 1996, P.18).

COMPONENT FIVE **A** Demonstrating a Personal and Professional Code of Ethics

COMPONENT FIVE **B** Understanding One's Impact on the School and Community

COMPONENT FIVE **C** Respecting the Rights and Dignity of All

COMPONENT FIVE **D** Inspiring Integrity and Ethical Behavior in Others

Without effective educational leadership, cries of injustice and inequity have opportunities to flourish in the schoolhouse. It is impossible for a school administrator to act as an educational leader without clearly understanding, enveloping, and practicing the components of Standard 5, which call for promoting the success of all students by acting with integrity, with fairness, and in an ethical manner.

The four components of Standard 5 entail a vision for success, a focus on teaching and learning, an involvement of all stakeholders, and a demonstration of ethical behavior as seen through the success of all students. These four components are sequential in application. First, the school leader must clearly demonstrate his/her personal code of ethics by modeling a highly developed code of morality in exchanges with others. Second, the school leader understands that the personal ethics of a leader affect the entire school community. Therefore, it is incumbent that all members of that community are treated with dignity. Only when these three components are in place can the school leader inspire others to act ethically and with integrity.

Component 5a, "Demonstrating a Personal and Professional Code of Ethics," is the basis for a school leader's foundation. As educators, we are in the business of continuously assessing and addressing human needs. Without a code of ethics to chart our way, we lend ourselves to the likes of a collision course where reasoning and integrity are left in the wreckage. School leaders are faced with making decisions on a daily basis that affect people. In order to promote student achievement and strengthen school communities, effective educational leaders must act in practice with integrity, fairness, and in an ethical manner. This in turn will aid in demonstrating that they truly care about the people entrusted to their leadership.

Component 5b, "Understanding One's Impact on the School and Community," is directly linked to 5a. Educational leaders must not only act but also be able to measure the cumulative effect of their decisions. School communities want to know that they can trust their leader. They look to him/her to set the standard for acceptable behavior. "Attitude reflects leadership," thus, school leaders in practice must continuously provide opportunities for meaningful discussion and use the information gained to bring about positive change.

Component 5c, "Respecting the Rights and Dignity of All," means that if a school is to be an ethical organization, then the dignity of all members of that organization is essential. Only through knowledge that the rights and freedoms of students, parents, and staff members are sacred can a school be organized to ensure the success of all students. Enlisting the support of other stakeholders as well as establishing and fairly supporting rules and routines provide the framework for how members of the community treat each other.

Component 5d, "Inspiring Integrity and Ethical Behavior in Others," is not something that can be taken for granted even when the first three components of this standard are in place. Whenever anyone in the school community fails to treat others with dignity, those instances must be confronted by the school leader. By first acting with integrity and then expecting the same level of ethical behavior from all within the school, the school leader has taken great strides towards promoting the learning of all.

Using Components 5a and 5b, Case Study 9 will demonstrate the challenge presented to a school leader when academic dishonesty is called into question. It will provide the framework for promoting the success of all students in a fair manner while taking into consideration compliance with school policies. It will question an administrator's integrity and test his/her ability to act in an ethical manner despite the lack of district support. The ramifications of this administrator's personal and professional code of ethics will heighten one's understanding of a school leader's potential impact on a school and its community.

Components 5c and 5d come under close scrutiny in Case Study 10 in which, due to the need for budget cutting, a principal must deal with the impact of losing successful programs which are meeting the needs of some of the hardest to serve students.

CASE STUDY 9

Roosevelt High School
9–12 Suburban School

As you read this case study, consider these two questions:

1. What plan could the principal present to the superintendent that might reverse the Board's decision?

2. How might the principal use the apparent support from the PTO and from the faculty to build more programs that would address the needs of all students?

Roosevelt High School has long held firm to its zero tolerance for unfair practices in the academic arena. It has served as a symbol of high moral standings, possessing a strong code of ethics for the members of its suburban school community to adopt and emulate. Traditionally, the high school has been praised for its strict compliance to rules and policies and for its positive impact on the school and community in upholding such standards. Recently, the very foundation of Roosevelt High School has been challenged. The tenth grade world history teacher discovers that the fifteen elaborately designed world culture projects presented at the semester multicultural exposition have been plagiarized directly from a Web site. The principal of Roosevelt High School goes with tradition and defends the teacher's actions to fail the fifteen students. This decision, however, is criticized by the students' parents and not supported by the first year Superintendent who has convinced the Bryant School District Board of Education to change the grades to passing.

OFFICIAL   CORRESPONDENCE

Roosevelt High School
Office of the Principal

March 1

Mr. and Mrs. (Parents)
Main Street

RE: Plagiarism of Multicultural Exposition Project

At the recent semester science fair, your child, Robert, submitted a project that was suspected as being plagiarized directly from a Web site. His world history teacher, guidance counselor, and I met with Robert to discuss and investigate this matter. Together, we discovered that Robert did, indeed, act with academic dishonesty in claiming to be the author of someone else's work.

As a student at Roosevelt High School, your child is held responsible for his/her own academic endeavors. The student handbook which you and Robert signed acknowledging receipt clearly states on page 77, rule 29 that "zero tolerance will be afforded to students found guilty of academic dishonesty/plagiarism." Staying in line with this rule, your child will receive a zero for his science project. Being that the project is worth 50% of Robert's grade, this zero will result in a failing grade for the course.

Your child will be afforded the opportunity to make up this loss of credit by attending summer school. Information pertaining to this program may be picked up in the counselor's office. As always, we appreciate your support and assistance in upholding Roosevelt High School's reputation for academic excellence. If you have any questions or concerns, feel free to contact me at 555–5555.

memo . . .

Superintendent — Bryant School District

To: Roosevelt High School Principal
From: Superintendent of Schools
Date: March 11
RE: Academic Dishonesty Policy

The Board of Education met on March 7 to discuss the recent infraction of academic dishonesty at the high school multicultural exposition. Although you acted within the purview of the student handbook and board approved policy, we have come to the conclusion that we cannot support your decision to fail the 15 students thus denying them credit for this course. We are directing you to change the grades to passing. The reasons behind our decision are as follows:

1) One infraction should not result in the loss of full course credit; thus, we are recommending that the multicultural exposition projects count no more than 25% of a student's grade allowing for individual success despite the single infraction that resulted in a zero.

2) We desire to seek feedback from the community and use it to strengthen relations between the school and the community; thus, our decision is based on the results of this joint effort.

3) Our vision is to promote the success of all students; thus, in changing the grades back to passing, we are providing an opportunity to foster this vision.

In speaking on behalf of the Board of Education, we appreciate your strict compliance with district policy, but we are directing you to uphold and carry out the decision of the Board to change the grades of the 15 world history students to passing.

𝕹𝖊𝖜𝖘𝖕𝖆𝖕𝖊𝖗

Bryant Weekly News

Breaking With Tradition

Suburban school, Roosevelt High, has been the center of much unwanted attention. Typically, a model for rigorous academic standings with zero tolerance for academic dishonesties, Roosevelt High School's firm foundation has suffered a severe blow, and the whole school community is watching, waiting patiently to see if the institution can survive the jolt.

It seems a world history teacher gave 15 of her tenth grade students zeroes for plagiarizing their semester multicultural exposition projects from a Web site, and the zeroes placed their grades on "course failure" status. Angered, parents of the 15 students insisted that the Superintendent and School Board do something. The Board caved in to the parents' demands and ordered the principal to direct the teacher, Susan Sloan, to change the grades to passing. Ms. Sloan, holding fast to her understanding of concepts like integrity and honesty, resigned in protest.

Her simple stand has shaken the school community. The main item of discussion on campus and around town is not the winning touchdown in last night's game but rather the topic of ethics. Now the residents are questioning the decision-making powers of the district asking what a grade means and who should determine it — angry parents or compliant School Board members.

The School Board should be celebrating educators like Susan Sloan for teaching her students how to conduct their lives rather than just using world history to study past life.

These students may learn a hard lesson in integrity from Ms. Sloan's class. Then again, they may learn what the School Board was promoting: That if enough of you bend the rules, get caught, and complain loud enough about being punished, you're wrong-doing will be overlooked.

The entire school community of Roosevelt High School may be learning a lesson, and not from those who put academic honesty on the back burner.

Roosevelt High School Parent Teacher Organization
Minutes of PTO Meeting
March 13

Danny Spadoni called the meeting to order at 4:05 PM. Those present included president Danny Spadoni, vice-president Hazel Mays, secretary Stacey Mallett, reporter Doug McClain, treasurer Keith Browning, and 250 parent/community members.

Minutes from the last meeting were accepted on a motion by Doug McClain and seconded by Stacy Mallett.

Old Business: chairs were appointed for the following committees:
Meeting Room Chair: Keith Browning
Agenda Chair: Hazel Mays
Activity Chair: Stacy Mallett
Refreshment Chair: Aimee Farley

The Agenda Committee met and prepared a draft for PTO members to distribute to solicit prospective members. The next scheduled PTO meeting will be April 10.

New Business: A heated discussion was held concerning the decision made by the Superintendent and Board of Education to change the grades from fail to pass of 15 world history students verified as plagiarizing. The high school principal and local press support the teacher's decision. The PTO wishes to show its support for dealing with violators of academic integrity in a fair and consistent manner that instills honesty and respect for hard work.

Amanda Slape made a motion for the PTO to support and encourage the principal to respond to the actions taken by the Board of Education. Glenda Fitzhugh made a second and the motion carried.

Craig Smith made a motion for the PTO to declare March 18 "Susan Sloan Day" in honor of her professional integrity and a second by Gloria Taylor adjourned the meeting at 4:55 PM.

Respectfully Submitted,

Stacy Mallett, PTO Secretary

THE PROBLEMS

Based on the information about this school presented through the scenario and documents, how should the principal respond to these two questions?

1. What plan could the principal present to the Superintendent that might reverse the Board's decision?

2. How might the principal use the apparent support from the PTO, local press, and faculty to build more programs that would address the needs of all students?

This case raises several issues within the school and greater community that reflect the principal's status as the school leader. There is clearly a lack of support at the district level for her decision to uphold the teacher's ruling to fail the fifteen students for plagiarizing. Because the district has overturned the principal's decision, the perception of her as being in the wrong is spreading like wildfire throughout the school community. The principal's reputation is at stake here. The newspaper article in support of the teacher's resignation further taints the principal's public image. The PTO is urging the principal to stand her ground. Thus, she has support; however, student discipline versus student success weighs heavily on the matter.

The principal decides to mobilize the PTO, using its influential status to confront the Board for failing to support her decision. She calls the PTO president and asks her to send a letter requesting a special Board meeting related to this decision. Because she knows that the Board will be reluctant to hold such a meeting, she suggests that the letter be signed by each officer of the PTO and that it be sent to the local newspaper as an "open letter to the School Board." The principal also asks the PTO President not to share that she has been urged to take this action by the principal. "Leaving me out of this," she explains, "will demonstrate that this is a community issue and not a personal one."

Principal A writes a letter to each member of the Board of Education clarifying her decision and elaborating on her present status in the community due to the overturned ruling. She explains to each Board member that her personal integrity and respect as a leader is now in question by the students, staff, and parents of Roosevelt High School.

She schedules a meeting with the counselor and the fifteen students along with their parents in an attempt to paint a picture of what the Board's decision will mean for the students on campus. She points out to them that since the teacher who resigned was so well liked by students and staff, the other teachers will have a difficult time treating these fifteen students fairly. The principal clings to the belief that Roosevelt High School's foundation is firmly rooted in being fair, firm, and consistent and that the high school will rise to that stature again. She also shares her belief that the Board will eventually overturn its decision so that it would be better for them if they volunteer to accept the consequences that were originally established.

PRINCIPAL B accomplished response

One major issue presented in this case is whether or not as a school leader the principal is ensuring the school's vision with great equitable and ethical consideration. Another issue pertains to modeling the expectation for appropriate behavior that has been predetermined for the principal by the school community. A third factor involves the principal evaluating herself and continuously assessing the needs of her constituents.

Principal B has always felt it was important to obtain frequent feedback and uses the knowledge gained to strengthen the school/community relationship. She goes directly to the power sources within the community (parents, business representatives, politicians). She collaborates with them, keeping them apprised of school events, and works to actively engage them in the school setting. Without the community's support, the rules mean nothing. She works to ensure that there is a buy in by all stakeholders by immersing them in the school culture through invitations to participate in academic, athletic, and extra-curricular ceremonies and activities.

She becomes well-immersed in the school's policies and procedures and is willing and able to stand up and fight for what is fair and right for all students, as well as remain open and receptive to change what is not. She has built a relationship with the community to such an extent that she can pinpoint whose voice rings the loudest and funnel that resource to expedite her endeavors for the high school. The principal reaches out and embraces the school community's expectations for effective leadership and acts in a personal and professional manner to promote opportunities for positive teaching and learning. She does not view the Board's decision as a personal blow. She knows that the overturned ruling is not about her reputation nor the teacher's resignation. It is about the students and what is best for them.

She takes the community's expectations to heart and uses them to grow and assist others in learning from this decision. She is immersed in the community. She understands their wants and needs, and she works with and among them to see that those wants and needs are satisfied. Principal B serves as the mirror through which the process is reflected; thus, she models appropriate behavior and is willing to rigorously confront inappropriate behavior.

To ensure the success of all students, the principal must continuously provide opportunities for open, honest, and constructive discussion in regard to her own impact on the school community. She should welcome and eagerly invite input from students, parents, and community members as it pertains to grading, handbook policies, discipline, and so forth. She should elicit input through surveys or questionnaires to drum up support and increase awareness. The principal must challenge herself to continuously assess the needs of her constituents asking for frequent feedback and use the information gained on an ongoing basis to bring about positive change that will strengthen the community/school relationship. She could set up strategic committees that are comprised of all stakeholders to ensure involvement on the front end, throughout processes, and in the finale.

The pages that follow outline the "Keys for Improved Performance." Specifically, they note:

a) the differences in the performance of rudimentary Principal A and accomplished Principal B;

b) the potential consequences of the continued performance of Principal A at the rudimentary level;

c) strategies and suggestions on how to move from one level of performance to another level.

Again, these pages specifically relate to the case outlined herein and the two focus questions:

1. What plan could the principal present to the Superintendent that might reverse the Board's decision?

2. How might the principal use the apparent support from the PTO and from the faculty to build more programs that would address the needs of all students?

 KEYS FOR IMPROVED PERFORMANCE

DIFFERENCES IN PRINCIPAL PERFORMANCE

One obvious difference between Rudimentary Principal A and Accomplished Principal B is clarity. Principal A seeks little or no evidence. She rarely thinks to assess and evaluate the needs of her constituents. She projects concern or seeks to understand, but vaguely models a true sense of caring. Principal B makes effective and consistent use of information gained to bring about positive change. She not only seeks, but rigorously pursues convincing ways to strengthen relationships and to provide opportunities for open and honest discussions. Both take into consideration the issues of teaching and learning and seek feedback to improve the process and one's own performance, but approach such issues from different angles and varied levels of thought and use of the information gathered.

Principal A is not actively involved or engaged in truly understanding her learning community and how to serve its needs; thus, she cannot clearly identify the needs of her constituents nor understand how the school's vision or her actions may be adversely affecting those needs. She does not have a feel for the situation nor the people involved which will keep her from providing others with a model to emulate. She is hiding under the auspices of the PTO, viewing it as her support network. This is not a healthy choice to make. She may hurt herself personally, professionally, and ultimately tarnish the efforts to ensure student success.

To alleviate such public scrutiny in the future, as the leader, she should first speak with the Superintendent prior to supporting teachers' decisions. She should work closely with the various chains of command reaching a decision that all levels will support in front of the Board. She must strive to ensure that teachers make parents fully aware of grading procedures and disciplinary sanctions and that she communicates with them at the building level in such a manner that will deter them from taking further measures. She should look into the grading policy across all disciplines to ensure that student success is possible for all students.

PRINCIPAL A
rudimentary response

TO

PRINCIPAL B
accomplished response

HOW DO YOU MOVE FROM RUDIMENTARY PRINCIPAL A TO ACCOMPLISHED PRINCIPAL B?

The path from Principal A to B is not an easy road to travel. One must first develop integrity in order to learn how to ensure the engagement of others and to promote such opportunities for equitable participation. The principal must foster the school community's vision, model it both professionally in school and personally out of school, keeping all constituents in mind as participation is monitored and injustices are confronted and remedied.

To reach the status of Principal B, A must learn to use the knowledge gained to address needs and to improve the overall atmosphere of the school community. In order for this to transpire, the leader must provide opportunities for disseminating information and opinions through open, honest discussions. She must develop a knack for seeking feedback and for using it in a significant way to strengthen the relationship between the school and the community.

10 CASE STUDY

Jackson Middle School
6–8 Suburban School

As you read this case study, consider these two questions:

1. What plan could the principal present to the Superintendent that might accommodate both the needs of the students and the decision of the Board of Education?

2. How might the principal use the apparent support from the high school principal and the middle school faculty to build more programs that would address the needs of all students?

Jackson Middle School, grades 6–8, has a school population that is highly representative of the small suburban community it serves: Jackson is nearly completely residential except for the small service and retail industry needed for a community of this size. Most adults, white-collar professionals, are employed in a nearby urban community known for its contributions to technological advances. The high cost of housing in Jackson makes it difficult for low-income families to live within the town limits. However, a plethora of new apartment construction built to meet the housing needs of this growing urban area is causing a slight change in demographics that is bringing Jackson closer to the wide diversity of ethnicity and income levels for which the region is known.

Jackson Middle School prides itself on its high academic standards. Statewide assessment results place it in the top 10% of middle schools in the state. However, not every Jackson student performs at these high levels. The long time former principal of Jackson Middle School was cognizant of demographic changes in the region and kept a close watch on the small, but growing numbers of students, most of whom lived in the new apartment complexes, that seemed to be having difficulty with the school curriculum. Realizing that these students did not enter school with the same cultural capital of long-time Jackson families, he successfully wrote and received a five-year grant from the Wide Foundation to provide an educational program to meet the specific needs of students who were at risk of not meeting grade level standards. This is the fifth year of the grant, and a general downturn in the economy has had its effect on the school budget. The School Board is not willing to continue funding this program. A search for alternative foundation support has hit a dead end as foundations have placed their more limited funds in communities with greater perceived needs.

memo . . .

Jackson Union School District
Superintendent's Office

To: Jackson Middle School Principal
From: District Superintendent
Date: March
Re: Budget cutbacks

As we have discussed in administrative staff meetings over the last six months the economic outlook for our state is bleak. It does not appear that we will be receiving any increases in state support for our schools. With increasing costs it has become necessary for us to eliminate all programs outside of what is considered a regular classroom. In our regular classrooms we will maintain a district-wide ratio of 25 students to every one instructor, with the exception of mandated special education services and classrooms.

To that end your special program, funded up until this year by the Educational Foundation, will have to end, and the students in this program will be served in a traditional classroom. I am confident that the high quality teachers on your staff, who have benefited from the professional learning experiences provided from your Educational Foundation grant, will rise to the challenge of ensuring that the students formerly in this program have their needs met.

I know it will be difficult for your staff to make this adjustment. However, it is an economic necessity. I'm counting on your strong leadership skills to counter any opposition to this move, as it is the only alternative in these difficult times.

The elimination of this program will cause a net decrease of three teachers at your school. The personnel office will be in contact with you to make you aware of any transfers that may need to be made. This may require several months due to the unknown factor of natural attrition from retirements or teachers leaving the area. Please be patient.

memo . . .

Jackson Area Education Association

To: Principal
From: JAEA President
Date: March
Re: Possible Budget Cutbacks

Except for the annual cries of budget woes, it would be hard to believe that it is nearly spring. We were so fond of our former principal, but we know that, in time, we will grow to have the same respect for you. This year is flying by.

As we hear rumors of possible budget cuts, I want you to know that there are some programs the Jackson Middle School faculty feels are "untouchable." Our salaries are, of course, untouchable, but so are the wonderful support services our students receive. They are, along with the talented faculty, the foundation of our greatly recognized student success.

The Educational Foundation Program is absolutely critical to our ability to maintain the high quality classroom environment for which our school is noted. If these students were not given the support Wide provides, we know that they would create both discipline and instructional problems beyond the capacity of an already over-burdened teacher to handle.

We want you to know that you have our full support to do everything you can to protect the special programs that make Jackson Middle such a wonderful school. If you need us to organize parents, write the district administration, circulate petitions, or storm a school board meeting, we will be right behind you.

I cannot express strongly enough how important our great tradition is to us. Without special support, especially the Educational Foundation Program, our school could become just another school rather than the exciting center of learning that it is.

Please let me know how I, as well as the JAEA, can be of help.

	Two Years Ago Language	Last Year Language	Current Year Language	Two Years Ago Math	Last Year Math	Current Year Math
Jackson Middle School Assessment Report **Language Arts and Math Norm-Referenced Test Results**						
% of all students above the 75th percentile	72	75	74	68	66	79
% of students below the 75th percentile	7	5	8	9	9	10
% of low SES students above the 75th percentile	4	5	6	8	6	6
% of low SES students below the 25th percentile	75	74	75	64	64	66
% of Hispanic students above the 75th percentile	3	3	3	6	9	7
% of Hispanic students below the 25th percentile	83	80	84	73	72	70
% of students in Educational Foundation Program above 75th percentile (after 2 years in program)	40	41	42	44	44	45
% of students in Educational Foundation Program below 25th percentile (after 2 years in program)	1	2	1	2	1	1

Note: All students who score in the 25th percentile or lower on the norm-referenced test in either language arts or math are eligible to participate in the Educational Foundation program. 80% of those students do participate.

DOCUMENT 4: STUDENT DEMOGRAPHICS

Student Demographics		
Ethnicity	Total School	Educational Foundation Program Participants
% White	80	4
% Hispanic	15	74
% Other	5	22
Socioeconomic status		
% of students on free or reduced lunch	6	81
Parent education level (highest level completed)		
% some high school	3	45
% high school graduate	8	27
% some college	14	11
% college graduate	41	15
% higher degree	34	2

Jackson-Wood Oaks Union High School District
Jackson High School

November

Principal
Jackson Middle School
Jackson

Dear Principal,

Congratulations on your appointment as the new principal of Jackson Middle School. You follow in a long tradition of quality principals, and I am certain that you have the courage, skill, and determination to make the School Board proud of its selection of you to head Jackson Middle.

For the past five years, Jackson High has benefited from an incredible program dreamed up and implemented by Jackson Middle's former principal. His farsightedness led him to seek the support of the Wide Foundation to provide a program to meet a small but growing number of students who were at risk of not meeting the high standards of our district.

Of course, not every student comes to Jackson High ready to learn and be successful, but those students who have participated in the Educational Foundation Program have, almost without exception, become outstanding high school students. I feel it is essential that you do everything possible to continue to provide this high level of service to these students, who without Wide Foundation support, would remain at risk of dropping out, drug use, and behavioral difficulty.

Keep up the great Jackson Middle School tradition. We are counting on you.

Sincerely,

Jackson High Principal

THE PROBLEMS

Based on the information about this school presented through the scenario and the documents, how should the principal respond to these two questions?

1. What plan could the principal present to the Superintendent that might accommodate both the needs of the students and the decision of the Board of Education?

2. How might the principal use the apparent support from the high school principal and the middle school faculty to build more programs that would address the needs of all students?

Principal A knows that the Educational Foundation Program cannot be abandoned. He can see that it clearly makes a difference for his students. He knows it has the backing of the staff and of the principal of the high school that his school feeds. He knows that, in particular, the Educational Foundation Program serves a population, primarily minority and low socioeconomic families, that is in many ways under-served in this region. His school knows how to meet the needs of these students. It could possibly serve as a model for other schools, which have failed to bring such students to a level where they can achieve success. Because Principal A knows that integrity and ethical behavior are important, he must do everything necessary to ensure the continuation of the Educational Foundation Program.

The first action he takes is to announce at a faculty meeting that the School Board is trying to cut the Educational Foundation Program and that the school staff must unite to stop this. He asks if the faculty is ready to take the high road to support his efforts. He asks if the Jackson Area Education Association would create and then have signed by all teachers a letter of support to present to the Superintendent.

At the next PTA meeting he makes the same announcement to the parents present. As only parents of successful students attend the meeting, he also shares that "those students" cannot be in our classrooms without support. He has a copy of the letter that teachers are circulating, and he asks the parents who are present to sign a similar letter.

He then calls the Superintendent to schedule a meeting where he can present these letters along with his plan to save the Educational Foundation Program. As he prepares for this meeting Principal A has another idea: he creates a class schedule based on the need to eliminate two regular classroom teaching positions by increasing class size so that the three Educational Foundation Program teacher positions can be saved. He realizes that if the School Board will only decrease the staff size by one rather than three he can increase the average class size by only three students and save the Educational Foundation Program.

Jubilant, he prepares the teacher letter, the letter from parents, and his request to raise the class size by three students (a move he knows his teachers will support) and drops all three into an envelope and sends it to the Superintendent. He also calls the Superintendent and leaves a voice mail message stating, "No need for us to meet. The problem is solved. I just put the solution in the intra-district mail."

Principal A has another job to do. Although the Educational Foundation Program is successful, it has not met the needs of every student. In order to be a successful principal, respecting the rights and dignity of all—as well as making sure all others do the same—he decides that every teacher and every program needs to create a program that will serve the students who score below the 25th percentile on the annual test.

Noticing that there are large failure rates in the foreign language and English departments, he writes a memo sharing the letter from the high school principal. As this letter speaks of the great Jackson

Middle School tradition, he informs the teachers of these departments to create a plan for helping all their students to receive scores of C or better. He ends this letter by saying, "I know that you'll want to join me in ensuring that no Jackson Middle School student is left behind, and that each and every one of our students will make Jackson High School proud."

Principal A also notices that the math and science departments have a very low fail rate. He calls the chairs of these two departments together and congratulates them for their success. He then tells them that he has arranged for the two of them to spend tomorrow meeting with the English and foreign language department chairs to show them how to do the same. He tells them that his vision for the school is for every student to succeed.

PRINCIPAL B accomplished response

Principal B also knows that the concept of the Educational Foundation Program should not be abandoned. He can see that it clearly makes a difference for Jackson Middle School students. He knows it has the backing of the staff and of the principal of the high school that Jackson Middle feeds. He knows that, in particular, the Educational Foundation Program serves a population, primarily minority and low socioeconomic families, which is in many ways under-served in this region. Jackson Middle School staff has created a program that is currently meeting the needs of these students and could possibly serve as a model for other schools, which have failed to bring such students to a level where they can achieve success. Principal B has the integrity and ethical courage to know that he must bring the community together in order to ensure that the fundamental concepts of the Educational Foundation Program will be preserved.

To remind the school community that the success of all students is paramount, Principal B ensures that all faculty members, parents, and students focus on the school mission statement. He has seen that it is attractively placed on the school letterhead as well as made sure that it is frequently displayed on the school marquee. A poster with the mission of the school has been placed on the door of every classroom.

It is now March and Principal B is aware that the economic crisis in the state will certainly trickle down to the school level. He is concerned that there may be pressure on his district Superintendent to eliminate many of the fine programs that have made the district so special. At a faculty meeting, he addresses the accomplishments of the staff and students as a way to introduce the main topic of the looming budget problem. He begins the meeting by asking his staff to share some of the specific tasks that they have done, or noticed others doing, that demonstrate that the staff at the school is living its vision. Teachers share moving stories of student successes, not just academic success, but also of their behavior, and involvement in the life of the school. Principal B uses these anecdotes to move the staff to the next item on the agenda. This agenda item addresses the looming budget cuts. Principal B shares all the information he currently has available (in written form) regarding the projected school budget for the following year. With the stated belief that the Educational Foundation Program is a critical component of the entire educational program, Principal B asks the faculty to consider two alternative strategies designed to save the Educational Foundation Program concept: (1) find a method to reallocate reduced resources to save the program or, (2) look for creative ways of maintaining the objectives of the program within the traditional classroom setting. Principal B understands that it is necessary to balance the need to assist the Superintendent and Board of Education in responding to the reduction of funding while, at the same time, sustaining initiatives that promote the learning of all students. Principal B uses the opportunity of this positive faculty meeting to rally the school community into action teams that will address the two strategies introduced by the principal.

The meeting agenda moves on to another item of business in which the most recent results of school-wide formative assessments are discussed. Each teacher is asked to work with others in the department to develop specific strategies for the students most at risk of failing a class. Teachers are asked if any of these students would benefit from a faculty member who would serve as a mentor by checking in with the student at least two times a week. The teacher coordinating the mentoring program (which was created after a process in which the teachers and administrators implemented, evaluated, and revised the shared vision for success of students, faculty, and parents) is recognized for his leadership of this effort.

As a follow-up to the faculty meeting, Principal B meets with many members of the community and local businesses to share the story of the special programs that the teachers have created for the at-risk students of Jackson Middle School. He explains the work of the teams who are exploring strategies to preserve the concept of the Educational Foundation Program and he invites community representatives to join these teams. He explains that the commitment to all students is one that is shared by the entire school community and clarifies how the mission of the school expresses this commitment. He shares his own excitement about a student council project to provide peer tutoring. With the assistance of the high school principal, it is proposed that high school students participate as volunteers in this project. This, he feels, is an example of how the school's mission is understood not just by adults, but also by the students in the district. The student who first thought of this program and steered it through the student council is introduced to share his story. A student who is now a senior at Jackson Senior High School also comes to school frequently to meet with community members to share the difference the programs of Jackson Middle School have made in her life. "So many of Jackson students, who came to the school failing, have learned that they have what it takes to be successful, and the best part is that their success has carried us through high school," is the way she concludes many of these conversations.

Principal B frequently invites successful graduates of Jackson Middle and High Schools to return to school and hold conversations with current students. In this way he is able to recognize and reward their efforts.

Word of the success of Jackson Middle School is widely known throughout the community. Many are astonished at the list of community service projects that have been completed by Jackson Middle students when they are published in the local paper.

Principal B refers calls from community and business leaders to teachers who can respond directly to the ideas that are being offered. He frequently will arrange to cover a portion of a class period so that a teacher can meet with a community volunteer.

A LOOK AHEAD

The pages that follow outline the "Keys for Improved Performance." Specifically, they note:

a) the differences in the performance of rudimentary Principal A and accomplished Principal B;

b) the potential consequences of the continued performance of Principal A at the rudimentary level;

c) strategies and suggestions on how to move from one level of performance to another level.

Again, these pages specifically relate to the case outlined herein and the two focus questions:

1. What plan could the principal present to the Superintendent that might accommodate both the needs of the students and the decision of the Board of Education?

2. How might the principal use the apparent support from the high school principal and the middle school faculty to build more programs that would address the needs of all students?

DIFFERENCES IN PRINCIPAL PERFORMANCE

PRINCIPAL A
rudimentary response

The contrast in style between Principal A and B is as obvious as Principal A's constant references to *his* school and Principal B's repeated reference to *our* school. Both Principal A and Principal B share a commitment to ensuring the success of all students. However, Principal A sees this success as his success whereas Principal B sees it as the only logical extension of the school mission.

Principal A rushes to use the opinions of staff members he happens to agree with or who will help to make his points.

Principal A believes it is important to act quickly to serve the changing needs of students.

PRINCIPAL B
accomplished response

Principal B demonstrates his respect for the school staff by honoring the time commitments he has made with them. He seeks the involvement of all because he knows that each teacher is worthy of respect and dignity and has much to offer not just in the success of the students in the classroom but for the success of the entire school. He seeks and acts on their opinions.

Principal B ensures that all actions taken are consistent with the vision and mission of the school and in support of the decisions of the Superintendent and Board of Education.

PRINCIPAL A Potential Consequences

Potential Consequences of the Performance of Principal A

Principal A's mistakes in this scenario are perhaps a bit too obvious. By acting alone he is sure to alienate his boss, his school board, and his staff. He is willing to present solutions without discovering if the people who must implement those solutions will support them or whether they might have better ones. The actions described in this chapter will lead to distrust. Certainly his ability to move his school steadily forward will be at risk; this will mean his job is at risk.

Principal A's Action	Probable Consequence
Asks staff to unite to stop budget cut.	Alienates school board.
Asks parents to petition school board to stop budget cut; in process advocates that "regular" students will be hurt by ending a successful program for "at risk" students.	Further alienates school board. Unwittingly promotes myth that low socioeconomic (SES) students can harm education program of high SES students, thereby dividing community.
Presents own proposal without consulting staff or Superintendent.	Diminishes opportunity for staff buy-in to solution. Alienates Superintendent.
Cancels meeting with Superintendent.	Effectively ends the opportunity for collaboration.
Orders teachers to create plans to assist students below the 25th percentile.	Disenfranchises those who must implement plan.
Orders interdepartmental meetings without determining all possibilities for difference in performance.	Increases jealousy between departments; increases opportunity to excuse low performance.

PRINCIPAL A   TO   PRINCIPAL B

rudimentary response   accomplished response

HOW DO YOU MOVE FROM RUDIMENTARY PRINCIPAL A TO ACCOMPLISHED PRINCIPAL B?

Principal B acts in a manner consistent with his beliefs and with the mission of the school, and works within the policies and directions of the Superintendent and Board of Education. Everyone is treated with dignity and respect. He is clear that the high standards he holds for himself will also be confronted when not held to by teachers or students. He fairly ensures that clear and consistent rules and routines are followed by confronting the offenders when they are not. He does this not with his own personal power, which is substantial, but through reminding people of the vision that is commonly held for the school.

Growing from Principal A to Principal B requires sustained monitoring and revision of the school mission. It requires an understanding that this cannot be done alone. It requires practicing interpersonal skills that bring people to work together to achieve a common goal. It requires an abiding faith in the people with whom one works to seek solutions. And, most of all, it requires acting with integrity and respect when working with students, teachers, parents, other administrators, and the wider school community.

A key to moving from Principal A to B involves a personal ethics base that demands one act for the good of students, family, and staff rather than for personal gain. Principal A seems more motivated to demonstrate his skills at problem solving than he does at meeting the needs of students. Principal B works continually with staff to articulate a shared understanding of the mission of the school. Principal A must work to ensure that the school mission is a shared mission by, in part, involving staff in meaningful decision making and acting with the highest ethical standards and professional expectations.

Some resources that may help school leaders to move from Principal A behavior to Principal B behavior include:

Making Sense as a School Leader (Ackerman, Donaldson, and Van der Bogert, 1996). Chapter 2 from this book, "Justice: Doing What's Right...But What is Right?" and Chapter 5, "Resources: Balancing Infinite Needs and Finite Resources," will provoke thinking as they share contrasting responses to dilemmas that arise when school leaders act with high ethical standards.

The Leadership Paradox (Deal and Peterson,1994). In "The Bifocal Principal," Chapter 3 of this book, Deal and Peterson describe the paradoxical nature of the work of school leaders. They suggest that by addressing contradictions it is possible to achieve balance and harmony and offer the analogy of bifocals as a means to accomplish goals. As Principal B balances student needs and real budget issues, bifocals will come in handy.

Michael Fullan, in the article, "Emotion and Hope: Constructive Concepts for Complex Times" (1997 ASCD Yearbook, *Rethinking Educational Change with Heart and Mind*) provides assistance to school leaders when he reminds them that "reformers are ill-advised to work only within the balkanized cocoons of like-minded individuals. We stand more of a chance of getting somewhere if we confront differences earlier in the process, working through the discomfort of diversity, than we do if we attempt to work in sealed-off cultures."

CHAPTER 7 SUMMARY

Society/life in general places many demands on educational leaders. Numerous temptations plague one's integrity in handling situations on a daily basis. Treating others fairly while choosing to do the right thing to maximize student success weighs heavily on the minds of administrators. Practicing, communicating, and addressing issues in an ethical manner will be the challenge that they will be forced to accept, struggle through, and overcome in order to survive in today's schools.

Educational leaders are on the forefront in the line of duty when it comes to setting an example for their school community constituents to observe and emulate. They define the curve in the eyes of those entrusted to their leadership. Everything they do and say is under close scrutiny and affects the lives and decision-making processes of so many. It is thus the educational leader's task as the administrator-in-charge to demonstrate a personal and professional code of ethics (Component 5a) and, in turn, to fully understand his/her impact on the school and community (Component 5b). This must be done while respecting the rights and dignity of all (Component 5c) and inspiring the integrity and ethical behavior of others (Component 5d).

It is our hope that our pictures of the two Principal B's in this chapter have illustrated how a principal, amidst a swirl of competing definitions of the right thing to do, can promote "the success of all students by acting with integrity, fairness, and in an ethical manner." This was certainly the intent as our Accomplished Principals:

- created opportunities for open, honest, and constructive discussion in regard to the impact on the school community

- welcomed and eagerly invited input from students, parents, and community members as it pertained to grading, handbook policies, and discipline

- elicited input through surveys to increase awareness

- created strategic committees comprised of all stakeholders to ensure involvement on the front end, throughout the process, and in the finale

- understood that an overturned ruling is not about one's reputation; but about the students and what is best for them

- ensured that the mission of the school was understood and supported by all

- became cognizant of economic trends in the wider community and predicted their possible impact on the mission of the school

- reviewed assessment data regularly to see if the school is implementing its mission and vision

- kept the wider community aware of the successes and needs of the school

Acting with personal integrity and in an ethical manner is but one part of the process of meeting Standard Five. The more difficult part is to constantly examine the school's efforts to achieve its mission by ensuring that all individuals in the school community act ethically and with integrity.

Notes

STANDARD 6: THE POLITICAL, SOCIAL, ECONOMIC, LEGAL, AND CULTURAL CONTEXTS OF LEARNING

The focus of the cases in Chapter 8 is on ISLLC Standard 6: The Political, Social, Economic, Legal, and Cultural Contexts of Learning. Chapter 8 introduces you to issues of concern at two suburban schools, Truman Elementary and Grant High School.

As you read through this chapter, you will find each case structured in a specific way.

First, you will be introduced to a specific Standard and to the case study scenario and its accompanying documents. Secondly, you will be given two focus questions to keep in mind as you read the case and as you analyze the two fictitious principals' responses: one principal at the rudimentary level, the second at the accomplished level.

As a reader, you will consider the core of the ISLLC standard and then apply this understanding to the rudimentary and accomplished principals' responses. We also invite you to consider other factors that could be built into each principal's response.

STANDARD **6**

A SCHOOL ADMINISTRATOR IS AN EDUCATIONAL LEADER WHO HAS THE KNOWLEDGE AND SKILLS TO PROMOTE THE SUCCESS OF ALL STUDENTS BY UNDERSTANDING, RESPONDING TO, AND INFLUENCING THE LARGER POLITICAL, SOCIAL, ECONOMIC, LEGAL, AND CULTURAL CONTEXT (CCSO, 1996, P. 20).

COMPONENT SIX **A**   Operating Schools on Behalf of Students and Families

COMPONENT SIX **B**   Communicating Changes in Environment to Stakeholders

COMPONENT SIX **C**   Working Within Policies, Laws, and Regulations

COMPONENT SIX **D**   Communicating with Decision Makers Outside the School Community

Leaders achieve their goals by influencing others. In order to promote student success, such influence is exerted in various forums, within the school environment and within the larger environment in which schools function. When a leader is successful, the larger environment understands and supports the school's vision, realizes the school's challenges and success, sees its effort to work within its legal framework, and is a partner in decision making.

Effective school leaders influence the environment for the benefit of students. They do not simply accept what is, they strive to create what can be. In order to make what can be a reality, leaders must know and be able to do certain things. Leaders:

- use a single-minded focus on the interests of students and their families to guide their work, always seeking to make schools places that better promote achievement

- make sure that all who are part of it, and/or can influence it, know the learning environment, both internal and external, of the school

- know, understand, and carry out policies, laws, and regulations that safeguard members of the school community from harm and neither succumb to expediency nor accept such from others

- identify those who have an effect on the school's environment from outside and effectively communicate with them in order to have a positive influence

The case studies that follow illustrate ISLLC Standard 6 in practice. The first case involves an elementary principal's effort to influence the school district to seek additional funding for a reading program. It focuses on the ability of a leader to rally others in support of the school and to communicate why it is important to the school to do so. In the second case, faced with a required and controversial high-stakes graduation test, a high school principal must simultaneously implement the regulatory framework while leading a school that questions its relevance and validity; in effect, to lead a group that is challenging a mandate the leader is bound to carry out.

 CASE STUDY

Truman Elementary School
Pre-K–8 Suburban School

As you read this case study, consider these two questions:

1. What are the instructional issues presented in the scenario and documents?

2. What are the short- and long-term actions the principal should take to gain the support of the Superintendent, Board of Education, and other appropriate stakeholders in addressing these instructional issues?

Truman Elementary School houses grades Pre-K–8 in a suburban community outside a medium-sized Midwestern city. The school district has four K–8 elementary schools ranging in size from 500 to 700 (Truman is the largest), two K–4 schools, one middle school (5–8), and a single high school. The school's 700 students are placed in three classes of each grade level and one pre-school. Grades 7 and 8 are divided into teams. Approximately 15% of the school's students qualify for free/reduced lunch and 5% speak a primary language other than English, typically Spanish. The principal has been in the school for two years and comes from outside the school, but within the district.

Of particular concern at Truman Elementary is the reading achievement of students. Standardized, national achievement test scores indicate that students at Truman: do worse in reading than they do in math; lose ground as a cohort moving through the school; and lose ground from grade to grade. Additionally, parents in the school have taken note of the test scores and commented negatively on their views of reading instruction. This dissatisfaction was evidenced in the request from the Parent Teacher Organization (PTO) to have the principal address the concerns at the next meeting.

The principal asked the district reading supervisor to visit classrooms in the school and create a reflection on the observations with recommendations for instructional improvement. While the principal had already made an assessment, the reading supervisor was brought in to provide an independent, second look. A recent grant announcement from the State Department of Education has provided an opportunity for the school to organize and support its effort to address its reading issues. The challenge for the principal is to organize the school and the district in support of a grant proposal.

OFFICIAL CORRESPONDENCE

State Department of Education
Office of the Commissioner
Department of Instruction

Notice of Grant Opportunity

March 20

Interested Parties:

The recent Federal reauthorization of the Elementary and Secondary Education Act (ESEA) has made available to states funds to support the implementation of research-based reading programs. Grants are available to districts in support of schools that house students in grades K–4. Total available funds for grants are $3,000,000. The department expects to award between 10 and 15 grants averaging between $200,000 and $250,000, but no grant is to exceed $350,000. A small number of awards of up to $500,000 may be made to consortiums of districts and schools. The grants will cover activities over a two year period.

Grant awards will be made according to the following criteria:

- Need: Determination of need will be made on the basis of student poverty and achievement history. The goal is to make awards where there are demonstrated gaps in student performance and in areas of high poverty.

- Preparation: Priority for awards will go to applicants who have conducted an analysis of their student achievement and instructional program. The goal is to make awards to applicants who have demonstrated a baseline of knowledge and awareness of the needs of their reading program.

... continued on next page

- Research Base: Awards will be made to applicants who demonstrate understanding of research-based programs and are making a commitment to implement research-based programs. A statement of commitment from the Superintendent of Schools is required for consideration.

- Budget Activities: Weight will be given to the suitability of the applicant's budget and proposed activities to the desired goals of the grant program. This will be determined by the applicant's explanation as to how the proposed activities are designed to reach the desired project goals.

Complete application packets with required forms are available from the Department of Education or may be downloaded (DOE.state.edu/instruction/reading_grant/application). Important dates in the application process are:

Grant Notice/Applications Available. . . . . This year — March 20

Deadline for Applications. . . . . This year — June 1

Notice of Award. . . . . This year — July 1

Grant Activities Commence. . . . . Next year — September 1

Interim Progress Report Due. . . . . In two years — August 31

Grant Period Ends. . . . . In three years — August 31

Final Report Due . . . . In three years — October 1

Questions may be addressed to:

Felix Almonzora
Federal Projects Director
Office of Instruction
State Department of Education

OFFICIAL CORRESPONDENCE

Truman Elementary School PTO

June 20

Dear Principal,

At the last PTO Board meeting our discussion turned to reading. A lot of parents are saying that we're not teaching reading anymore in Truman. There's no spelling program and the teachers don't correct our kids' spelling mistakes when they make them. When we tell our children to sound out words, they say their teacher told them not to do that. Bright kids are bored because they have to wait for slower kids to catch up, and they end up reading books that are way too easy. The state test scores in the paper show that our kids can't read well.

At the next PTO meeting can you present to us why we're not teaching reading at Truman and what we can do to change it? An article in a magazine says that research has found that you have to teach phonics for kids to learn to read and it doesn't seem that we're doing that.

Sincerely,

Mary Ellen Sarcozzi
President

memo...

Consolidated School District #27
Office of Instruction

Memorandum

TO: TRUMAN PRINCIPAL
FROM: READING SUPERVISOR
DATE: JANUARY 24
RE: CLASSROOM OBSERVATIONS

As you requested, I spent last week in your primary grade classrooms observing reading instruction and seeking reasons behind weak reading test scores in the district and your school. I compared the observations to recent research on effective reading instruction. My findings and recommendations are outlined below. Overall, the issues you mentioned to me that arose from your observation reports are valid. What I saw supports your proposed direction and, I hope, provides some additional detail and focus.

Findings

1. In general, teachers are using the basal reading program and following the curriculum. At least one hour is spent each day in language arts instruction, often more, but not always. This time is typically in the morning, but not always. It is not always in one block, as the classroom days are broken up by special area instruction, recess, and lunch.

2. Instruction is almost always whole group. There is little individualized or small group skill development. Where there are small groups, each group tends to be instructed on the same thing. In a typical lesson, the classroom is introduced to a story, the story is read by class (sometimes by the teacher, sometimes by students in turn, and sometimes chorally) and the students then complete workbook pages individually.

3. Skill development occurs solely in the context of basal instruction. Spelling instruction also occurs only in basal context and within writing. The entire class receives the same skill instruction regardless of performance level.

4. In only a few classes was there any discussion of strategic reading. Most classroom instruction did not include direct lessons regarding what strategies students can and should use when reading, especially when running into difficulty. Those classrooms that did teach strategic reading seemed to appear randomly, as if those teachers had learned to teach that way on their own.

5. In sum, reading instruction at Truman is not aligned with recent research on what is effective. This includes both the content of what is taught as well as the delivery of instruction.

Recommendations

1. Curriculum standards need to be revised to include balanced attention to: phonemic and phonetic skills, reading comprehension, and integrated reading and writing. Also, one hour a day of language arts instruction is inadequate.

2. Classroom instruction needs to include attention to all the balanced elements of reading. Students should spend time working with words (phonemic and phonetic skills), read both books that are within their ability and that challenge them, learn strategies to improve their comprehension, and write about what they read.

3. The delivery of instruction needs to focus on the needs of the individual as well as the needs of the class. Instructional organization should be flexible, provide the teacher with diagnostic information about students, and allow the teacher to individualize instruction to student performance level.

4. This will require a comprehensive professional development program for your staff. For some, this will be a major shift in teaching, and others are well on their way. For those for whom the shift is major, extensive support will be needed.

DOCUMENT 4: STANDARDIZED-TEST RESULTS

Truman Elementary School
Standardized-Test Results
The Past Three School Years

Reading

Grade	Median Percentile			Cohort Change			Grade to Grade Change			Math Versus Reading Matrix [Reading-Math]		
	Last year	Two years ago	Three years ago	Last Year	Two years ago	Three years ago	Last year	Two years ago	Three years ago	Last Year	Two years ago	Three years ago
1	55	60	52							-3	+1	-1
2	52	52	58		-3	-2	-3	-8	+6	-3	-4	0
3	50	49	51		-3	-1	-2	-3	-7	-1	-4	-6
4	53	47	50		-3	+1	+	-2	-1	0	-4	-4
5	47	52	48		-1	+1	-6	+5	-2	-3	-3	-3
6	49	46	51		-1	-1	+2	-6	+3	0	-4	-2
7	50	48	47		-1	+1	+1	+2	-4	-2	-2	-5
8	48	49	46		-1	-2	-2	+1	-1	-4	-2	-3

Mathematics

Grade	Median Percentile			Cohort Change			Grade to Grade Change		
	Last year	Two years ago	Three years ago	Last Year	Two years ago	Three years ago	Last year	Two years ago	Three years ago
1	58	59	53						
2	55	56	58		-2	-1	-3	-3	+5
3	51	53	57		-2	-1	-4	-3	-1
4	53	51	54		0	+1	+2	-2	-3
5	50	55	51		+2	0	-3	+4	-3
6	49	50	53		0	-2	-1	-5	+2
7	52	50	52		+1	+2	+3	0	-1
8	52	51	49		-1	-1	0	+1	-3

Based on the information about this school presented through the scenario and the documents, how should the principal respond to these two questions?

1. What are the instructional issues presented in the scenario and documents?

2. What are the short- and long-term actions the principal should take to gain the support of the Superintendent, Board of Education and other appropriate stakeholders in addressing these instructional issues?

PRINCIPAL A rudimentary response

A rudimentary principal:

> tells the community what its vision of reading instruction should be
>
> shares an analysis of needs with the community to defend the vision
>
> focuses the vision on the problems faced by the school in teaching reading
>
> creates a plan for the improvement of reading
>
> seeks desired ends and develops strategies to achieve them

A rudimentary principal reacts to the pressure of poor achievement with defensiveness. Principals at this level seek to assign blame for problems and look for obstacles to cite as evidence of why the problems have not been overcome. In creating a response, the principal looks no further than what is in plain view and does not consider those problems faced by families and community; develops a plan and defends it staunchly; and, believes that solutions lie within the scope of responsibility of others.

A rudimentary principal calls on parents to spend more time at home working with their children to assist in their reading development. This is done without context, without any determination of what parents do and do not know about how they can support learning at home, and without any attempt to understand the context and capacity of families to carry out an ill-defined assignment. A meeting with the PTO becomes confrontational and accusatory. Parents, alienated from the school, put pressure on the principal to change things. The principal, casting about for scapegoats, adds lack of central office support, the influence of unions, and inadequate staffing for the current state of affairs. When meeting with the faculty, the list of those to blame is similar, but not identical.

Principal A announces that the scores received by Truman Elementary students are low because teachers in the school won't use the teaching techniques they're supposed to and students don't come to the school prepared. Cited is the memo from the reading supervisor as evidence of problems in teaching. There is no attempt to find what is right about teaching in the school; there is no attempt to assume responsibility as leader of the school.

Principal A now must work with the faculty to develop improvement strategies, and they prove unwilling to openly discuss their concerns and uncertainties about their teaching strategies, fearing further assignment of blame. As a result, the principal is unable to accurately assess their needs and develop an effective professional development plan. Their reaction is the same as the principal's, to defend what they do and seek to place blame elsewhere. Since they have not been substantively engaged in an analysis of the data about student learning in the school, no basis for a common dialogue has been formed.

The rudimentary principal creates a barrier between herself and the faculty, publicly blaming the faculty for low reading scores and excluding herself from any responsibility. In a discussion with teacher Y, she tells him that according to the reading supervisor he is not using the appropriate teaching strategies. He responds that he is, that he has too many students in his class demanding attention to individualize, and with all the special needs students in his class he can't expect much progress. The opportunity to probe what strategies he is using now and how he individually determines and addresses need is missed, and he is simply told that he'll have to improve regardless.

Attendance and participation in the school improvement plan lags. The alienation of parents and the faculty results in few volunteers and less investment. The principal is reinforced in the belief that she must do it all. With pressure to take action continuing to mount, the memo from the State Department of Education arrives as a last minute salvation.

Without a clear vision of improving instruction for the students and families in the school, and without having communicated to all stakeholders the environmental context of reading instruction, the rudimentary principal turns to the Superintendent and central office. The principal has identified the reading grant opportunity as the last best hope to improve the school.

The rudimentary principal lacks a clear understanding of what is internal and what is external to the school. District curriculum standards, materials, and resource allocation are no different than parent involvement and stakeholder communication. There is no identification of audiences, stakeholders, and participants, much less the role of each in her school with improvement planning.

The approach to the central office is to tell the Superintendent and school committee what is needed and what they need to do. Principal A asks for a meeting with the Superintendent and explains that the school's test scores are low, teachers don't consistently use best practice, and parents are not involved. Additionally, the obstacles faced in overcoming these problems and why it would be unfair to expect the principal to overcome them, are listed. The grant will provide Truman with the resources to improve. The specific request is that the central office submits a grant for Truman that addresses the problems identified. Lacking is a data analysis to determine need, a carefully developed professional development plan, and an identification of the instruction desired with a budget plan to get there. What is provided is basic and lacking in development. Through the eyes of the Superintendent, much work and preparation is foreseen.

PRINCIPAL B *accomplished response*

An accomplished principal:

creates within the community a common vision of a quality reading program

builds the vision on a documented analysis of student and community needs

incorporates the challenges faced by students and families into the plan to improve the reading program

brings community groups together to create a plan to address reading in the school

works with integrity, openness, and honesty in developing and realizing the plan

An accomplished principal begins by assuring that the community understands the data regarding the school's reading program. Teachers, parents, and community take part in the data analysis and a discovery of the story of reading at Truman Elementary School. The analysis continues in considering what student and family factors impact reading. Parents' knowledge and understanding of how children learn to read and what is effective instruction are considered.

Principal B makes sure that all parents have an opportunity to be heard about the school's reading program, asks the reading supervisor to present to parents what has been learned about effective instruction, and invites parents to share their perceptions of how the Truman program does and does not stack up to what they have just learned. This skillful mixture of learning and surveying shares information about effective programs and places the concerns of parents in the context of, "Are we effective?" rather than simply providing an opportunity to share what people don't like without context or focus.

The analysis creates a picture of how reading is taught at Truman Elementary School and the challenges and supports that surround the instructional program. An accomplished principal compares the picture of what is, with the picture of what can and should be. This requires open, honest discussion and comparison. Principal B models behavior for others, assuming ownership of and responsibility for the current program, and refusing to engage in finger pointing. By accepting responsibility, the principal allows others to take similar steps without fear of being "hung out" and encourages honest and open dialogue.

The analysis of classroom reading instruction provided by the reading supervisor provides opportunity and challenge. It lays out how current instruction is not aligned with best practice. It provides insight into classrooms where best practice is in place, and it is the principal who will determine if that practice finds its way into every classroom. An accomplished principal creates an environment where teachers can examine their practice in light of best practice and develop individual plans of improvement.

The discussion with a second grade teacher begins with a look at what the teacher thinks is and isn't going well. These ideas are tested against achievement data. The teacher's initial reluctance is overcome by probing questions that assume positive performance and stretch thinking. The discussion leads to a support plan for improving student achievement in the classroom. A support plan that, when combined with support plans of other teachers, becomes the school's professional development plan.

The comparison of what is and what can be provides an action plan for the school's reading program. The open dialogue allows each stakeholder to understand their role in the plan and what they need to do to support it. The plan explains how instruction needs to change in the school, the requirements of the change, community education, identification of the groups and individuals that still have to become involved, and how those steps will be accomplished.

Some of what needs to change is solely within the power of the school. Due to the nature of reading instruction, the communication with and support of parents are internal factors. Factors that impact reading are district curriculum standards, choice of materials, and resource allocation. The school can influence these, and influencing them in a way that supports the achievement of students is what accomplished principals do.

The memo from the Department of Education announcing a reading grant provides the principal with an opportunity to secure the resources and support to make the school's plan a reality. To this point, the principal's efforts have been focused on the environment within the school. Now, in order to bring the vision to life in the larger environment, the one in which the school exists, must be influenced as well. The school district, specifically the Superintendent and school committee, must become partners in the plan developed to transform reading instruction at Truman Elementary. Issues within a school also exist within a district. Solutions for a school are also solutions for a district. An accomplished principal brings the school committee and Superintendent into partnership with the school.

Principal B invites the Superintendent to the next meeting of the school improvement team. The team is planning to review its data analysis and test solutions against current research to assure that the plan is internally consistent. The principal hopes the Superintendent will function as an outside pair of eyes and find the strengths and weaknesses of their work. Principal B will also ask the Superintendent what else they need to prepare to have all the necessary prerequisites complete for the grant application, and what the school committee will look for in the request for support. This strategy has the effect of expanding the partnership to include the central office, making external forces feel as if they were internal. It is hard to say "no" to your partner. The principal also demonstrates to the Superintendent that the school is one that can be counted on. Should the grant be awarded, Truman is a school that is organized for the work to be done.

The pages that follow outline the "Keys for Improved Performance." Specifically, they note:

    a) the differences in the performance of rudimentary Principal A and accomplished Principal B;

    b) the potential consequences of the continued performance of Principal A at the rudimentary level;

    c) strategies and suggestions on how to move from one level of performance to another level.

Again, these pages specifically relate to the case outlined herein and the two focus questions:

    1. What are the instructional issues presented in the scenario and documents?

    2. What are the short- and long-term actions the principal should take to gain the support of the Superintendent, Board of Education and other appropriate stakeholders in addressing these instructional issues?

 KEYS FOR IMPROVED PERFORMANCE

An accomplished principal identifies areas of improvement in order to enrich the lives of students and families in the school. This driving goal ends up reflected in the strategies chosen to unite the school community in influencing the larger environment. In contrast, a rudimentary principal has a narrower, less family-centered goal: improve reading scores. As a result, the focus and strategies are narrow. This difference shows up in the inclusion of stakeholders: the accomplished principal does so because such action grows out of a core belief; the rudimentary principal involves others when they are needed for a purpose.

Similarly, the willingness of the accomplished principal to accept responsibility frees up others to do the same. The effect of good role modeling cannot be overstated and reflects the moral, ethical core of the leader. Poor role modeling is as consequential — it just yields different and undesirable behavior. Over time, principals set the tone for the school. Family-centered principals beget family-centered schools. Where the principal engages in dialogue with stakeholders, stakeholders engage in dialogue with each other.

The manner in which each principal communicates with stakeholders about the educational environment illustrates differences in rudimentary and accomplished principals, as well as how others react to the differences. Parent dissatisfaction with the reading program, low reading scores, weak curriculum and instruction, new evidence about best practice in reading instruction, and the state's grant opportunity comprise internal and external forces that impact the work of the school. An accomplished principal creates an effective working team, while the rudimentary principal isolates stakeholders while building defenses.

How did this happen? The accomplished principal shared with parents what has been learned about effective reading instruction while simultaneously letting them know that their concerns are valued. Parents were asked to share their observations about how Truman's reading program stacked up. This principal simultaneously informed parents and united them with the school's mission. This also forged the bond between the principal and the parents through working toward a common goal.

In contrast, the rudimentary principal alienated parents by telling them what needed to be done and placing blame for the reading scores on the preparedness of students. Parents learned nothing about what their children's school should be like; they only had reinforced what they did not like about it. The defensiveness communicated to parents that there would not be an open and thorough analysis and improvement plan was only the effort of others trying to escape responsibility. Furthermore, when members of different stakeholder groups have an opportunity to compare messages, and find that the rudimentary principal has blamed different people to different groups, credibility is eroded and ethical behavior found lacking.

The principal's goal in this scenario is to influence the Superintendent and Board of Education to seek, and ultimately be awarded, a grant to improve reading instruction in the school. The manner in which the accomplished and rudimentary principals approach these audiences affects not only the likelihood of a positive response, but also the likelihood of a successful grant proposal being submitted. The accomplished principal creates a partnership with the central office and comes to the table prepared. The rudimentary principal looks to the central office for salvation and comes to the table, not prepared, but with hands outstretched.

The accomplished principal invites the Superintendent to join the work of the school in designing the grant application, and shares how the school is positioned to create a successful application in partnership with the district. The need is established, the school is well prepared, and the research base established. The overriding philosophy in bringing the grant opportunity to the district level is that solutions, not problems, are the principal's currency. To the Superintendent, the grant, if awarded, will facilitate and accelerate what will likely happen anyway.

In contrast, a rudimentary principal is not well prepared. There is no evidence that the principal has done preparatory work in advance of the grant application. This requires others to do much work if a successful grant is to be developed. The rudimentary principal has brought problems to the Superintendent and school committee and is seeking solutions. Even if the grant application is successful, it is not clear that a school led by a rudimentary principal has the capacity to carry out the planned activities. It is not clear that the grant will be successful in changing practice in the school.

CASE STUDY 12

Grant High School
9–12 Suburban School

As you read this case study, consider these two questions:

1. How should the principal respond to the concerns of the school community over the issues raised in the state-testing plan?

2. What steps should the principal take to enlist the support of the local school stakeholders in communicating these concerns to the state decision makers?

Grant is a high school of 950 students in a suburban district in a "ring city" outlying a major metropolitan area. The school exists within a large county school system of 25,000 students. The school is seven years old in a community that has seen explosive growth over the past two decades. The resulting school community is comprised mostly of families who relocated to the area and lack a strong sense of community. Fifteen percent of the school's students receive free/reduced lunch. Less than a dozen students speak a language other than English, and those students typically are from professional families working in the area's technology industry. The school's graduation rate has fluctuated between 85% and 90%, and approximately 70% of the school's graduates attend post secondary institutions. Both numbers are stable. The current principal has been in the school since it opened. Most of the staff is new to the school, district, and profession within the last ten years.

Grant High School faces internal resistance to the implementation of a state requirement that all students pass an exit exam as a requirement for graduation. The minutes of the faculty meeting detail the concerns of the faculty and those of the students are explained in a letter from the student council. Opposing these viewpoints is a newspaper editorial articulating the broad public support received by measure. The district has outlined the expectations for the school in responding to the mandate, and the principal faces the challenge of pulling these disparate elements together.

Newspaper

GRANT DAILY NEWS

High School Graduation Exams: It's About Time!

Last week the Governor signed into law the requirement that all students pass an exam before graduating. Our state has joined the other 23 states in the country that require similar exams, and our public school systems will be better off for it. For too long we've been handing out diplomas to students who couldn't read and sending off to universities and colleges graduates needing basic remedial education. The new law is an effective balance. It gives ample warning to students, taking effect with this year's entering freshmen. It requires schools to identify students early at risk of not passing and to provide remediation. More intensive remedial opportunities await students who fail on their first attempt. We applaud the Legislature's and Governor's courage in standing up to those who sought to water down the tests and grant exemptions.

Exit exams cannot be arbitrarily or capriciously imposed. They must be fair, they must measure what is taught in school, they must be challenging so curriculum does not become watered down, and they must be given early enough so students have a chance to learn where they stand and take corrective action. Our state's test meets these standards. It begins in tenth grade and students can retake it until they pass. It is based on rigorous English and mathematics coursework that is equivalent to a college preparatory program, and it includes rigorous field-testing.

The opponents of exit exams offer the usual litany of excuses and tales of woe. In the end, they remain afraid of accountability and remain willing to merely pass students along for sitting in class and behaving well, regardless of what they have or have not learned. We suspect that what scares the exams' opponents the most is fear of having to provide remediation to failed students. Parents and communities will now expect schools to effectively prepare students for the graduation exam and we encourage them to hold schools' feet to fire. We note that nations that have rigorous exit exams outscore those that do not by one to two grade levels.

Students who began as freshmen this year will be the first that must pass the exam to graduate. When they leave school, the citizens and businesses of the state will know that they have mastered challenging curricula. Our colleges and universities will know that their incoming students will not need remedial education, and the parents of our students will know how prepared their children were. Graduation exit exams were a long time coming, but now that they are here we welcome them and the era of accountability they bring with them.

GRANT HIGH SCHOOL STUDENT COUNCIL

October 28

Dear Principal,

The student council is very concerned about the new testing law. The state passed a new law saying that we have to pass an exam to graduate, but no one asked any of us what we thought. Myself, I'm council president, play on two sports teams, am a member of the Honor Society, and get good grades. It doesn't seem fair that one single test will outweigh everything else I do in school. Several of us have been looking up information on graduation exams as part of our current events class and some things need to be brought to light.

- Classes like band, drama and art will be eliminated so that more English and math classes can be added.

- If I pass the exam as a sophomore, can I graduate then? It would seem so, since I've met the graduation criteria.

- If I'm in a class with students who failed the exam, will it just be exam prep, even if I passed already?

- We have students from foreign countries in our school; will they be able to pass the exam even if their English isn't very good?

- What if somebody's teacher is out sick or a student misses a lot of school? Will anything be done to help them get ready for the test?

We think that before the state passes a law about graduation, they should find out what students think. Some states have had their exams challenged with lawsuits. We would like to find out what we can do to change this law, even though it won't affect many of us on the student council now.

Sincerely,

Student Council President

memo...

Consolidated School District #27
Office of Instruction

Memorandum

TO: DISTRICT HIGH SCHOOL PRINCIPALS
FROM: SUPERINTENDENT
DATE: JANUARY 24

RE: GRADUATION EXAMINATIONS

The state legislature has recently enacted legislation requiring that every student pass a qualifying examination in order to receive a diploma. The requirement takes effect with this year's freshmen and this is not an optional requirement. It is now state law that unless the exam is passed there is no diploma. There are several important state requirements and local steps all district high schools will take.

1. The examination is first administered in grade 10. Students who fail the examination or enter the school system afterward are required to retake the examination in grade 11 and again in grade 12 if necessary. The examination is administered once annually, in March.

2. The examination has reading and mathematics components. The standards are set so that a student in a college preparatory program should be able to pass the examination in tenth grade. It is a performance-based test with multiple choice, short answer and an extended answer section in the reading component. The entire test takes four hours to complete and is administered over four days.

3. There are no exclusions, waivers, or accommodations for the test. It applies to every student, regardless of disability, language competence, or any other reason.

4. A copy of the complete regulations for the test is being sent under separate cover.

It is expected that the performance of schools and district will be measured by success on this test. The school committee has approved an action plan for the district in responding to the examination requirement. The following plan steps apply to high schools.

1. All programs of study, most critically in English and mathematics, are to be revised to assure that students have access to instruction that will prepare them for the examination. Specifically, low-level courses, typically below college preparatory, are to be eliminated and replaced with instruction targeted at examination aligned levels.

2. Courses that provide remedial intervention are to be added for grade 11 and 12 students who did not pass the examination. Earlier test results and a count of students enrolled in non-college preparatory coursework will provide a working estimate of students not expected to pass the examination. These courses are to be mandatory.

3. A specific remedial intervention plan shall be developed for each student who fails the examination in grade 10 or 11. This plan should include required remedial courses, but need not be limited to it. Special education and limited English services as well as other support should be applied on a case-by-case basis. The district is acquiring an examination aligned with the state test that can be used for planning and preparation purposes in remediation plans.

4. The district will host a facilitated work session with high school and district instructional personnel to develop shared strategies for creating high student success on the state examination. This will occur at the close of school.

DOCUMENT 4: FACULTY MEETING MINUTES

**Grant High School
Consolidated District #27**

Faculty Meeting Minutes
November 17

The topic of today's meeting was the new state graduation exam. The principal reviewed the Superintendent's memo outlining the requirements of the exam.

1. The exam requirement is in effect beginning with this year's freshmen.

2. They will first take the exam in March of grade 10.

3. The exam will be offered once annually in March.

4. Remedial plans are required for at-risk and failing students.

5. The exam covers English and mathematics.

Several faculty members wondered if there was anything that could be done to stop the exam. Several concerns were expressed about the exam.

1. There is a lot more that students learn in high school than can be covered in a single exam. It doesn't seem fair that one test alone determines whether or not someone graduates.

2. The exam only covers English and mathematics. Those two subjects are only about a quarter of what students take in high school now. Other subjects will be cut in order to prepare students for those two subjects, narrowing the curriculum.

3. Our bright students can pass the exam easily. What will challenge them to keep working when they pass as sophomores?

4. The legislation says the exam will be comparable to college prep courses. Many of our students are not in those classes and won't be able to pass the exam.

5. Students who come from different cultural backgrounds will be disadvantaged on the test, especially the English test, and will fail.

6. The test doesn't have any consideration for special needs students who don't test well; it discriminates against them and they need an exception.

7. Our classes will turn into just "teaching to the test." We do a lot of creative things in our classes and those will have to go to get kids ready for the exams.

8. A lot of our students don't care about education and doing well in school. They won't try on the exam and, when they fail, the newspapers and school committee will blame us. There's nothing we can do with unmotivated kids and parents who aren't involved.

THE PROBLEMS

Based on the information about this school presented through the scenario and the documents, how should the principal respond to these two questions?

1. How should the principal respond to the concerns of the school community over the issues raised in the state-testing plan?

2. What steps should the principal take to enlist the support of the local school stakeholders in communicating these concerns to the state decision makers?

PRINCIPAL A rudimentary response

A rudimentary principal:

- does little or no examination of the **policy** background behind the State's new requirement for an exit exam nor its relationship to the school's current vision

- focuses mostly on listening to the internal concerns, but keeps the concerns of the school community internal, without developing a communication network with outside decision makers

- accepts without question the commonly held assumptions that the requirement will result in diminished curricula and that some students cannot pass the test

- articulates the possible problems, but misses the opportunity to use the new requirement as an opportunity to communicate about increasing demands on graduates and to use the mandate as a vehicle to promote higher levels of success for all students

The new testing requirement and the Superintendent's memo requiring remediation plans for all failing students create both challenge and opportunity for Grant High School. A rudimentary principal reacts to the challenge without seizing the opportunity.

The concerns of others are accepted and perhaps listed, but without an analysis of the requirement's possible beneficial effects and its relationship to the vision of the school. Furthermore, the school community's concerns are kept within, allowed to fester and multiply, and not addressed. As a result, negativity grows, and faculty and students approach the new requirement without positive support or an effective, meaningful intervention plan so necessary for many of them to pass and graduate.

The faculty has expressed their reservations about the requirement, concerned that the curriculum will be limited. This may or may not occur, depending, to a large degree, on the actions of the school's educational leader.

A rudimentary principal agrees that the result is likely to be a narrowing of the curriculum, denying his or her own authority to make sure it does not. Furthermore, there is no push to be sure that the assessment system becomes a vehicle to improve both the curriculum and instructional program for the benefit of students. Rather than focus on the requirement as a force for positive change in teaching and learning, only its negative aspects are analyzed, reported, and commented upon.

The faculty also questions the ability of many students, stating they just cannot pass the test. This assumption is left unchallenged, missing an opportunity to reinforce the belief in the capacity of all students to achieve at high levels and the vision of the school to promote their success.

The memo from the Superintendent requiring remedial plans for all failing students becomes a paperwork exercise to the rudimentary principal. Remedial plans are not based on the assumption that, with effective intervention, all students can pass the test. In fact, they are based on the assumption that many cannot, and remedial plans are an exercise in compliance that the school must go through as those students repeat their failure. Lacking a clear vision of success for students, the rudimentary principal allows this belief system to exist in the school, and it becomes the underlying vision, whether written or not.

The negative beliefs about the assessment system could be challenged and scrutinized if they were subject to a broader, more open dialogue. Similarly, stated concerns could be the vehicle for both public examination and eventual improvement of the testing requirement, district remediation plans, and curriculum if they are brought into the light of a larger context. Under the leadership of a rudimentary principal, this does not occur.

What communication does exist is narrow and reactive and lacking in reflective analysis. Such communication takes the form of complaints, such as: we don't have the staff to remedy all of these failing students; we can't be expected to get these kids to pass; until the lower grades do a better job of preparing kids this isn't fair to high schools; and, this test isn't a good indicator of what our kids can do. Such communication is not focused in either message or audience. It is not designed to build networks of internal and outside stakeholders. It is not designed to create open, honest dialogue. It is not designed to communicate the work that is ongoing in the school. It is designed to cultivate reinforcement among an internal audience that is opposed to the initiative without regard to its larger impact or effect on students or teaching and learning.

The requirement that all students pass an examination before graduating, whether it is agreed with or not as a policy initiative, was born of a genuine public concern for failing and under-performing students. The district memorandum requiring intervention plans for all failing students, whether it is agreed with or not as a policy initiative, was born of a genuine interest in seeing the students of the district be successful in the face of the mandate. A rudimentary principal does not bring to light within the school the important public policy interests behind the requirement and does not include them in the internal and external dialogues that involve the school. The clear spirit of the policy is that it will be a catalyst to improving student success. It will not only be an accountability measure for schools, but a motivator for students as well. A rudimentary principal not only does not abide by this spirit, but also fails to use it to make Grant High School a better place for the students that attend it.

An accomplished principal:

- leads the internal stakeholders, students, parents, and faculty in an examination of the **policy** background behind the State's new requirement for an exit exam and actively articulates its relationship to the school's current vision

- listens to internal concerns, assists in drafting professional expressions of those concerns, and develops and uses a communication network with outside decision makers

- encourages all stakeholders to question commonly held assumptions, especially the assumption that the requirement will result in a diminished curriculum and that some students cannot pass the test

- articulates the possible problems, but uses the new requirement as an opportunity to communicate to internal stakeholders about the increasing demands on graduates and as a vehicle to promote higher levels of success for all students

A stable framework of beliefs, directions, and high priority best practices mutually developed at the school level and shared by all stakeholders guides the accomplished principal. He or she uses the requirement for an exit exam to advance and promote the pre-existing agenda toward high levels of performance for all students.

The framework used by the accomplished principal is already strong, locally adapted from the state accreditation model and the nationally recognized school improvement models such as those derived from the Effective Schools Research (ESR) and/or National Study of School Evaluation (NSSE). Therefore, the new requirement for a specific remedial intervention plan is used to bring about positive change in teaching and learning for all students and staff.

Far from simply reacting, as does the rudimentary principal, the accomplished principal leverages the new mandate to strengthen both internal commitments to push higher levels of achievement, but to also empower the local stakeholders. This happens through improved communication, understanding, and, while working within policies and regulations, actually increasing the possibility of influencing decision makers outside the school community.

First, the accomplished principal seeks to understand, then to be understood (Covey). He or she ensures that internal stakeholders understand exactly what is required, and why. This is done in a purposefully open manner, to ensure that external policy makers are well aware of the local respect for the policy and their knowledge of the rationale for it. The policy makers also become aware of the fact that Grant High School stakeholders know the policy well, share the rationale for it, and are, in fact, pushing toward even higher levels of student achievement. This is to ensure that any concerns and suggestions are well-grounded, not only in accurate knowledge of the regulation but also in a well-constructed plan fostering high levels of achievement in all subject areas.

Second, the accomplished principal listens to internal stakeholders, demonstrably emphasizing and collecting the more informed input from those who understand the regulation. This is done with the explicit understanding that several opportunities will be created for shaping the concerns into a professional and useful format and then sharing the concerns and suggestions directly with the Superintendent and with several decision makers outside the school community.

Emphasis is placed on Grant's higher expectations for all students, accurate understanding of the actual regulation, internal identification and questioning of any assumptions being made, and on the generation of specific suggestions for practical ways of improving the regulation.

Since the higher expectations for all students follow from the shared mission, beliefs, and framework of high priority best practices, these elements are a focus for the internal discussions and for the external communications.

The main concern of faculty and students, that the curriculum will become limited, is addressed head-on; that the curriculum at Grant High School will continue to be aimed at their locally determined curriculum and standards, in all subjects, not only in English and mathematics as tested by the State. The accomplished principal might use this opportunity to act on the thought that all Grant seniors might be invited to present an exhibition or project that demonstrates high-level mastery of the curriculum in an integrated fashion. (See the Thomas Higgins example in the "References and Actual Examples" section at the end of this chapter.)

Alternatively, the accomplished principal might address the faculty and student concern that some students will have difficulty with the test. This is done by first challenging the assumption that this has to be true, and then by actually exploring that the school might volunteer to help create and pilot early versions of the test — insuring that Grant students know and are prepared for the eventual test, and that Grant teachers can confidently address the test content and well beyond. (See the Athena Vachtsevano example in the "References and Actual Examples" section.)

The accomplished principal will effectively use the requirement to provide remediation to failing students as an opportunity to mobilize the internal stakeholders to do exactly that, and to do it early enough that failure is not only addressed, it is avoided as much as possible. Staff members are provided opportunities to visit exemplary schools — some of which engage in study groups to collaboratively analyze student work and teacher lessons to prevent failure. Some of these schools actually regroup students frequently during the semester, based on achievement of particular standards, rapidly intervening with corrective instruction at an early point.

The emphasis of the accomplished principal in all cases is to demonstrably listen to informed concerns and forge realistic ways to successfully address them in ways that both do and do not involve influencing outside decision makers.

The accomplished principal helps internal stakeholders to forge complaints into professional, useful, informed communications to outside decision makers. He or she uses the mandate to strengthen already shared commitments to higher levels of student performance by involving internal stakeholders and creating opportunities for them to directly articulate their concerns and practical suggestions.

The newspaper editorial is met by an internal stakeholder op-ed piece clarifying the actual mandate, clearly embracing the well-intentioned rationale for the mandate, and offering practical, well-reasoned suggestions for improvement. Many of these suggestions can be implemented without any approval from outside decision makers since they actually involve aiming much higher than the state, providing stretch for high-achieving students at Grant, and describing well-constructed ways to intervene early with at-risk students. The op-ed piece is written by a team of internal stakeholders and is a model of communication with stakeholders and decision makers outside the school community.

The accomplished principal identifies and articulates the spirit of the mandate and abides by it, and leverages the mandate to make Grant a better high school.

A LOOK AHEAD

The pages that follow outline the "Keys for Improved Performance." Specifically, they note:

a) the differences in the performance of rudimentary Principal A and accomplished Principal B;

b) the potential consequences of the continued performance of Principal A at the rudimentary level;

c) strategies and suggestions on how to move from one level of performance to another level.

Again, these pages specifically relate to the case outlined herein and the two focus questions:

1. How should the principal respond to the concerns of the school community over the issues raised in the state-testing plan?

2. What steps should the principal take to enlist the support of the local school stakeholders in communicating these concerns to the state decision makers?

DIFFERENCES BETWEEN PRINCIPAL A AND PRINCIPAL B

The accomplished principal models the acceptance of responsibility while the rudimentary principal reacts with defensiveness, both to the mandate and to the concerns of the staff and students.

The accomplished principal uses the new mandate specifically, and policies and regulations generally, to promote and enhance the mutually developed vision of the school, especially toward high levels of achievement for all students, while the rudimentary principal reinforces fears that the new mandate will restrict the curriculum and isolate low-achieving students even more and, consciously or not, uses the new mandate as an excuse for lower levels of student achievement.

The accomplished principal strongly communicates to both outside decision makers and, internally, with faculty and students and arranges for direct communication between them. As a key communicator, the principal first ensures that the mandate and its rationale are well understood by all parties, and that concerns are professionally forged into a constructive response addressing the spirit of the mandate and the local shared vision of high achievement for all students. The rudimentary principal neglects to learn the actual provisions or the rationale of the new mandate and reflects the fears and unchecked assumptions of students and faculty, without forging them into a professional response and assisting in the communication of the resulting response to decision makers outside the school community.

PRINCIPAL A   Potential Consequences

Potential Consequences of the Performance of Principal A

The rudimentary principal neither improves learning at his or her school nor builds capacity for future positive steps, either internally to achieve a vision or externally to influence decision makers outside the school community. As a result, policies are not understood, or respected, or followed in a productive manner, and there is little useful communication to decision makers external to the school community and, there is little chance that learning will be improved either because of the new mandate or in spite of it.

HOW DO YOU MOVE FROM RUDIMENTARY PRINCIPAL A TO ACCOMPLISHED PRINCIPAL B?

Forging a mental model of a stable framework of beliefs, directions, and high priority best practices and mutually refining that framework with stakeholders at the school level to be sure the resulting vision and understanding is shared by all stakeholders is a fundamental step.

In this regard, it is important, in becoming an accomplished principal, to learn the strengths of existing accreditation models, and national school improvement frameworks — such as effective schools research, quality improvement approaches, systems thinking and learning communities, and national educational reform models — to build a personal and local school framework of high priority best practices within which to address external mandates.

Working to understand the total system — the systems within the system, the parts, and especially how the parts relate to and influence one another — is vital to becoming an accomplished principal. Knowing the elements of a learning community and creating one is a singular step in the transition to an accomplished principal.

Taking care to model respect for people and policies, and working within policies, laws, and regulations while creating formats to share concerns and practical suggestions of internal stakeholders for improvement, will build external respect and internal empowerment.

It is important to know and model effective communication practices which start with an unfailing visible desire to respect and thoroughly understand both internal and external stakeholders. A clear commitment to assist others in formulating professional, practical, user-friendly methods of directly communicating concerns and suggestions at the student, teacher, school-wide, school system, and state levels, if done consistently, will foster respect and build the kinds of relationships necessary for a rudimentary principal to grow into an accomplished principal.

The accomplished principal puts into practice the knowledge that communication with decision makers external to the school community, as well as many other facets of effectiveness, depends on the quality of the personal relationships. Relationships in turn depend on character — notably honesty, respect, responsibility, fairness, and empathy. Showing respect for the letter and the spirit of the policy, and building the relationships needed to assist internal stakeholders to directly communicate effectively with external decision makers is the mark of the rudimentary principal becoming an accomplished principal.

The transformation from a rudimentary to an accomplished principal will be facilitated by inner growth and the development of a strong, non-defensive, personal and professional identity characterized by respect for others, as much as by increasing knowledge of practical best practices at the student, classroom, and school levels.

Both the inner growth and the gaining of knowledge and perspective are important and possible with focus, and each reinforces the other. The accomplished transformational leader takes conscious responsibility for his or her personal and professional transformation, as well as for the transformation of the school.

References and Actual Examples

Thomas Higgins (Principal of Walton High School) initiated project-study exhibitions by graduating seniors at Walton High School to encourage high levels of integrated learning, going well beyond state-mandated graduation tests and system required end-of-course assessments.

Athena Vachsavanos (Principal of Sprayberry High School) encouraged teachers to volunteer to develop and pilot the first draft of the system level end-of-course assessments, to both tighten the instructional alignment and to influence the rigor and applicability of the anticipated state-mandated end-of-course exams. Sprayberry also volunteered to help develop and pilot a planned teacher evaluation instrument aligned with the principles in *Enhancing Professional Practice: A Framework for Teaching* (ASCD, 1996) and the National Board of Professional Teaching Standards. Efforts such as these and others assisted Sprayberry recently to win the Professional Staff Development Award.

Susan Galante (Principal of Daniell Middle School, former Assistant Principal of Campbell High School) encouraged high school teachers to address the barriers to higher math achievement, over which they had some control. This resulted in assessing and moving students after each math unit to ensure that both corrective and "stretch" activities were available as appropriate. Frequent regrouping based on achievement, not ability, was unusual for high school and led to improved student performance at all levels. Susan continually demonstrates the ability to listen carefully to teachers as they find ways to do better by every student.

Cheryl Hunt Clements (Principal of Shallowford Falls) makes sure her teachers are listened to, and that their voices makes a difference, as long as the bottom line is academic growth for each student. They look carefully at data and search together for "best practices" so teachers see several initiatives as focused on the same goal. Efforts such as these and many more helped Shallowford Falls to win the National Award for Model Professional Development in 1998 (given to a few schools where professional development is demonstrably related to improved student achievement).

Sandra McGary (Principal of Harmony-Leland Elementary School) encouraged staff to adapt and adopt a National Reform Model focusing on developing high levels of student engagement linked to rigorous curriculum standards, and to personally engage in curriculum mapping and vertical and horizontal curriculum-instruction-assessment alignment. Such efforts have led to remarkable gains in student achievement in a high poverty elementary school.

NEXT STEPS

It is now time to reflect on the actions taken by our fictional principals in responding to the twelve case studies presented in this book. Practitioners can find valuable insight in improving their own professional practice by reflecting on these actions. Further, by examining the responses of these principals to all too familiar situations, practitioners and educational decision makers can begin to look at the role of the principal through the lens of the ISLLC Standards. Doing so will provide them with some insight on the behaviors of true instructional leaders. What do the responses to these case studies tell us about how effective school principals go about their daily work? How are these responses aligned with current views and research on effective school leadership? Let's first examine a brief summary of some views of effective leadership presented by our contributing practitioners.

Lessons Learned From the Field

To see how our accomplished, fictional school leaders responded, let's take a snapshot of their behaviors and actions created by our contributing practitioners. What are the common threads that weave through the actions and decision-making processes of the accomplished principal in each of our case studies? Listed below are but a small sample of the commonalities, identified as "Keys to a Successful Principalship," which will be described in more detail later in this chapter:

- ensure the inclusion of all members of the school community in creating the school vision (Chapter 3)

- celebrate accomplishments and the reaffirmation of the school's vision and mission statement (Chapter 4)

- allocate resources linked to values delineated in the vision of the school (Chapter 5)

- communicate directly with the community to gain an understanding and appreciation for its diverse needs (Chapter 6)

- demonstrate integrity by promoting opportunities for equitable participation of all members of the school community in all school programs (Chapter 7)

- seek areas in need of improvement to enrich the lives of students and families (Chapter 8)

- reflect on other steps one could take to move from rudimentary to accomplished (Add them to this list.)

What begins to emerge is that these accomplished principals are:

guided by a vision

committed to the involvement of stakeholders

focused on making ethical decisions that are
based on what is best for children

pledged to seek success for all students

reflective about their actions

Now let us compare these selected "Keys" to a sample of best practice research.

Harvard Professor Richard Elmore (2000) has stated that in many schools there is "no expectation that individuals or groups are obliged to pursue knowledge as both an individual and collective good. Unfortunately the existing system doesn't value continuous learning as a collective good and does not make this learning the individual and social responsibility of every member of the system" (p. 20). He contends, therefore, that "leaders must create environments in which individuals expect to have their personal ideas and practice subjected to the scrutiny of their colleagues, and in which groups expect to have their shared conceptions of practice subjected to the scrutiny of individuals" (p. 20). "Leadership is the central force that drives the guidance and direction of instructional improvement" (p. 13).

To see Elmore's conceptual framework of leadership put into practice, one can examine the work of Cawleti and Protheroe (2001). They studied six school districts in an attempt to determine how they became transformed into high performing systems. All districts in this study shared these characteristics:

1. They had leaders who developed and nurtured widely shared beliefs about learning, including high expectations, and who provided a strong focus on results.

2. They restructured their system in order to decentralize management and budgeting at the building level. This change increased accountability by linking people to results, with the school staff working in teams using feedback about performance to plan for improvement.

3. They worked extensively on curriculum alignment, ensuring that the local curriculum matched the state framework and doing item-by-item and student-by-student analyses of student response to test items.

4. They saw the need for instructional processes that enabled teachers to accomplish three things on a daily and weekly basis: (1) organizing instruction to regularly administer interim assessments of skills taught before moving on to new material; (2) providing tutoring or extra help for those students who fail to master the skills taught and enrichment learning activities for those who have mastered the skills; and (3) providing frequent practice throughout the year to ensure retention for students who have initially mastered the skills needed.

5. They recognized the importance of sustaining multiple research-based changes over a period of years that actually have a positive effect on the daily instructional lives of students (p. 98).

Clearly, these researchers identified a leader's focus on teaching and learning: using data to inform decisions; and collaborative, shared decision making. Further, they state that, "We cannot stress enough the importance of leadership and vision. Although this can come initially from one person, the superintendent, a key to the success of the improvement efforts is that person's ability to develop a cadre of committed, hardworking people — in both the central office and the schools — who share that vision and who will do everything they can to see that teachers and every school reaches the goal of high achievement for all students" (p. 102).

This vision of instructional leadership is reaffirmed in the report, *Leadership for Student Learning: Reinventing the Principalship* (October 2000), published by the Institute for Educational Leadership. This report shows that principals today must serve as leaders for student learning. Today's principals must know academic content and pedagogical techniques as well as how to work with teachers to strengthen skills. They must collect, analyze, and use data to inform decisions and they must know how to rally the school and the larger community around the common goals of raising student performance (p. 2). This report emphasizes that the bottom line of schooling is student learning and that everything principals do must be in service of student learning (p. 4).

In another recent report, *The Principal, Keystone of a High-Achieving School: Attracting and Keeping the Leaders We Need* (2000), principals in effective schools initiated several programs that focused on improved student achievement. The effective schools were student-focused. This was demonstrated by the principals' ability to marshal limited resources in the service of student learning by taking such action as organizing the time of instructional staff to decrease the pupil-teacher ratio during instruction in the core courses of reading, writing, and math. Further, they used teacher evaluation and staff development to improve teaching and so raise the level of student learning (p. 9). In this report it was found that no principal was seen as being singularly responsible for the attainment of the school's goals. The principal, however, had an increased responsibility to rally stakeholders and to build consensus among constituencies (p. 18). This report continues by stating,

> The effective principals are often characterized as being good communicators and listeners, able to relate to others and to recognize their contributions, and adept at fostering relationships among those in the school community. These effective supporters of school change are seen as forward-looking and proactive—they anticipate changes in the school's environment and then take the initiative to adapt to these. If necessary, they are willing to take risks when these are viewed as necessary to improve educational opportunities for students. Finally, the effective principal finally believes that a school's purpose is to meet the instructional needs of all its students (p. 19).

Hoyle, English and Steffy (1985) summarize their prerequisites for success succinctly by listing the following:

- Create an equitable allocation of resources.

- Embrace a future-focused school system.

- Utilize the entire community.

- Share a common vision (pp. 272-273).

Murphy and Hallinger (January/February 1988) believe that high performing school districts and schools are goal-driven. They feel that goals were a major vehicle used to maintain excellence and promote improvement in the school districts they studied. By closely aligning school objectives with district goals, successful districts were able to more closely evaluate principal performance, implement new programs, and allocate resources. Furthermore, curricular and instructional goals were predominant in the overall goal structure (p. 177).

Joe Murphy (2001) and his colleagues restate the importance of clear goals as a critical element in successful schools. They believe that, "...one of the strongest features found in successful high schools is a clear focus on learning as the primary goal of the institution" (p. 141). Furthermore they believe that,

> Successful high schools have at their core an understanding of and dedication to learning and teaching. It is this vision or mission that allows the school to achieve academic excellence for its students. This focus on learning is evidenced in effective high schools by the presence of a shared purpose, mission, or vision; goal consensus and shared values; well articulated goals; a focus on learning and teaching; instructional and cultural leadership; and a common academic core of courses (p. 141).

And,

> Having a vision and clear goals is only effective if they are communicated throughout the school. Statistics show that more than 50% of exemplary high schools regularly communicated goals to staff, students, and parents, and that the goals are understood, supported, and followed. Discussions among staff members at faculty meetings, in-service or professional development sessions, and department meetings serve as a forum in which teachers can understand and internalize the developing school vision.... Beyond discussion, in productive high schools goals are written and distributed to parents and students in handbooks, letters, memos, and manuals (p. 143).

Thus, it is their belief that well-articulated and clearly communicated goals, vision, and mission are core, fundamental precepts of quality schools.

Murphy and his colleagues go beyond goals, however, and focus on an enlightened school leadership. In their model, this leader is one who is confident and astute enough to enlist a cadre of stakeholders to participate in the planning and decision-making process.

A key factor in schools being able to implement a school wide approach to problem solving is the support and encouragement of the administration. If the principal is not willing to move from the more traditional leadership role and allow others to be involved in decision making, faculty discussion about school problems have little impact. In all the schools in which collective problem solving has been successful, the principal has been able to give up some typically visible leader behaviors and allow staff members to be responsible for running meetings and programs, to have input in policy decisions, and to develop solutions to school problems (p. 151).

In successful high schools, the climate is welcoming and inclusive of its students. It is this inclusive climate that allows students to feel membership in the school and encourages participation in the life of the school. Adults in the school care for and nurture students when they have the opportunity to be involved in the students' academic and personal growth. In effective high schools, this inclusive environment is denoted by student involvement in extracurricular activities, increased per interaction through shared experiences, schoolwork relevant to students' lives, students' feeling of belonging, transitional programs for new students, and appreciation for multicultural perspectives (p. 162).

Elmore (2002) provides us with an effective and provocative summation of these observations on effective schools and their leaders. He believes that bringing about positive change in school requires that three things must be fundamentally and simultaneously addressed:

- the values and beliefs of people in schools about what is worth doing and what is possible to do

- the structural condition under which the work is done

- the ways in which people learn to do the work (p. 30)

Elmore believes that,

> We are now at the stage of understanding that schools and school systems have very different responses to pressure for performance, depending on the knowledge and skill embodied in their teaching and administrative staff, their capacity to create a strong normative environment around good teaching, and their ability to muster and manage the resources required to begin the long process of training the level of practice. The issue is what we will do with this knowledge, whether we will use it to, once again, affirm the self-fulfilling prophecy that some schools and their students in them are "better" than others, or whether we will enable all schools to become competent and powerful agents of their own improvement (p. 33).

With these observations from the field and with the challenge laid before us by Elmore, how do we proceed? What are the "Keys" to successful practice?

The Keys to a Successful Principalship

The responses by fictional, accomplished principals to the case studies created by our team of practitioners mirror the research on effective school leadership. What the contributors succeeded in creating in Chapters 3–8, however, was the placement of these behaviors in the context of the ISLLC Standards conceptualized as our framework for school leaders. In our first book, *A Framework for School Leaders: Linking the ISLLC Standards to Practice* (2002), we created a framework made up of 24 components. These components served to organize and consolidate the six ISLLC Standards around their numerous indicators of knowledge, disposition, and performance statements. Our contributors to Volume 2 created principal responses to the case studies through the lens of these components. These specific behaviors that emerge now become our "Keys to a Successful Principalship" and they can be organized and summarized in the following tables. The tables are arranged so that each ISLLC Standard can be related to its framework components, which are then in turn related to its relevant "Keys." These "Keys" give school leaders a representative view of the actions of accomplished principals.

Table 1. The Keys of a Successful Principalship, Standard 1

THE ISLLC STANDARD	Framework Component	Accomplished school principals:
Standard 1: The Vision of Learning	1a. Developing the Vision	• ensure the inclusion of all members of the school community in creating the school vision • examine their own personal beliefs, assumptions, and practices • believe in continuous school improvement
	1b. Communicating the Vision	• employ communication that is broad-based • stimulate positive and critical discussion for improvement
	1c. Implementing the Vision	• challenge values and promote discussion and dialogue on beliefs • build leadership capacity and create commitment of high standards for all
	1d. Monitoring and Evaluating the Vision	• consider information from a variety of sources that includes student achievement data, demographic data, and other sources of relevant data • focus on improved student learning and success

Table 2. The Keys of a Successful Principalship, Standard 2

THE ISLLC STANDARD	Framework Component	Accomplished school principals:
Standard 2: The Culture of Teaching and Learning	2a. Valuing Students and Staff	• celebrate accomplishments and the reaffirmation of the school's vision and mission statements • use the school's strengths to support growth in areas in need of improvement • recognize the efforts of staff in bringing about positive change
	2b. Developing and Sustaining the Culture	• advocate the school's vision • model the vision for staff, students, parents, and the community • enlist teachers to become catalysts for change
	2c. Ensuring an Inclusive Culture	• develop positive connections with the community and use this relationship to sustain the culture • provide opportunities for all members of the diverse school community in shaping the school climate • believe in the importance of professional development in the creation of a positive school climate • provide leadership opportunities for teachers and other members of the school community • engage the school community in assuring that all students are enrolled in challenging, high level courses
	2d. Monitoring and Evaluating the Culture	• use climate surveys to monitor culture • analyze student indicators of success such as attendance, course enrollment patterns, and grades

Table 3. The Keys of a Successful Principalship, Standard 3

THE ISLLC STANDARD	Framework Component	Accomplished school principals:
Standard 3: The Management of Learning	3a. Making Management Decisions to Ensure Successful Teaching and Learning	• allocate resources linked to values delineated in the vision of school • engage members of the school community in the decision-making process
	3b. Developing Procedures to Ensure Successful Teaching and Learning	• engage in a process of continuous learning designed to gain greater understanding of effective teaching and learning • remain current with the latest research in areas such as how students learn, curriculum, and assessment
	3c. Allocating Resources to Ensure Successful Teaching and Learning	• explore creative avenues to obtain resources needed to support teaching and learning • seek creative ways to increase leadership capacity among the staff related to resource allocation • engage all appropriate members of the school community in the management of resources • involve all appropriate stakeholders in ongoing decisions related to resource management
	3d. Creating a Safe, Healthy Environment to Ensure Successful Teaching and Learning	• establish channels of collaboration within the school and community to create a positive and safe learning environment • empower the members of the school community in creating and sustaining high academic standards • demonstrate a commitment for the creation of a safe environment that supports effective learning • build partnerships with local law enforcement and other community groups eager to share the common vision of school safety

Table 4. The Keys of a Successful Principalship, Standard 4

THE ISLLC STANDARD	Framework Component	Accomplished school principals:
Standard 4: Relationships with the Broader Community to Foster Learning	4a. Understanding Community Needs	• communicate directly with the community to gain an understanding and appreciation for its diverse needs • actively solicit the assistance of the superintendent in clarifying the needs and goals of the community
	4b. Involving Members of the Community	• enlist the assistance of members of the community to collect and analyze data related to the needs and goals of the larger community • model trust in the judgment of the members of the community • demonstrate an appreciation for the efforts of the community on behalf of the school • maintain a directory of community resources and agencies that are available to support the school
	4c. Providing Opportunities for the Community and School to Serve Each Other	• include representatives of the community in the design, development, and implementation of educational programs • become proactive, rather than reactive, in addressing community issues • seek ways to engage the community in school issues by actively demystifying the educational process • establish procedures and expectations that encourage community involvement in school programs • maintain relationships with the community designed to create financial support for instructional programs • provide opportunities for community business and political leaders to attend and participate in school activities and programs • create and maintain effective avenues of communication between the school and members of the community
	4d. Understanding and Valuing Diversity	• create a school culture that is based on respect for all • ensure collaboration and consultation with the superintendent by sharing facts and data in responding to sensitive and, potentially, crisis situations • take full advantage of the diversity within the community to gain a deeper understanding of divergent points-of-view • rely on multiple data sources to gain a clearer understanding of community issues and goals • ensure that the curriculum and related school programs are inclusive of and sensitive to the diversity that exists in the larger community

Table 5. The Keys of a Successful Principalship, Standard 5

THE ISLLC STANDARD	Framework Component	Accomplished school principals:
Standard 5: Integrity, Fairness, and Ethics in Learning	5a. Demonstrating a Personal and Professional Code of Ethics	• demonstrate integrity by promoting opportunities for equitable participation of all members of the school community in all school programs • act in a manner consistent with the vision of the school • treat everyone with dignity and respect • establish expectations of high standards for all
	5b. Understanding One's Impact on the School and Community	• foster the school vision both in the school and in the community by including all constituents and confronting and remedying injustices • provide opportunities for disseminating information and opinions through open, honest discussions • seek feedback from the community to strengthen the relationships between school and community
	5c. Respecting the Rights and Dignity of All	• seek the involvement of all stakeholders • establish procedures that ensure that everyone's rights and dignity are preserved
	5d. Inspiring Integrity and Ethical Behavior in Others	• demonstrate an obvious desire to understand the needs of the learning community and to serve those needs • identify and confront injustices that occur in the school community • hold oneself to the same standards established for the school community

Table 6. The Keys of a Successful Principalship, Standard 6

THE ISLLC STANDARD	Framework Component	Accomplished school principals:
Standard 6: The Political, Social, Economic, Legal, and Cultural Contexts of Learning	6a. Operating Schools on Behalf of Students and Families	• seek areas in need of improvement to enrich the lives of students and families • seek to understand the elements of the learning community and how they influence each other in support of the school's mission • take responsibility for one's professional growth and development
	6b. Communicating Changes in Environment to Stakeholders	• engage in dialogue with stakeholders to encourage communication among the stakeholders • create working teams comprised of stakeholders • share effective instructional strategies with the community to build support and demonstrate sensitivity to their needs • ensure that external stakeholders have a clear understanding of the school's changing context
	6c. Working Within Policies, Laws, and Regulations	• demonstrate an awareness of how to use policies and regulations to promote the success of all students • demonstrate a respect for the individuals, policies, and regulations that shape and govern the school • understand the importance of adhering to existing policies and regulations to ensure the safety of all members of the school community
	6d. Communicating with Decision makers Outside the School Community	• create opportunities for communication between the school and outside decision makers • create an awareness of the school's vision and goals among outside decision makers • model effective communication practices by demonstrating respect and awareness for needs and values of external stakeholders • build relationships with external stakeholders and decision makers based on character, honesty, fairness, and respect

Lessons Learned From the Research

While the "Keys to a Successful Principalship" have been culled from the work of actual principals and school leaders in response to case studies, it has been shown that they closely parallel the views expressed in the literature about school leadership. But, are we able to generalize, or transfer, these "Keys" to the general universe of leadership?

What makes a good company great? Jim Collins (2001) investigated this phenomenon and discovered some interesting parallels between corporate leaders and accomplished school principals. First he found that bringing about this transformation to greatness was not a mechanical or technical process. "Technology and technology-driven change has virtually nothing to do with igniting a transformation from good to great. Technology can accelerate a transformation, but technology cannot cause a transformation" (p. 11). Further he found that none of the great companies in his study were in particularly great business sectors. He found that, "Greatness is not a function of circumstance. Greatness, it turns out, is largely a matter of conscious choice" (p. 11). And, the people who led these companies were not superstars or in the headlines. "They are more like Lincoln and Socrates than Patton or Caesar" (p. 13). The leaders he found had unwavering faith that you can and will prevail and they proceeded as if "relentlessly pushing a giant heavy flywheel in one direction, turn upon turn, building momentum until a point of breakthrough, and beyond" (p. 14).

Kouzes and Posner (1987) looked at inspired leadership from the perspective of challenges met and the willingness to take risks. They found these common traits in great leaders:

Inspiring a shared vision — Leaders spend considerable effort gazing across the horizon of time, imagining what it will be like when they have arrived at their final destinations. Some call it vision; others describe it as a purpose, mission, goal, even a personal agenda (p. 10).

Enabling Others to Act — They encourage collaboration, build teams, and empower others (p. 10).

Modeling the Way — In order to lead by example, leaders must first be clear about their business beliefs. Managers may speak eloquently about vision and values, but if their behavior is not consistent with their stated beliefs, people ultimately will lose respect for them (p. 12).

Encouraging the Heart — People become exhausted, frustrated, and disenchanted. They often are tempted to give up. Leaders must encourage the heart of their followers to carry on (p. 12).

Kouzes and Posner have reconfigured these traits as the Ten Commandments of Leadership:

Challenging the Process

    1. Search for Opportunities

    2. Experiment and Risk

Inspiring a Shared Vision

    3. Envision the Future

    4. Enlist Others

Enabling Others to Act

    5. Foster Collaboration

    6. Strengthen Others

Modeling the Way

    7. Set the Example

    8. Plan Small Wars

Encouraging the Heart

    9. Recognize Individual Contribution

    10. Celebrate Accomplishment (p. 14)

THE TEN COMMANDMENTS OF LEADERSHIP

1. Search for Opportunities
2. Experiment and Risk
3. Envision the Future
4. Enlist Others
5. Foster Collaboration
6. Strengthen Others
7. Set the Example
8. Plan Small Wars
9. Recognize Individual Contribution
10. Celebrate Accomplishment

Kouzes and Posner

In a later work, Kouzes and Posner (1993) explore successful leadership from the context of credibility and integrity. According to this model, effective leadership requires *clarity, unity, and intensity*. *Clarity* involves the clarification of the leader's and constituents' needs, interests, values, vision, and aspirations. *Unity*, on the other hand, is related to being united in a common cause—credible leaders are able to build a community of shared vision and values. Finally, *intensity* exists when principles are taken seriously when they reflect deeply felt standards and emotional bonds, and when they are the basis of critical organizational resources allocation (pp. 47-48.) The authors aver that the six disciplines of credibility are:

- Discovery of yourself

- Appreciating constituents

- Affirming shared values

- Developing capacity

- Serving a purpose

- Sustaining hope (pp. 49-59)

Ulrich, Zenger, and Smallwood (1999) have identified what they call the Key Elements of Leadership Attributes. They describe these as the need to:

Set direction — Leaders define the future of a company in ways that excite participation and allocate resources to make the future happen.

Mobilize individual commitment — Leaders must build collaborative relations. Leaders must help individuals see and feel how their contributions aid in accomplishing the goals of the organization.

Engender organizational capability — Leaders facilitate the process, practice, and activities that create value for the organization.

Demonstrate personal character — Leaders with character "live" the values of their firm by practicing what they preach; they possess and create in others a positive self-image, and they display high levels of cognitive ability and charm (pp. 6-15).

While each of these authors has established unique (and in some cases, not so unique) perspectives on corporate leadership, they all seem to echo those qualities found in accomplished principals: vision, collaboration, goal-driven, and integrity.

THE SIX DISCIPLINES OF CREDIBILITY

1. Discovery of yourself
2. Appreciating constituents
3. Affirming shared values
4. Developing capacity
5. Serving a purpose
6. Sustaining hope

Kouzes and Posner

KEY ELEMENTS OF LEADERSHIP ATTRIBUTES

1. Set direction
2. Mobilize individual commitment
3. Engender organizational capability
4. Demonstrate personal character

Ulrich, Zenger and Smallwood

Putting Lessons Learned Into Practice

The "Keys" presented in this book are offered as a way to travel the road to improved practice; to reach toward the goal of becoming an accomplished school principal. How might the school principal or the district decision maker put these "Keys to a Successful Principalship" into practice? One must, in all probability, consider these basic and fundamental steps:

Reflect — Look at one's current practice through the lens of the ISLLC Standards and the "Keys to a Successful Principalship." What is the current fit? Can immediate changes be made in one's practice?

Promote — Encourage discussion about the ISLLC Standards and the "Keys to a Successful Principalship." Use the vocabulary of the Standards as you rally the forces to promote the success of all students.

Model — Demonstrate those behaviors that you would like to see in others as delineated in the "Keys to a Successful Principalship."

Mentor — Guide new leaders (and potential future leaders) to create a cadre of successful, effective principals and to ensure lines of succession to perpetuate this vision of leadership.

Collaborate — Develop meaningful partnerships with stakeholders, both internal and external, to firmly establish the vision of leadership that will promote the success of all students.

Assess — Use the Standards and "Keys" in benchmarking school leader performance as a way of, ultimately, promoting the success of all students.

Conclusion

As we have discovered in our research and confirmed by the work of contributing practitioners, school leaders have learned that leadership must be shared if innovative school change and improved student performance are to result. Shared leadership requires the redistribution of power and authority, both among the immediate leadership team and, ultimately, to the staff and the community. It is a Herculean challenge to master and invoke each of the "Keys to a Successful Principalship." But, through the redistribution of authority and by building leadership capacity, we can advance the ideas that are essential if we are to develop sustainable, self-renewing schools.

Components of Professional Practice for School Leaders*

STANDARD 1: THE VISION OF LEARNING

1a. Developing the Vision
1b. Communicating the Vision
1c. Implementing the Vision
1d. Monitoring and Evaluating the Vision

STANDARD 2: THE CULTURE OF TEACHING AND LEARNING

2a. Valuing Students and Staff
2b. Developing and Sustaining the Culture
2c. Ensuring an Inclusive Culture
2d. Monitoring and Evaluating the Culture

STANDARD 3: THE MANAGEMENT OF LEARNING

3a. Making Management Decisions to Ensure Successful Teaching and Learning
3b. Developing Procedures to Ensure Successful Teaching and Learning
3c. Allocating Resources to Ensure Successful Teaching and Learning
3d. Creating a Safe, Healthy Environment to Ensure Successful Teaching and Learning

STANDARD 4: RELATIONSHIPS WITH THE BROADER COMMUNITY TO FOSTER LEARNING

4a. Understanding Community Needs
4b. Involving Members of the Community
4c. Providing Opportunities for the Community and School to Serve Each Other
4d. Understanding and Valuing Diversity

STANDARD 5: INTEGRITY, FAIRNESS, AND ETHICS IN LEARNING

5a. Demonstrating a Personal and Professional Code of Ethics
5b. Understanding One's Impact on the School and Community
5c. Respecting the Rights and Dignity of All
5d. Inspiring Integrity and Ethical Behavior in Others

STANDARD 6: THE POLITICAL, SOCIAL, ECONOMIC, LEGAL, AND CULTURAL CONTEXT OF LEARNING

6a. Operating Schools on Behalf of Students and Families
6b. Communicating Changes in Environment to Stakeholders
6c. Working Within Policies, Laws, and Regulations
6d. Communicating with Decision Makers Outside the School Community

* From *A Framework for School Leaders: Linking the ISLLC Standards to Practice*. Available at:
http://www.ets.org/pathwise/slsframework.html

Notes

REFERENCES

Ackerman, R., Donaldson, G., & Van der Bogert, R. (1996). *Making Sense as a School Leader*, Jossey-Bass.

American Association of School Administrators. (2002). *Using Data to Improve Schools*. Arlington, VA: American Association of School Administrators (AASA).

Bambino, D. (2002). Critical friends. *Educational Leadership*. Alexandria, VA: Association of Supervision and Curriculum Development (ASCD) 59(6), 25-27.

Barth, R. (1988). "School as a Community of Leaders." In A. Lieberman (ed.) *Building a Professional Culture in Schools*. New York: Teachers College Press.

Bellamy, G. T., Holly, P., & Sinisi, R. (1997). *The Cycles Of School Improvement*. Oxford, OH: National Staff Development Council.

Bernhardt, V.L. (1994). *The School Portfolio*. Larchmont, NY: Eye on Education.

Bernhardt, V.L. (1998). *Data Analysis for Comprehensive Schoolwide Improvement*. Larchmont, NY: Eye On Education.

Calhoun, E. (1994). *How to Use Action Research in the Self-Renewing School*. Alexandria, VA: ASCD.

Calhoun, E. (Winter, 1999). The singular power of one goal. Interviewed by Dennis Sparks. *Journal of Staff Development*, National Staff Development Council. 54-58.

Calhoun, E. (2002). Action research for school improvement. *Educational Leadership*. Alexandria, VA: ASCD. 9(6), 18-24.

Cawleti, G & Protheroe, N. (2001). *High Student Achievement: How Six School Districts Changed into High-Performance Systems*. Arlington, VA: Educational Research Services.

Collins, J. (2001). *From Good to Great*. Harper Business: New York, NY.

Cook, W (1999). *Strategic Planning*. Colonial Cambridge Group.

Council of Chief State School Officers (November, 1996). *Interstate School Leaders Licensure Consortium: Standards for School Leaders*. Washington, D.C.

Danielson, C. (1996). *Enhancing Professional Practice: A Framework for Teaching*, Alexandria, VA: ASCD.

Deal, T. (1995). *Leading with Soul*. San Francisco: Jossey-Bass Publishers.

Deal & Peterson. (1994). *The Leadership Paradox*. Jossey Bass.

DePree, M. (1993). *Leadership Jazz: The Art of Conducting Business through Leadership, Fellowship, Teamwork, Voice, and Touch*. New York: Dell Publishing Group.

Elmore, R. (2000) *Building a New Structure for School Leadership*. Washington, DC: Albert Shanker Institute.

Elmore, R. (2002). *Bridging the Gap Between Standards and Achievement*. Washington, DC: Albert Shanker Institute.

REFERENCES

Elmore, R. (January, 2002). Building capacity to enhance learning: In Conversation. *Principal Leadership*. 2(5), 39-43.

Fiero, D. (February 28, 2002). Presentation at Educational Testing Service: English Language Assessments Advisory Group Meeting, Princeton, NJ.

Forsythe, L.K. (1997). *The Transformation of Leadership through Quadrant Thinking: Fostering a Sense of Power for School Improvement*. Symposium Paper. University of Northern Iowa.

Fullan, M. (1993). *Change Forces*. London: The Falmer Press.

Fullan, M. (1997). Emotion and hope: Constructive concepts for complex times. *Rethinking Educational Change with Heart and Mind, 1997 ASCD Yearbook*. Edited by Andy Hargreaves. Alexandria, VA: ASCD.

Garmston, R.J. & Wellman, B.M. (1999). *The Adaptive School: A Sourcebook for Developing Collaborative Groups*. Norwood, MA: Christopher-Gordon Publishers, Inc.

Gardner, J.W. (1963). *Self-Renewal*. New York: W. W. Norton.

Glickman, K. (2002). *Leadership for Learning: How to Help Teachers Succeed*. Alexandria, VA: ASCD.

Hall, G. & Hord, S. (1987). *Change in Schools: Facilitating the Process*. Albany, NY: State University of New York Press.

Hessel, K. & Holloway, J. (2002). *A Framework For School Leaders: Linking the ISLLC Standards to Practice*. Princeton, NJ: Educational Testing Service.

Holcomb, E.L. (1999). *Getting Excited About Data: How to Combine People, Passion, and Proof*. Thousand Oaks, CA: Corwin Press, Inc.

Holly, P.J. (1997). *Introduction to School Improvement*. Training Materials. New Iowa Schools Development Corporation.

Holly, P.J. (2002). *Introduction to Data Coach Training*. Training Materials. The Learning Group.

Holly, P.J. & Forsythe, L. Kay. (1996). *Quadrant Thinking*. Training Materials. New Iowa Schools Development Corporation.

Holly, P.J. & Southworth, Geoff. (1989). *The Developing School*. London: The Falmer Press.

Hoyle, J., English, F., & Steffy, B. (1985) *Skills for Successful School Leaders*. Arlington, VA: AASA.

Joyce, B. & Showers, B. (1988). *Student Achievement through Staff Development*. White Plains, NY: Longman.

Joyce, B., Wolf, J., & Calhoun, E. (1993). *The Self-Renewing School*. Alexandria, VA: ASCD.

Lange, M. (1998). *Change and the Grief Cycle*. Workshop Presentation. New Iowa Schools Development Corporation.

Leadership for Student Learning: Reinventing the Principalship (October 2000). Washington, DC: Institute for Educational Leadership.

Levesque, K. et al. (1998). *At Your Fingertips: Using Everyday Data to Improve Schools*. National Center for Research in Vocational Education/American Association of School Administrators.

Kouzes, J. & Posner, B. (1987). *Challenging the Process*. San Francisco: Jossey-Bass.

Kouzes, J. & Posner, B. (1993) *Credibility*, San Francisco: Jossey-Bass.

McCreery, K., Association of California School Administrators (2002). The Principals' Center. 1575 Bayshore Highway, Burlingame, CA 95814. (800) 672-3494, e-mail: rmontoya@acsa.org

Mislevy, R., Steinberg, L., & Almond, R. (January 1999). *On the Roles of Task Model Variables in Assessment Design*. CSE Technical Report 500. National Center for Research on Evaluation, Standards, and Student Testing and the Center for the Study of Evaluation. Graduate School of Education & Information Studies, University of California, Los Angeles.

Murphy, J. & Hallinger, P. (January/February 1988). Characteristics of instructionally effective school districts. *Journal of Educational Research*. 81(3), 175-181.

Murphy, J., Beck, L., Crawford, M., Hodges, A., & McGughy, C. (2001). *The Productive High School: Creating Personalized Academic Communities*. Thousand Oaks, CA: Corwin Press.

National Association of Elementary School Principals. (2001). *Standards for What Principals Should Know and Be Able To Do*. NAESP.

National Association of Secondary School Principals. (2002). *Teacher Talk: Conversation That Improves Practice*. Principal Leadership, March.

National Staff Development Council. (2000). *Data*. Journal of Staff Development. Winter 21(1).

Noyce, P., Perda, D., & Traver, R. (2000). Creating data-driven schools. *Educational Leadership*, Alexandria, VA: ASCD. 57(5). 52-56.

Pearlman, M. (March 14, 2001). *Practical Applications of Evidence-Centered Design*, unpublished presentation at the Educational Testing Service Constructed-Response Forum.

Richardson, J. (May 2001). Shared culture. *National Staff Development Council*.

Sagor, R. (2000). *Guiding School Improvement with Action Research*. Alexandria, VA: ASCD.

Saphier, J., Bigda-Peyton, T., & Pierson, G. (1989). *How To Make Decisions That Stay Made*. Alexandria, VA: ASCD.

Schmoker, M. (1996). *Results: The Key to Continuous School Improvement*. Alexandria, Virginia: ASCD.

Schmoker, M. (2001). *The Results Fieldbook: Practical Strategies from Dramatically Improved Schools*. Alexandria, VA: ASCD.

Sparks, D. & Hirsh, S. (1997). *A New Vision For Staff Development*. Oxford, OH: NSCD/Alexandria, VA: ASCD.

REFERENCES

The Principal, Keystone of a High-Achieving School: Attracting and Keeping the Leaders We Need. (2000). Arlington, VA: Educational Research Service.

Tuckman, B. (1965). Developmental sequence in small groups. *Psychological Bulletin*, 63, 384-399.

Ulrich, D., Zenger, J. & Smallwood, N. (1999) **Results-Based Leadership**. Boston, MA: Harvard Business School Press.

Wahlstrom, D. (1999). **Using Data To Improve Student Achievement**. Virginia Beach, VA: Successline Inc.

Walsh, J., Saltes, B., & Wiman, E. (March 2001). A quickie check-up—Gauging school improvement. *Kappan*.

Wang, M. & Walberg, H. (editors). (2001). **Tomorrow's Teachers**. Richmond, CA: McCutchan Publishing Corp.

Wisconsin Center for Educational Research. (Spring, 2001). Using data for educational decision making. *The Newsletter of the Comprehensive Center-Region VI*, 6(1).